The Elizabethan Hamlet

The Elizabethan Hamlet

Arthur McGee

YALE UNIVERSITY PRESS
NEW HAVEN AND LONDON
1987

Designed by Faith Brabenec Hart

Set in Linotron Bembo by Best-set Typesetter Ltd., Hong Kong
Printed in Great Britain by The Bath Press, Avon

Library of Congress Cataloging-in-Publication Data

McGee, Arthur, 1922–
  The Elizabethan Hamlet.

  Includes index.
  1. Shakespeare, William, 1564–1616.
Hamlet. I. Title.
PR2807.M47   1987   822.3′3   87–13271
ISBN 0-300-03988-3

To Kay

Acknowledgements

My GRATITUDE is due first to Professor L.C. Knights and Professor E.A.J. Honigmann for their encouragement when I first began this book and for their help in the earlier stages. Then in the pre-publication phase the Yale University Press adviser made valuable suggestions as to both form and content with a gusto and candour which was positively refreshing – if I am not free entirely from the taint of original sin it is not his fault.

Then too I was fortunate in contacting John Nicoll in the first place; his combination of plain speaking and tact has made him a pleasure to deal with. I have also good reason to be grateful to Faith Hart for her meticulous editing.

In my enquires into the world of the medieval nun I have been ably assisted by Father Paul Hackett S.J., by Father Howard Docherty O.F.M., and by Sister Loyala O.S.F. who is secretary and archivist of her Order. I should add that while I do not share their faith I respect their integrity and am grateful for their kindness. I am also solely responsible for the conclusions I have drawn from the information they gave me.

My thanks also to the patient, polite and long-suffering library staff at Glasgow University in whose corporate flesh I have been more than a seasonal thorn. I am also grateful to Patricia Kelly who employed her skills in word-processing on my behalf, often at very short notice.

Finally, I ask myself what I would have done without my wife Kay, to whom this book is dedicated, at my side. Above all she has convinced me of the reality of love – without which we all drift into the nightmare darkness where Hamlet and Fortinbras would destroy the very stars.

Contents

Introduction

A.C. BRADLEY, in 1904, when considering 'the question regarding the tragic world and the ultimate power in it', assumed that his readers would agree that

> this question must not be answered in 'religious' language. For although this or that *dramatis persona* may speak of gods or of God, of evil spirits or of Satan, of heaven and of hell, and although the poet may show us ghosts from another world, these ideas do not materially influence his representation of life, nor are they used to throw light on the mystery of its tragedy. The Elizabethan drama was almost wholly secular.

But he felt obliged to add in his concluding remarks on *Hamlet*:

> While *Hamlet* certainly cannot be called in the specific sense a 'religious drama', there is in it nevertheless both a freer use of popular religious ideas, and a more decided, though always imaginative intimation of a supreme power concerned in human evil and good, than can be found in any other of Shakespeare's tragedies.[1]

In 1940 however Fredson Bowers rejected the notion that the Elizabethan drama was secular; for in its attitude to revenge tragedy

> one may sum up the Elizabethan critical view by saying that tragedy portrayed violent action – deeds of lust, villainy and murder – but these deeds were always punished at the close. The firm object of Elizabethan tragedy, therefore, was the exacting not only of poetic, but, more important, of divine justice.

And he says later:

> The great tragic theme of the sixteenth – and seventeenth – century is this theme of God's revenge for sin. Writers of tragedies, both dramatic and non-dramatic tragedies, were necessarily preoccupied with this fundamental teaching.[2]

1

Eleanor Prosser in 1966 agreed that Elizabethan tragedy was not secular:

> We have not recognized the familiar ethical and religious
> foundation upon which the plays were constructed because it is
> buried so deep. I would agree with Ornstein that the ethical
> question of revenge is rarely central in Elizabethan and Jacobean
> drama, but it is not central, I submit, because it is not a
> 'question' to the average playwright or to most of his audience.
> The issue was settled. Revenge was a sin against God, a defiance
> of the State, a cancer that could destroy mind, body, and soul –
> and that was that.[3]

In Britain there had also been a drift away from 'secular' tragedy.
H.D.F. Kitto in 1956 insisted that Greek tragedy was 'religious'
drama and that *Hamlet* should be regarded similarly. And in 1960
L.C. Knights published lectures given some years earlier in
which he applauded Kitto's approach but found the play 'religious
in a different way from that defined in Kitto's account of Greek
tragedy', and then went on to outline an approach to *Hamlet*
which questioned the ethical basis which Bradley had taken for
granted.[4] Then we may also note G. Wilson Knight's uneasiness
about the Ghost in his *An Essay on Hamlet*:

> The Ghost may or may not have been a 'goblin damned'; it is
> certainly not a 'spirit of health'.[5]

Most recently (1983) Philip Edwards has said:

> I personally cannot see a way forward in any discussion of
> *Hamlet* that does not take as a point of departure that it is a
> religious play.[6]

I wish therefore to begin by looking at the State religion in
Shakespeare's time in its most basic form – the form in which it
was transmitted to the people. From the appearance of the Prayer
Book of 1552 it becomes obligatory that:

> The Curate of every Parish shall diligently upon Sundayes and
> Holydayes, after the second Lesson at Evening Prayer openly in
> the Church instruct and examine so many children of the Parish
> sent unto him, as he shall think convenient, in some part of his
> Catechism.

And Richmond Noble also quotes Professor Foster Watson (*The
English Grammer Schools to 1660*):

It may be safely asserted that the Statutes of Schools much more frequently include the teaching of the Catechism, primer and A B C than they explicitly name the Bible. The most important consideration was that the child should know the articles of the faith.[7]

The 'Little Catechism', as it was called, the form of the Catechism taken from the Book of Common Prayer, was thus drummed into children either at school or on Sundays at church or both. In essence what they received was instruction in the Ten Commandments, the first 'table' defining man's duty to God and the second 'table' defining man's duty to his fellow man.

The influence of this religious teaching is observable for instance in Francis Bacon, as Caroline Spurgeon mentions:

> Thus when speaking against the propagation of religion by wars, the forcing of men's consciences by sanguinary persecutions, he says that to put the sword in the people's hands tends to the subversion of all government, of God. 'For this', he cries, 'is but to dash the first table against the second', and we realize that the mention of God's law has called up instantly before him the figure of Moses in the Wilderness with the two tables of stone in his hands, one containing man's duty to God, the other man's duty to man.[8]

As early as 1561, as A.L. Rowse records, there was a royal order to set up the Ten Commandments in the churches for the people to read. So it is clear that the Ten Commandments were part of the religious training, call it indoctrination if you will, that every Elizabethan, however great, however humble, underwent.

If in particular we look more closely at the Sixth Commandment as presented by the catechists of the time we find that the condemnation of revenge is categorical:

1. God in this commandment forbiddeth not only the murder done with the hand, but also the murder of the heart and of the tongue. Matt. v. John iii. In the murder done of the hand is forbidden all private revenging between private persons, that will be judges in their own cause. (A Declaration of the Ten Commandments by Bishop Hooper. This appeared in 1549 and in 1550, and again in 1588.)[9]
2. After this manner ought all Christians to be affected, not to revenge, but ready to forgive; not to curse, but to bless; not to render evil for evil, but to overcome evil with goodness,

leaving all vengeance to God, which saith: 'Vengeance is mine: I will reward'. (The Catechism of Thomas Becon, 1560)[10]

3. M. Now rehearse the sixth commandment.
   s. 'Thou shalt not kill.'
   M. Shall we sufficiently fulfil this law if we keep our hands clean from slaughter and blood?
   s. God made his law not only for outward works, but also and chiefly for the affections of the heart. For anger and hatred, and every desire to hurt, is, before God, adjudged manslaughter. Therefore these also God by this law forbiddeth us.
   M. Shall we then fully satisfy the law if we hate no man?
   s. God in condemning hatred requireth love towards all men, even our enemies, yea, so far as to wish health, safety, and all good things to them that wish us evil, and do bear us a hateful and cruel mind, and us much as in us lieth, to do them good.

4. A wreakful mind and revengeful of injuries the word of God doth surely condemn. (Both 3 and 4 from Nowell's *Catechism*, 1570)[11]

5. To bear no malice nor hatred in my heart. (The 'Little Catechism' – as an adjunct to the Sixth Commandment)

It is also obvious that revenge meant revenge and not justice. There is no ambiguity in the basic religious instruction of the Elizabethans. God was Justice and only He could revenge. Thus in human terms there was no such thing as 'just revenge'.

There is no contemporary evidence of such confusion arising except in the minds of various revengers in the drama, whose motives were demonstrably evil. For instance Hieronimo exclaims:

> The mother cries on righteous Rhadamanth
> For *just revenge* against the murderers.
>
> (3.13.141–2)

In *The Massacre at Paris* the Guise gives instructions about the body of the Admiral thus:

> Away with him, cut off his head and hands,
> And send them for a present to the Pope;
> And when this *just revenge* is finished,
> Unto Mount Faucon will we drag his corse,

And he that living hated so the cross
Shall, being dead, be hang'd thereon in chains.

In *Faustus* we have Benvolio who thinks he has murdered Faustus:

First, on his dead, in quittance of my wrongs,
I'll nail huge forked horns, and let them hang
Within the window where he yoked me first,
That all the world may see my *just revenge*.

(4.3.55–8)

In *Bussy d'Ambois* Monsieur says:

Justice will soon distinguish murtherous minds
From *just revengers*: had my friend been slain
His enemy surviving, he should die,
Since has added to a murthered fame,
Which was in his intent, a murthered man.

(2.1.168–73)

Henry's attitude however negates this sophistry. Then there is the fiendish Cutwolfe, Nashe's revenger:

Revenge is the glorie of armes, & the highest performance of valure: *revenge is whatsoever we call law or justice*. The farther we wade in revenge, the neerer we come to the throne of the almightie ... All true Italians imitate me in revenging constantly and dying valiantly.[12]

In Tourneur's *The Revenger's Tragedy* the Second Lord tells the villainous Vindice:

our wrongs are such
We cannot *justly be revenged* too much.

(5.2.9–10)

Othello too before killing Desdemona persuades himself that he is acting in the cause of 'justice' (5.2.17), and he tells Emilia afterwards that he 'did proceed upon just ground to this extremity'.

In *The Captives* by Thomas Heywood (1624) Friar Richard says:

it might be thought the Knight in jealousy
had done this murder in a *just revenge*.

(4.2.53–4)

Then in *The Witch of Edmonton* (Act 2, Sc. 1) we find the following conversation between Mother Sawyer and Satan in the form of a dog:

5

M. SAWYER. Bless me! the devil?
DOG. Come, do not fear; I love thee much too well
  To hurt or fright thee; if I seem terrible,
  It is to such as hate me. I have found
  Thy love unfeigned; have seen and pitied
  Thy open wrongs; and come, out of my love
  To give thee *just revenge* against thy foes.

From these examples it is evident that the Elizabethan audience cannot be presumed to have shared the moral confusion of the revengers they saw on the stage. Fredson Bowers records that:

> Bishop Hall (1612) predicts for the revenger a double death, of body and soul. The religious writers denounced the fact that men could 'thinke that God is fauorable ... when as they imagine, that the reuenge they pursue is iust, and that they haue beene vnworthelie abused.' No private revenge could ever partake of justice.[13]

It is little wonder then that James I said 'Revenge and murder come coupled together', for he too probably learned this as a child.[14] Catholics also in Shakespeare's audience would have taken the same view, for their attitude to revenge was similar. Catholic children today receive the same teaching as their Elizabethan ancestors: '[This] commandment forbids anger, and still more, hatred and revenge.'[15] So too, as we have seen, playwrights could talk of 'just revenge' without placing audiences in an ethical dilemma, because they took this as a kind of diabolic double-talk which tempted the revenger to follow the road to damnation. Perhaps the source of our confusion is that so many of us no longer accept the literal existence of God and the Devil – in the latter case in particular 'Hell is a fable' as it was for Faustus. The result is that while we may attempt to see the play in terms of religion we are still prone to translate the religious symbols into metaphors.

Robert Bolt sums up our problem in discussing Sir Thomas More:

> The English Kingdom ... was subservient to the larger society of the Church of Christ, founded by Christ, extending over Past and Future, ruled from Heaven. There are still some for whom this is perfectly simple, but for most it can only be a metaphor. I took it as a metaphor for that larger context which we all inhabit, the terrifying cosmos. Terrifying because no

laws, no sanction, no mores obtain there, it is either empty or occupied by God and Devil nakedly at war.[16]

Hamlet too inhabits our cosmos and on that scale the issues of revenge and justice indeed become blurred, but if the Elizabethans had shared our view they would not have pinned the label of 'just revenge' solely on the avenger who had embraced evil. As Anne Barton says:

> Elizabethan dramatists enlisted powerful emotional support for the virtuous avenger, up to a point, but they almost invariably turned on him in Act V. In doing so, they acknowledged that the man who persists and actually does the deed must be contaminated by it, that he cannot really be approved of or saved.[17]

Thus too if we can use our modern cosmic scale we cannot but agree with Harold Jenkins.

> In his first words after the Ghost has left him, 'O all you host of heaven! O earth!', Hamlet acknowledges both the force of nature and the power that governs nature. But he ominously goes on, 'What else? And shall I couple hell?' Later he does precisely that when, in the soliloquy on the Player at the end of the second act, he says he is
>
> > Prompted to my revenge by heaven and hell.
>
> Those who maintain that the prompting is wholly diabolical and so to be resisted are confuted by the text.[18]

But this, with respect, is not 'Elizabethan', for no version of the Catechism required Satan to add his signature to the Ten Commandments. On the contrary, as Bacon said, 'vindictive persons live the life of witches: who, as they are mischievous, so end they unfortunate'. Revenge and witches went together – Satan was supposed to command them to revenge themselves when a coven was convened.

Then again, as Philip Edwards points out,

> Three times during the course of the play Shakespeare brings the story of Cain and Abel to our minds. There is the mention of 'the first curse' in 1.2; 'the primal eldest curse ... A brother's murder' in 3.3; and 'Cain's jawbone, that did the first murder' in 5.1. *Hamlet* is the story of two royal brothers, a kingdom and a queen, given to us as a reflection of the primordial disintegration of the human family in the first

7

murder which resulted from and betokened man's separation from God.[19]

This was the 'archetype of fratricide' to the Elizabethans as J.H. Walter says and he goes on:

> It was available not only in its biblical form, but in dramatic form in the play cycles of Chester, Coventry, Towneley, York, and the Cornish play of the Creation. Some of these made use of the legends that had accumulated round the figure of Cain, legends current in verse and in sermons during the Middle Ages.[20]

Thus for centuries people had had held up before them the disastrous consequences of murder within the family and they were constantly reminded of God's prohibition of vengeance – presumably by his kin – against him:

> Therefore whosoever slayeth Cain, vengeance shall be taken on him sevenfold. And the Lord set a mark upon Cain, lest any finding him should kill him. (Gen. 4:15)

It seems therefore to me that arguments which claim an ambivalence in the Elizabethan attitude to blood revenge miss the point, for while Sir William Segar's *Book of Honour* (1590) has been quoted in support of this view he could not uphold the right of a revenger against a fratricide when the revenger was the son of the murdered man. Revenge within the family was abhorrent to the Elizabethans. In *Horestes* for example the Vice Revenge is a Vice who persuades Horestes that he is a 'messenger of heavenly gostes' and incites him to murder his mother Clytemnestra – as in Aeschylus.

If then we look again at Hamlet's words:

> Yea, from the table of my memory
> I'll wipe away all trivial fond records,
> All saws of books, all forms, all pressures past
> That youth and observation copied there,
> And thy commandment all alone shall live
> Within the book and volume of my brain,
> Unmixed with baser matter – yes, by heaven!
> O most pernicious woman!
> O villain, villain, smiling, damnèd villain!
> My tables, meet it is I set it down
> That one may smile, and smile, and be a villain,

At least I am sure it may be so in Denmark ...
So, uncle, there you are. Now, to my Word,
It is 'Adieu, adieu, remember me.' ...
I have sworn't.

(1.5.98–112)

It is rather odd that the collocation 'revenge' – 'tables' – 'commandment' has produced no religious comment from editors although there are annotations on the writing tablets or tables that the Elizabethans used. Then too Hamlet's behaviour at this point has been seen as more or less bizarre. Eleanor Prosser for instance, whose Hamlet is always sane, suggests that Hamlet 'jabbed the picture into his brain with a rigid finger', for to produce his notebook and 'frantically write down Claudius's villainy would strongly suggest that he had gone mad'. If however we wish to portray a mad Hamlet it may be observed that a 'table' could also be the palm of the hand. Launcelot Gobbo uses the word in this sense as does Dekker's Bellafront, in *The Honest Whore*, in which contexts the expression must have been intelligible even to groundlings.[21] So too we may wish to note the traditional belief recorded by Noble, that God scratched the Ten Commandments on the Tables with his nails, and this in turn had given rise to the colloquial usage whereby the Ten Commandents meant 'the two hands with whose fingers and thumbs an offender was scratched, usually with reference to women, as for instance "my wife's ten commandments"'.[22] C.T. Onions glosses the expression as 'fingers' and stresses its frequent use c.1600.[23]

But would an Elizabethan audience fail to see a blasphemous parody of God giving the Tables of the Law to Moses? How could they when they in 'youth' had used an 'Absey book' – a spelling book with the Catechism attached – and so probably copied out the Ten Commandments as an exercise? How could they fail to understand that Hamlet is being egged on to commit murder in defiance of the Sixth Commandment that had been impressed upon the 'tables of their memory'? If we are right to suppose that they saw no ambiguity in 'just revenge' then they surely saw that the Ghost's command was an unambiguous command to Hamlet to commit murder, the murder of a fratricide – a crime to which a special divine prohibition was attached, and which had been part of their religious training for centuries. Nigel Alexander rightly asks 'how a Ghost which condemns all murder as "foul" can demand vengeance, since vengeance will almost certainly involve

9

the act of murder'[24] – when, in addition, Shakespeare's audience could quote the Sixth Commandment that they may have learned at school using the sort of mnemonic technique involving the use of key words which Alexander describes.[25]

The revenger was, in Elizabethan eyes, 'playing God'. In Marston's *The Insatiate Countess* Isabella, inciting Sago to commit murder, says:

> Be God on earth, and revenge innocence
> O worthy Spaniard, on my knees I beg,
> Forget the persons, think on their offence.

To which Sago replies:

> By the white soul of honour, by heaven's Jove:
> They die if their death can attain your love.

But the ladies too, as we have seen, took their turn at 'writing' their Ten Commandments. In *Richard III* Anne threatens Gloucester:

> If I thought that, I tell thee, homicide,
> These nails should rend that beauty from thy cheeks ...
> It is a quarrel just and reasonable,
> To be revenge'd on him that kill'd my husband.
>
> (1.3)

Today, we may share the perplexity of which Anne Barton speaks when we contemplate a Hamlet who

> altogether avoids the issue of God's prohibition of revenge, although he has a good deal to say about what there may be in the afterlife, and about the Christian sanction against suicide. This silence seems odd in a play where even the unreflective Laertes admits that to exact revenge for a father's death is to 'dare damnation' (IV.5.135). But it must be intentional.

Professor Barton goes on to point out that Hieronymo 'had explicitly weighed the biblical text forbidding private revenges against his own extremity and frustration before deciding to act', and that even in 'the non-Christian Rome of *Titus Andronicus* ... the idea that vengeance belongs to heaven and that Titus ought to wait patiently for divine retribution was painstakingly expressed'. Andronicus is 'so just that he will not revenge' (IV.1.129).[26]

We may also agree with Nigel Alexander that

The questions of heaven and hell, death and judgment, were answered, but scarcely solved by the Elizabethan theologians. The Ghost, however, is more powerful and primitive than the careful catalogues of the theologians. Fundamentally its appeal is pre-Christian and prehistoric. It is not an appeal that the most sophisticated audience can ignore.[27]

But we cannot therefore suppose that the Elizabethan audience would have reacted similarly – that they also would have been perplexed by Hamlet's attitude to revenge and would have found their religion less than 'cosmic'. And the consequence is that we are liable – and perhaps we are right – to read into the Ghost and Hamlet himself ambiguities which for the Elizabethans simply did not exist.

It seems to me that at heart we still agree with Bradley on the total imaginative effect of the play although as this century has progressed there is increasing evidence that we, like Bradley, have misunderstood at least some of the play, particularly the true nature of the Ghost. The effect has been a gradual shift towards annotations which appear to restore religious connotations we have previously missed. For my own part I am acutely aware of the antinomy in my own position – on the one hand I feel drawn to Bradley even though his knowledge of things Elizabethan is woeful, while on the other hand I think the research into the religion and ghost lore of the time is productive and indeed has not gone far enough. I also feel, paradoxically, that this awareness is a help rather than a hindrance because it makes me distrust my own intuition – I think I have learned more about the Elizabethans by realizing that what seems obvious to me was not obvious to them, and vice versa. I am unsure, like Robert Bolt, of my 'cosmos' but I am sure it was not the same as that of the Elizabethans. And because of my uncertainty I have taken the investigation of Elizabethan religion a stage further – or rather I found it could be taken a stage further – and found that we cannot talk about religion without talking about sectarian conflict. So my own proneness to turn the religious symbols into metaphors as Bradley did, and as I still tend to do, is restrained by the fact that these symbols were the source of bitter conflict in word and deed and that if Shakespeare had not presented his symbols in a manner acceptable to the authorities, who were Protestants, *Hamlet* might never have appeared and Shakespeare might have ended up in jail.

Throughout however there are some certainties. For example,

11

there is no doubt that the Elizabethans relished their revenge tragedies – the religious prohibitions added spice to the drama. If there was also a lay approval of blood revenge, as has been claimed, it would not have fundamentally altered this basic attitude. Revenge was all the more entertaining precisely because it was forbidden and because at the end it led to Hell and damnation. Far from reducing the dramatic effect for the Elizabethans their religion, which presented them with the prospect of damnation, was 'box office' – *Faustus* was the most popular Elizabethan play. They enjoyed their forbidden fruit and we may therefore ask ourselves why we are so keen to turn it, as it were, into a Newtonian apple – for them the sin of revenge had to have 'no relish of salvation in it'.

1

The Revenge Ghost

JOHN DOVER WILSON in his *What Happens in Hamlet* quotes Pierre
Le Loyer, a French lawyer, and a Catholic, who had written *IIII
Livres des spectres ou apparitions et visions d'esprits, anges et demons se
monstrans sensiblement aux hommes* in 1586:

> Of all the common and familiar subjects of conversation that
> are entered upon in company of things remote from nature and
> cut off from the senses, there is none so ready to hand, none so
> unusual, as that of visions of Spirits, and whether what is said of
> them is true. It is the topic that people most readily discuss
> and on which they linger the longest because of the abundance
> of examples, the subject being fine and pleasing and the discus-
> sion the least tedious that can be found.[1]

This book was a counterblast to a Protestant book by Ludwig
Lavater, published in Zurich in 1570, which in translation ran to
two editions, the latter being published in 1596 under the title
of *Ghosts and Spirites walking by Nyght*. The points of doctrinal
difference are not immediately of concern, although they will be
referred to later; it is enough to say that people in Shakespeare's
time, whatever their religion, thought about and talked about
ghosts.

About 1560 developments began in the English drama which
were to lead to the production of what we now classify as Revenge
Tragedy: the tragedies of Seneca began to appear in translation,
the most comprehensive collection being that of Thomas Newton
– *Seneca, His Tenne Tragedies* – in 1581. Newton claimed that
Seneca's

> whole writings (penned with a peerless sublimity and loftiness
> of style) are so farre from countenancing vice, that I doubt
> whether there bee any amongst all the Catalogue of Heathen
> wryters, that with more gravity of Philosopicall sentences,
> more waightyness of sappy words, or greater authority of
> sound matter beateth down sinne, loose lyfe, dissolute dealinge,
> and unbrydled sensuality.

13

This insistence upon the moral value of the plays is important because the Elizabethans were acutely aware of the religious code, even if they chose to disobey it.

The importance of this Christian background to revenge tragedy cannot be underestimated because, while the revenge ghost had its origin in Seneca, it was always clearly labelled by dramatists as demonic. 'Vengeance is mine' was the divine ruling and ghosts were subject to it just as much as men – and there was no disagreement between Protestant and Catholic on this central issue. For example, Jasper Heywood (a Catholic who was later to flee from England) added the revenge ghost Achilles to his translation of the *Troas* (1559) and this apparition threatens 'the furies wrath' and seeks to appease 'the sprightes and hell' and 'the wrath of Hel'. Similarly in his *Thyestes* Megaera is 'one of the Hellish furies' and 'the grysly Ghosts of hell' dwell in 'blackests Tartare'. Heywood also refers to the 'fowlest fiends of hell' and the 'hollowe hell' where lie 'the lothsome Lymbo lakes'. Other translations in *Seneca, His Tenne Tragedies* show the same identification of the classical Underworld with the Christian Hell. In *Hercules Furens* the Eumenides are 'upraysed of lowest hell', Megaera is invoked to 'bring out of hell ... a huge and direful brand'; and there are 'spryghts of hell' and 'ghosts of hell'. Medea muses on 'vengenaunce fell' and she calls on 'dampned Ghosts', the 'Lady dyre of Hell', the 'hellish hagges' and 'divelish Feendes', and she 'intreats' the 'Goblins grym of Hell'. It is evident therefore that revenge, Hell and the Furies went together in the minds of the translators. Some other points to be noted are the synonyms for Hell used by the translators and also employed by the writers of revenge tragedy: 'the Chaos of eternal nyght of hell' (for 'noctis aeternae chaos') the 'dungeon darke', 'the most dreadful den of everlasting night', etc.

This hybridization of classical and Christian symbolism can also be seen in *The Misfortunes of Arthur* (1587) in which alternative lines by William Fulbecke were preferred to those of Thomas Hughes. The association of Gorlois, the revenge ghost, with Hell is clearly indicated:

> Death hath his conquest, hell hath had his wish,
> Gorlois his vow, Alecto her desire;
> Sin hath his pay, and blood is quit with blood:
> Revenge in triumph bears the struggling hearts!
> Now Gorlois, pierce, the craggy rocks of hell,

> Through chinks whereof infernal sprites do glance,
> Return this answer to the furies court.

'Revenge' and the ghost of Don Andrea in *The Spanish Tragedy* of Thomas Kyd are influenced by Seneca and they in turn are, according to Fredson Bowers, 'presumably influencing the action of the characters in much the same fashion in which the ghost of Tantalus casts his malign influence over the house of Pelops in *Thyestes*'.[2] But while Seneca is not the only influence, as Bowers points out, the ghost's demand for vengeance for his own death may be derived from Italian – hybrid symbolism is again in evidence. Charon is 'the ferryman of hell', and 'bloody Furies' shake 'their whips of steel' in 'the deepest hell'. Lorenzo vows to send Horatio's soul into 'eternal night' and Hieronimo in his distraction cries:

> I'll down to hell, and in this passion
> Knock at the dismal gates of Pluto's Court
> Getting my force, as once Alcides did,
> A troupe of furies and tormenting hagges,
> To torture Don Lorenzo and the rest ...
> Till we do gaine that Prosperine may grant
> Revenge on them that murdered my Sonne.

Other signs that 'Revenge' and Don Andrea's ghost are demonic are that they come from 'depth of vnderground' and that Hieronimo mistakes Bazulto for 'a furie sent from the emptie kingdom of black night', but Bazulto replies that he is not a ghost. Hieronimo is determined to have justice, but he feels that he has to descend to the judges of Hell to find it. And 'Revenge' promises Don Andrea that

> This hand shall hale them downe to deepest hell
> Where none but furies, bugs, and tortures dwell

The ghost of Pompey in Kyd's *Cornelia* shows the same Christianization of classical symbolism. The Chorus warns Cornelia that the ghost of Pompey is evil:

> None but inevitable conquering Death
> Descends to hell, with hope to rise againe;
> For ghosts of men are lockt in fiery gates,
> Fast-guarded by a fell remorceless Monster.
> And therefore thinke not it was Pompey's spryte,
> But some false Daemon that beguild your sight.

Kyd's attitude to ghosts, therefore, although influenced by Seneca, was consonant with Christian doctrine which precludes the appearance of a malign ghost from Heaven, and there is no trace of the Catholic belief in Purgatory; for although his Underworld has three parts it is still Hell, Tartarus being 'deepest Hell', and his Pluto and the infernal judges have a satanic aura.

In the anonymous *Locrine* (1594) Humber invokes the 'ugly ghosts' from 'Puryflegiton', the 'fierce Erinnis, horrible with snakes' and the 'vgly Furies, armed with whips':

> You threefold iudges of black Tartarus,
> And all the armie of you hellish fiends

Then the ghost of Albanact appears shouting:

> Revenge! revenge for blood!

And when Humber drowns himself Albanact's ghost exults:

> Backe will I post to hell moth Taenarus,
> And passe Cocitus, to the Elysian fields,
> And tell my father Brutus of these newes.

These lines follow the last despairing words of Humber:

> You gastly divels of the ninefold Stickes,
> You damned ghoasts of ioylesse Acheron,
> You mournfull soules, vext in Abissus vaults,
> You coleblack divels of Avernus pond,
> Come with your fleshhooks rent my famisht arms.

While Greene did not write revenge tragedy his attitude to ghosts conforms to Anglican doctrine and also has a trace of anti-Catholic satire – a trend which began to affect the revenge ghost proper. In *Alphonsus, King of Arragon* Medea conjures the ghost of Calchas in a white surplice and a cardinal's mitre from 'Pluto's loathsome lake', 'stinking Styx and filthy Phlegethon'. Calchas retorts:

> What mean'st thou thus to call me from my grave?
> Shall ne'er my ghost obtain his quiet rest?

Medea orders him back to Pluto to enquire of the Destinies 'How Amurack shall speed in these his wars', and Calchas unwillingly hastes 'to hell' to do her bidding. In *Friar Bacon and Friar Bungay*, in which the ghost of Hercules is conjured, Vandermast claims that it is 'The fiend, appearing like great Hercules'. And just as significant, although they are not points of dramatic importance,

16

are several miscellaneous references to ghosts. The clown in *A Looking Glass for London* is not afraid of the spirits that haunt the city: 'Turne me loose to all the divels in hell', he says. And in the same play the usurer, tempted by an Evil Angel to commit suicide, thinks he sees

> the bleeding ghostes
> Of those whom my corruption brought to nought.

It may be added that as Greene associates revenge with Tisiphone, one of the Furies, in his *Orlando Furioso* he thereby, as his classical symbolism is demonic, associates it with Hell.

George Peele's attitude to ghosts is similar. The three ghosts which cry 'Vindicta !' in *The Battle of Alcazar* (c.1589) are associated with Nemesis whose drum awakes the Furies lying 'In cave as dark as hell and beds of steel'. And the transplanting of classical figures into the Christian Hell can be seen in this passage:

> But may I never pass the river, till I be
> Revenged upon thy soul, accursed Abdelmelec
> If not on earth, yet when we meet in hell,
> Before grim Minos, Rhadamanth, and Aeacus,
> The combat will I crave upon thy ghost,
> And drag thee thorough the loathsome pools
> Of Lethes, Styx, and fiery Phlegethon.

Also in *The Old Wives' Tale* (1591–4) Sacrapant dies of fright when the ghost of Jack (whom he regards as a Fury, come to take his soul to Hell) takes the wreath from his head and the sword from his hand. Jack's ghost, it may be remarked, 'leaps down in the ground' at the end of the play – the setting is comic, but the demonic nature of the ghost is made evident.

The plays we have so far considered antedate the appearance of the First Quarto (QI) of *Hamlet*, and it is evident that not only are revenge ghosts uniformly evil but that ghosts generally were considered evil by the dramatists – even when the context was comic. Charles Edward Whitmore's view in *The Supernatural in Tragedy* was:

> The desire for revenge which appeared sporadically in the classical ghosts becomes the dominant trait of their English successors, to such a degree that we may fairly say that the developed revenge ghost is the creation of the Elizabethan age. Naturally this eagerness for revenge involves a close connection of the ghost with the plot; he either actually sets in motion a

17

train of events which will bring about the downfall of his enemies, or is deeply interested in the action, even if he does not personally affect its course.[3]

When therefore one considers the influence of the revenge ghost on the moral tone of the play it is fair to say that it supplied a motivation that was demonstrably evil.

By c.1599, if we take the Introduction to *A Warning for Fair Women* as evidence, audiences were growing a little tired of the Senecan–Christian hybrid ghost:

> Then, too, a filthy whining ghost,
> Lapt in some foul sheet or a leather pilch,
> Comes screaming like a pig half-sticked,
> And cries, 'Vindicta! Revenge, Revenge!'
> With that a little resin flasheth forth,
> Like smoke out of a tobacco pipe or a boy's squib.

Yet to this decade, or a little earlier, we must assign the so-called *Ur-Hamlet* which Kyd may have written. Dover Wilson quoting 'the ghost which cried so miserably at the Theatre like an oister wife, Hamlet reuenge' from Lodge's *Wits Miserie* (1596) concludes 'that the ghost of the pre-Shakespearean *Hamlet* was of the Senecan brand'.[4] If then we substitute 'Senecan–Christian' for 'Senecan' it follows that the *Ur-Hamlet* had a revenge ghost from Hell and that there was also either direct or indirect demonic motivation of the plot. From Bowers we learn also that the Kydian form of revenge tragedy – blood revenge, a ghost, hesitation in the avenger, madness as a dramatic device (the main ingredients) – still held the stage and continued to do so until about 1607. It is obvious therefore that if the Ghost in Shakespeare's *Hamlet* is good it defied the tradition of the evil revenge ghost which still held the stage at that time, and it also contravened the moral code of the audience, whether Protestant or Catholic.

Perhaps a change from the Senecan–Christian ghost was felt to be necessary by the end of the last decade of the sixteenth century, but judging by the plays of John Marston, there was an increasing interest in Italy as a location for revenge drama – not the contemporary Italy but the 'world of competing petty princelings, bearing names like Sforza, Gonzaga, d'Este, and Medici which belongs to the period portrayed in Guiccardini's *Storia d'Italia*', as G.K. Hunter observes.[5] And with Marston there are introduced

touches of anti-Catholic satire. In *Antonio's Revenge* (1599) the
ghost of Andrugio is Kydian, as is the madness of Antonio, but as
the church of St. Mark is the setting for the ghost's appearance,
the child Julio is murdered there, and Antonio after his revenge
decides to enter a monastery, one feels that Antonio's Catholicism
is being satirized. Julio is so brutally killed and Antonio is so
devoid of guilt that his religion is being ridiculed by the dramatist.
In *The Insatiate Countess* (c.1610) Guido ridicules

> Gallant prodigals
> When they have consum'd their Patrimonies wrongfully,
> They turn Capuchins for devotion.

The presentation of a Kydian ghost in an obviously Catholic
setting therefore brought the religious beliefs of the revenger into
question and diminished the tragic status of Marston's hero, and
the satire made the action melodramatic. Don Sago in *The Insatiate
Countess* is quite ridiculous. Don Sago shoots Massino who had
greeted him with:

> I know thee valiant Spaniard, and to thee
> Murder's more hateful, than is sacriledge.
> Thy actions ever have been honourable.

Marston's ghosts, in keeping with his attitude, are as evil as those
of his predecessors. When the ghost of Asdruball rises in
Sophonisba (1606) Syphax says:

> What damn'd ayre is form'd
> Into that shape?

When we turn to the plays of George Chapman we find the
ghost of Bussy in *The Revenge of Bussy d'Ambois* (1604) is a devil
which rises 'up from the chaos of eternal night', recalling the early
translations of Seneca, and as Bowers says it is capable of a
sophistry which no Elizabethan audience would accept:

> To be His image is to do those things
> That make us deathless, which by death is only
> Doing those deeds that fit eternity;
> And those deeds are the perfecting that justice
> That makes the world last, which proportion is
> Of punishment and wreak for every wrong,
> As well as for right a reward as strong
> Away then! Use the means thou hast to right
> The wrong I suffer'd. What corrupted law

Leaves unperform'd in kings, do thou supply
And be above them all in dignity.

(V.1.89–99)

It may be added that the dance of the ghosts round the body of
Montsurry – 'dances dire and of infernal state' – is a 'patterned
action', as M.C. Bradbrook points out, similar to the dances of the
Furies in other plays.[6] Furthermore, Clermont's own speculations
about the nature of spirits at V.5.133–8, as Thomas Marc Parrott
indicates, follow closely Plato's comments on the souls of the
wicked which 'prowl about tombs and sepulchres, near which . . .
are seen certain ghostly apparitions':[7]

> That spirits should rise in these times are fables;
> Though learnd'st men hold that our sensive spirits
> A little time abide about the graves
> Of their deceased bodies, and can take
> In cold condens'd air the same forms they had
> When they were shut up in this body's shade.

As in Marston there is anti-Catholic satire. Tamyra thinks of
her head as covered with snakes, like the Furies, and yet
contemplates entering a nunnery:

> Hide, hide thy snaky head! to cloisters fly,
> In penance pine! Too easy 'tis to die.

Clermont commits suicide – and so damns his soul – in order to
join the Guise who had played an infamous part in the massacre of
Protestants on St. Bartholomew's day. In *Bussy d'Ambois* the Friar
is a pander to the adultery of Bussy with Tamyra and is able to
conjure devils. He is a hypocrite in life and a hypocrite in death,
for he has the gall to preach to the wronged husband. Yet Bussy
always shows him respect and seems oblivious of the Friar's
shortcomings as a priest.

In Cyril Tourneur's *The Atheist's Tragedy* (c.1607) at first glance
there seems to be a 'good' ghost because it counsels Charlemont:

> Return to France, for thy old father's dead
> And thou by murder disinherited.
> Attend with patience the success of things,
> But leave revenge unto the King of Kings.

But the musketeer on guard duty whom it has disturbed has
different ideas:

20

> Nay, then the Devil's dam
> Has broke her husband's head, for sure it is spirit.
> I shot it through, and yet it will not fall.

If our sole criterion of the ghost's goodness is telling the truth then we fall into error. The Elizabethans believed the Devil could cite scripture for his own evil ends – the Witches in *Macbeth* speak the truth, but only to urge on Macbeth to his own destruction. Charlemont is thus plunged into a situation which brings him to the verge of despair. He resists the temptation but it is torment for him:

> You torture me between the passion
> My bloud, and the religion of my soule.

I maintain therefore that instead of the typical revenge ghost we have a demonic tempter.

The Protestant attitude to ghosts is in fact represented by the Musketeer and by the Puritan, Languebeau Snuffe. Charlemont makes a sudden appearance, pretending to be a ghost:

> CHARLEMONT. The spirit of Charlemont
> D'AMVILE. O stay. Compose me. I dissolve.
> L. SNUFFE. No, 'tis profane. Spirits are invisible.
> 'Tis the fiend in the likeness of Satan.
> I will have no conversation with Satan.
>
> (3.2.19–23)

In *The White Devil* (1607–12) and *The Duchess of Malfi* (1613–14) of John Webster the combination of the evil ghost and anti-Catholicism which we found in Marston and Chapman continues. For instance, in *The White Devil*:

> FRANCISCO. Come, dear Lodovico;
> You have ta'en the sacrament to prosecute
> Th' intended murder?
> LODOVICO. With all constancy.

Then the ghost of Brachiano, dressed in a cassock, appears with the object of driving Flamineo to despair.

> What's that? O fatal! He throws earth upon me
> A dead man's skull beneath the roots of flowers.
> I pray speak sir: our Italian churchmen
> Make us believe dead men hold conference

21

With their familiars, and many times
Will come to bed to them, and eat with them.

Exit GHOST.

He's gone; and see, the skull and earth are vanished.
This is beyond melancholy.
I do dare my fate
To do its worst.

(5.4.138 ff.)

In this play also the Last Rites of the Catholic Church are not only parodied but make an ironic prelude to the murder of Brachiano.

Finally, in Thomas Heywood's *The Captives* (1624) in which there are a couple of villainous friars, Dennis says, seeing Friar John's body which he hid in the convent garden, and which Friar Richard has returned to Averne's garden:

Help, help! His murdered ghost is come from hell
On earth to cry 'Vindicta!'

(4.2.112–13)

It would seem therefore that the revenge ghost in the Elizabethan drama went through three stages of development. (1) There was the Senecan–Christian ghost of the translators and the early playwrights. (2) There was the Kydian revenge ghost, a ghost modified by the influence of Italian tragedy and in plays set closer in time to the Elizabethans. (3) There was the revenge ghost more subtly conceived as a demonic tempter, in contexts which became increasingly Italianate and more obviously Catholic. But in all stages the revenge ghost was recognizably evil and its connection with Hell was constant. And we can reach this conclusion without a detailed knowledge of theology or a consideration of rival Christian doctrines.

If we restate this conclusion in dramatic terms we may then say that the revenge ghost came from the 'Hell' which lay under the Elizabethan stage, following a tradition that goes back to the Morality plays – Satan and his demons came from there. As G.R. Kernodle reminds us, the stage was 'a symbol of social order and of divine order'.[8] Thus too Dover Wilson says: 'the cellarage was commonly called "Hell", a name derived from the Miracle plays'. He also quotes Dekker's *News from Hell* (1606):

Marry the question is, in which the Play houses He [the Devil] would haue performed his prize ... Hell being vnder euerie one of their Stages, the Players (if they had owed him a spight) might with a false Trappe door haue slipt him downe, ande there kept him, as a laughing stocke to all their yawning spectators.[9]

We must also add that there was no such equivalent on the stage for Purgatory, nor indeed in any known play does any dramatic figure appear from there.

Thus a ghost from Purgatory would be an innovation in the writing and stage presentation of Elizabethan revenge tragedy, especially if the ghost were supposed to be 'good'. Eleanor Prosser reaches a similar conclusion:

In only one instance in Elizabethan and Jacobean plays (and nowhere, so far as I have read, in popular literature) is there even a hint that a ghost may have returned from Purgatory. That play, of course, is *Hamlet*.[10]

But if we also add 'revenge' to the ghost from Puratory no one in Shakespeare's audience could believe in its goodness – in its demand for 'just revenge' – because it would have been seen in the same light as its human counterpart, the 'just revenger' who broke the Sixth Commandment. No knowledge of the finer theological points was necessary; the teaching of the Catechism, in any of its Elizabethan forms, would have sufficed.

In addition, as the Catholicism of the revenge ghost in the drama had become increasingly obvious we now have to consider what Protestants would have thought of the development. Dover Wilson remarked: 'Obdurate Protestants would refuse to admit him [the Ghost] anything but a Devil even after the play scene had proved the truth of his story'.[11] So let us now turn to the activities of a group of the 'obdurate Protestants' in England, the 'correctors', the ecclesiastical censors through whose hands *Hamlet*, with its Catholic Ghost from Purgatory, had to pass.

2

The Censorship

THAT ELIZABETHAN PLAYS had first to be submitted to censorship by a high-ranking member of the Church is a fact that editors have largely ignored unless, as in the case of *Doctor Faustus*, textual problems arise. But that these 'correctors' had a decisive effect upon the development of the drama will shortly be apparent. In the revenge drama not only is there an absence of 'good' ghosts, there is also a complete absence of Protestant avengers. Nor is there a single revenge play in which Anglican doctrine is questioned. On the other hand Catholicism is freely used by the dramatists, and the Puritans are fair game for ridicule. In addition there is no discussion of contemporary political issues or matters of state. The Elizabethan drama indeed shows displacements in time, place and religion from the contemporary scene. The historian can learn a good deal about the social history of the Elizabethans from their plays but even there caution is necessary, for as we shall see *Hamlet* was intended to be old-fashioned. The censorship was much stricter than ours and continued so until at least 1640, and much ink has been spilled over the question of Shakespeare's religion as evidenced in the plays without considering that his work would have been banned if it had not been in accord with the state religion, which he could not, in any circumstances, have criticized.

A study of the Elizabethan censorship was made by Sir Edmund Chambers from which I now quote:

> The Act of Supremacy received the royal assent on 8th May 1559, together with the Act of Uniformity which established the Book of Common Prayer, and made it an offence 'in any interludes, plays, songs, or by other open words to declare or speak anything in the derogation, depraving, or despising of that book'. In the course of June followed a body of Injunctions, intended as a code of ecclesiastical discipline to be promulgated at a series of diocesan visitations held by commissioners under the Act of Supremacy. One of these Injunc-

tions is directly concerned with the abuses of printers of books. It begins by forbidding any book or paper to be printed without an express written licence either from the Queen herself or from six of the Privy Council or after perusal from two persons being either the Archbishop of Canterbury or York, or the Bishop or Archdeacon for the sake of printing. One of the two must always be the Ordinary, and the names of the licensers are to be 'added in the end' of every book. This seems sufficiently to cover the ground, but the Injunction goes on to make a special reference to 'pamphlets, plays and ballads' from which anything 'heretical, seditious, or unseemly for Christian ears' ought to be excluded; and for these it prescribes a licence from 'such her majesty's commissioners, or three of them, as be appointed in the city of London to hear and determine divers causes ecclesiastical'. These commissioners are also to punish breaches of the Injunction, and to take and notify an order as to the prohibition of 'all other books of matters of religion, or policy, or governance'.[1]

In practice a twofold censorship developed. Plays for performance were, from 1581 to 1610, censored by Edmund Tilney, the Master of the Revels, whereas printed plays were at first mainly the concern of the Wardens of the Stationers' Company. When however in 1583 Whitgift became Archbishop the licensing of printed books became more stringent. In 1586 the Star Chamber Act, for which Whitgift was responsible, concentrated the censorship 'of all ordinary books, including plays, in the hands of the archbishop and bishop' and on 31 June 1588

an official list of deputies was issued by the archbishop, and amongst these were several who had authorized books before and after 1586. These deputies, and other correctors whose names appear in the register at later dates, are as a rule traceable as episcopal chaplains, prebendaries of St. Paul's, or holders of London benefices. Occasionally laymen were appointed. The main work of correction now fell to these officials, but books were still sometimes allowed by the archbishop or bishop in person, or by the Privy Council or some member of that body.[2]

By 1593, Chambers continues,

the proportion of cases submitted to the ecclesiastical deputies sensibly begins to slacken, although the continuance of conditional entries shows that some caution was exercised. An intervention of the prelates in 1599 reversed the tendency again. As regards plays in particular the wardens received a sharp reminder 'that noe playes be printed except they be allowed by such as haue authority'.

Antonio's Revenge, it should be noted, received a conditional licence in that year; so that it must have been passed in the end by one of Whitgift's deputies.

This first decade of the seventeenth century is of crucial importance, for it saw the publication of the first two quartos of *Hamlet* in a period of stringent censorship. The average number of censors per year rose to about thirteen; and between 1604 and 1607 (omitting 1603 because there were many state publications) the number rose to sixteen.[3] This increase in the number of censors was perhaps occasioned by the growth of the book trade. Certainly the figures reveal an upward trend – from about 110 publications annually in 1601–2, to about to 130 in 1604–5, and then to 150-odd in 1606. The number drops to 137 in 1607, but if we add the seventeen plays licensed separately in 1607 by the Revels Office, which thereafter assumed responsibility for the licensing of printed plays, it seems to suggest that the task of censorship had become so heavy that this wider delegation of responsibility had become necessary, and was an improvement on the older system – which had caused a play to be censored for public performance by Tilney and again by the ecclesiastical correctors if the play was printed subsequently. When we consider also the increasing vigilance exemplified by the Act of Abuses in 1606, there are no grounds for believing in a relaxation of the censorship of plays in the first decade of the century. Sir Walter Greg's study of *Doctor Faustus* in which he attests his belief in the stringency of the censorship at that time – as does F.S. Boas – is a further indication that the argument is sound.[4] The Kydian revenge drama, and the Italianate phase which followed it, developed under the watchful eyes of the correctors.

One corrector in particular engages our attention because he issued a licence for the printing of *Hamlet* (i.e. Q1) on 26 July 1602. He was Zacharias Pasfield, a prebendary of St. Paul's, who acted as censor between August 1600 and December 1610.[5] That he was a trusted member of the establishment is evident from his licensing some 38 per cent of the total corrected in 1601, 37 per cent in 1602; 19 per cent in 1603 (ten other censors were at work in this year); 50 per cent in 1604; 18 per cent in 1605; 9 per cent in 1606; and 16 per cent in 1607. He, in 1604, was also responsible, together with the Bishop of London and another ecclesiastic, for allowing the published report on the Hampton Court Conference. When we consider also that the Wardens in 1601–2 licensed only ballads, music and non-controversial works which constituted about 25 per cent of the quota in those years, Pasfield's contribution was about 50 per cent annually.

Now it is certain that Pasfield would not have passed *Hamlet* if it in any way conflicted with the teachings of the Anglican Church; so it is pertinent to ask what exactly the Church's teaching about ghosts actually was. The general Protestant position was, as Dover Wilson says,

> that ghosts, while occasionally they might be angels, were generally nothing but devils, who 'assumed' – such was the technical word – the form of departed friends or relatives, in order to work bodily or spiritual harm upon those to whom they appeared.

Dover Wilson also adds that James I

> expressly dissociates himself from those who believe in angelic apparitions, on the ground that since the time of Christ the age of miracles has ceased.

Roman Catholics also believed that Satan and his devils could appear as ghosts, but they believed in addition that the souls of the dead might, in special circumstances, return from Purgatory. Such an occurrence according to Le Loyer was however relatively rare:

> Souls do not appear so often as do Angels and Demons.[6]

The Church of Elizabeth denied the existence of Purgatory and considered its rejection of this essential part of Roman Catholic doctrine so important that one of the Articles of Religion specifically deals with it. In 1553 Article XXIII of the Forty-Two Articles read as follows:

> The doctrine of Scholeaucthores concerning Purgatorie, Pardones, worshipping, and adoration as well of images, as of reliques, and also inuocation of sainctes, is a fonde thing vainlie feigned, and grounded vpon no warraunt of scripture, but rather repugnant to the woorde of God.

27

By 1563 what had become the Thirty-Eight Articles were ratified, Article XXIII of the original Articles now becoming Article XXII, the only change being that 'The Romish doctrine' was substituted for 'The doctrine of Scholeaucthores' – and it has continued in this form until this day.[7] In contrast, the Roman Catholic position on Purgatory is no different now from what it was in Elizabethan times:

(a) Purgatory is a place or state in which souls suffer for a time after death until they are purified from the effects of their sins.
(b) Those souls go to Purgatory who depart this life in venial sin, or who have not fully paid the debt of temporal punishment due to those sins of which the guilt has been forgiven.
(c) Hell is the place or state of punishment in which the wicked who die in mortal sin suffer forever with the devil and his Angels.[8]

No Elizabethan corrector therefore would have accepted for publication a play which contained a 'good' ghost from Purgatory. Samuel Harsnett, from whose *A Declaration of Egregious Popish Impostures* (1603) Shakespeare took the names of his devils in *King Lear*, was a corrector and a prebendary of St. Paul's like Pasfield when *Hamlet* was licensed, and was, predictably, wholly antagonistic to Purgatory:

> whereof there is not one sparkle to the seene in all the booke of God: which fire the pillers of Gods Church have alwies held for an Heathenish dreame, and a Platonick fiction, whose coles, brands, and skorching flames haue beene purgatives for mens purses, houses and lands, and have annihilated more mettall, and euaporated it into smoake, then all the conceited fire-works of our Chymicall Impostors have done ... And the conceited opinion of this imaginarie fire hath brought more sooty-soiled souls into hell, in a fancied hope of a purge after this life, which they can never meete withall, then any one cheating devise besides in all the Popes budget.[9]

The Church indeed took such a serious view of the heresy of Purgatory that William Allen, formerly Principal of St. Mary Hall, Oxford, a recusant who later became a cardinal, fled to the continent and published at Antwerp in 1565 *A Defense and Declaration of the Catholicke Churches Doctrine, touching Purgatory, and prayers for the soules departed.* He was ordered to be arrested, apparently in the belief that he had returned to England. The date of the order is 21 February 1576, and he is described as 'Alen, who wrote the late booke of Purgatory'. Again, a Proclamation of March 1569 ordering the surrender of 'seditious bookes' specifically names the works of eight recusants, Allen's being among those singled out. His tract appears yet again in a catalogue of Popish books compiled by William Fulke (who became Vice-Chancellor of Cambridge in 1581) in three successive publications during 1579–80. Fulke's list had apparently the same function as the Catholic Index and provides invaluable evidence of the activities of English recusant writers who had fled overseas. It can be seen, for example, that Richard Bristow, a former Fellow of Exeter College, Oxford, strongly supported Allen's book and had attacked in 1577 a reply which Fulke had made to Allen.[10]

Further evidence of the censorship's close watch upon works dealing with ghosts and Purgatory in the important first decade of the seventeenth century can be seen in the following:

(a) A book in answer to Bellarmine's *De Purgatorio Disputatione* was licensed in 1600 by Archbishop Whitgift himself.[11]

(b) Deacon and Walker's *Dialogical Discourses of Spirits and Devils* received the attention of Richard Bancroft, Bishop of London, and Pasfield in 1601.[12]

(c) Le Loyer's *A Treatise of Specters* (1605), to which reference has already been made, in its complete form included a defence of the Catholic Church's attitude to Purgatory, but only the first non-controversial book of the original four appeared in the licensed translation. May Yardley, having summarized the contents of this first book, asks, 'Can we guess that it was not his (the translator's) intention to end here, but that when he came to examine the later books he found them far different from what he expected and too heretical to offer to the Protestant monarch?[13] I suggest that it is easier to imagine that Jones, the translator, knew very well what he was about and had no intention of colliding with the censor – who in this case was Pasfield himself.'[14] Jones was indeed so sensitive to the official attitude that when Le Loyer at one point speaks disparagingly of Lavater he adds a marginal note craving the reader's indulgence, and further covers himself in his introduction by asking the reader to excuse Le Loyer's 'Romish' upbringing – which apart from the reference just noted is not at all evident.

It is clear then that ghosts in the Elizabethan age were not just old wives' tales or pieces of unimportant dramatic mechanism or literary embellishments – they were part of the religious doctrines of the times and their place of origin was a matter of bitter controversy. What, for example, of Protestants who fell into the hands of the Spanish Inquisition?

> And being put down well near dead, and very faint of this torment of the stappado, they asked me in particular, What other things touching the church of Rome I believed not in? I told them, that I had confessed in all things in faith as it was taught in England. Then, said they, say on, what it is. I told them, that there could be no remission of sins bought for money, as was in Spain by the Pope's bulls. But that all sins were forgiven only by the death of Christ. And that this doctrine was taught in England. Wherein I believed. What sayest thou of confession? said Licientado Gasco. I told them, that it was not necessary for salvation. Nor purgatory was there none; and holy water a ceremony not good for any thing.[15]

The Protestant record is no less black. A very strict watch was kept at ports to ensure that no recusant literature was smuggled in, as A.C. Southern records in his *Elizabethan Recusants Prose*, and the penalty was death. Thomas Alfield was hanged at Tyburn on 6 July 1585 for bringing in and distributing copies of Allen's *True Sincere and Modest Defence*. 'He admitted at his trial that he had brought five or six hundred copies of the book in and had managed to distribute a few of them before he was apprehended.'[16] This vigilance, it may be added, continued till at least 1640.

The Catholic doctrine of Purgatory was no abstract theological matter to be argued in the study or in the cloisters. It could as we have seen become a matter of life and death. But it could also become a joke. Richard Tarlton was the most famous clown at the end of the sixteenth century. He was one of Elizabeth's private jesters and 'an ordinary Groom of her Majesty's Chamber'. His protégé, Robert Armin, became one of Shakespeare's clowns. Tarlton died in 1588 and on 20 August 1590 there appeared in the Stationers' Register the following entry:

> Allowed vnto them for theire Copie vnder the hande of the Bisshop of London, and bothe the Wardens, TARLTONS newes

out of Purgatory, or a caskett full of pleasant conceiptes stuffed with delightfull devises and quaint myrthe as his humour maye afoorde to feede gentlemens fancies.

In this pamphlet[17] the author falls asleep under a tree and dreams that 'the verye ghoast of Richard Tarlton ... pale and wan, sat him down by me on the grasse'. Tarlton comforts him, for he is frightened:

> for although thou see me heere in likenes of a spirite, yet thinke me to bee one of those Familiares Lares that were rather pleasantly disposed then endued with any hurtfull influence, as Hob Thrust, Robin Goodfellow and such like spirites ... Theerefore sith my appearance to thee is in the resemblance of a spirite, think that I am as pleasant a goblin as the rest.

But the author is still scared and he reacts to the apparition as an orthodox Elizabethan Protestant would:

> In nomine Jesu, avoid Sathan, for ghost thou art none, but a very divell, for the soules of them which art departed, if the sacred principles of theologie be true, never returne into the world againe till the generall resurrection, for either are they plast in heaven, from whence they come not to intangle themselues with other cares, but sit continuallye before the seat of the Lambe, singing Alleluia to the highest; or else they are in hell. And this is a profound and certain aphorisme, Ab inferis nulla est redemptio. Upon these conclusive premises, depart from me, Sathan, the resemblance of whomsoever thou doost carrye.

Tarlton's ghost replies:

> why you horson dunce, think you to set Dick Tarlton non plus with your aphorismes ... what doo you make heaven and hell contraria immediata – so contrarie, that there is no meane betwixt them, but that either a mans soule must in poste haste goe presently to God, or else with a whirlewind and a vengeance goe to the divell! yes; yes, my good brother, there is a quoddam tertium, a third place that all our great grandmothers have talkt of, that Dant hath so learnedly writ of, and that is purgatorie. What, sir, are we wiser then all our forefathers? and they not onlye feared that place in life, but found it after their death: or els was there much land and annuall pensions given in vaine to morrowe – mass priests for dirges, trentals and such like decretals of devotion, whereby the soules in purgatorie were the sooner aduanced into the quiet estate of

31

heaven Nay, more, how many popes and holy bishops of Rome whose cannons cannot erre, have taught us what this purgatory is: and yet if thou wert so incredulous that thou wouldest neither believe our olde beldames, nor the good Bishops: yet take Dick Tarlton once for thine authour, who is now come from purgatory, and if any upstart Protestant deny, if thou hast no place of Scripture to confirme it, say as Pithagoras scolllers did (ipse dixit) and to all bon companions it shall stand for a principle.

The author 'could not but smile at the madde merrye doctrine of my freend Richard, and therefore . . . I praied him to tell me what Purgatory is and what they be that are resident there; as one willing to doo me such a favour, he sat him down and began thus'.

The ghost then describes his journey to Purgatory, where finally he enters a great hall where sit the Popes,

except the first thirtie after Christ, and they went presently to heaven: and the reason was, because Purgatorie was then a-building, and not fully finished. In those seates, I say, the popes sit triumphantly with their pontificalibus, and their triple crowns, and yet a-biding paines of purgatorie as well as the meanest in all the house, equallye proportioned according to the measure of their sinnes; some for false wresting the scriptures, others for ambition, some for covetousness, gluttonie, extortion, symonye, wrath, pride, envie, many for sloth, and idleness, and some I can tell you have come hither for wenching matters.

The pamphlet continues in the same tone of mockery, and becomes increasingly scurrilous.

A few months later another piece, *The Cobler of Caunterburie*, appeared.[18] In this a cobbler sets himself up as a 'corrector', to which 'Robin Goodfellow' in his introductory epistle says: 'A cobler become a corrector! ho, ho, ho; . . . tush, what of higher powers, what of Vniversities?' The author's intention apparently was to continue the Purgatory joke, while scoring off the earlier pamphlet. These pamphlets are important because they seem to be the first writings in which a ghost from Purgatory appears in Elizabethan literature. The first, as we have seen, was licensed by the Bishop of London and the second by three officiating wardens. And it is also obvious from the second that Purgatory was certainly regarded as a matter for a corrector. It is also worthy of note that Tarlton's pamphlet was so popular that it was reprinted twice. Also, a reprint of *The Cobler of Caunterburie* is recorded in the Stationers' Register (June 1600) and reads thus: 'Provided yt be not printed without bringing better Auctoritie'. Thus re-publication was not automatic and required a fresh scrutiny by the correctors.[19]

So far then it has been demonstrated that Elizabeth's censors diligently carried out her orders as to printed books and pamphlets, but similar evidence about plays was less easy to come by because no dramatist was fool enough to produce an anti-Protestant play. Recusants did indeed produce Catholic books and pamphlets but for the most part they fled the country before doing so. The only course open therefore was to read most of the Elizabethan drama and extract from it references to Purgatory, for it was just possible that the censor's attitude was more lenient towards Purgatory in plays. As we shall see, however, this hypothesis was proved to be false. What follows therefore is based upon a study of the works of at least twenty-five of the most important Elizabethan dramatists, to which are added Dodsley's collection of old plays and the collection of Brandl.

In order to clear the ground we may first put aside the purely metaphorical use of Purgatory to describe a trying experience, often used in a jocular context without any satire or ridicule being intended. Such usage was common in Catholic England and it continued after Elizabethan times. But let us look first at John Pikeryng's play *Horestes* (1567). It contains a Vice called 'Revenge' who incites 'Horestes' to revenge himself, and as the Vice is manifestly evil as well as comic the moral confusion of the hero is plain when he accepts Revenge as a 'Messenger of heuenly gostes'. Horestes is reluctant to act but Revenge goads him on and eventually Horestes symbolically hands over Clytemnestra to the Vice, who, we are to assume, helps to kill her. Revenge rejoices in the remorse which Horestes will feel and courts 'Fame':

A new master, a new! naye I wyll go;
Tout, tout, Horestes is be com a newe man.
Now he sorroweth: to bad that his is so;
Yet I wyll dresse him, by his oundes, and I can.
Who, Saintie amen, God morrowe, mystres Nan!
By his oundes, I am glad to se the so trycke.
Nay, may I be so bould at your lyppes to haue a lycke?
Jesus, how coye do you make the same!

33

You neauer knew me afore, I dare saye:
In fayth, in fayth, I was to blame,
That I made no courchey to you by the waye.
Who, berladye, Nan, thou art trym and gaye;
Woundes of me, she hath winges also;
Who, wother, with a myschefe, doust thou thinke for to go?
Heauuen? or to hell? to purgatorye or spayne?
To Venys? to pourtugaull ...

The association of Purgatory with Catholic countries is clearly
marked, and so is revenge, the implication being that only in such
ungodly countries will Horestes' deed be approved. By seeking a
new master the Vice means that he will look for another victim,
and he echoes the popular sentiment that women were specially
prone to revenge themselves:

I wyll seke a new master, yf I can him finde:
Yet I am in good comfort, for this well I knowe,
That the moste parte of wemen to me be full kynde.

We should also note that Purgatory is a Vice's joke, for we shall
encounter this again.

Next there is the late Morality play *New Custom* (1573) which is
markedly anti-Catholic. The characters include 'Perverse Doctrine' – an old Popish priest; 'Ignorance' – 'another but elder'; and
'New Custom' – 'a minister'. Ignorance says:

They haue revoked divers old heresies out of hell.
As against transubstantiation, purgatory, and the mass.

Perverse Doctrine agrees and refers to a 'young upstart lad' who
'teacheth that All our doings are naught'. New Custom is
scornful:

Then brought they in their monsters, their masses, their lights,
Their torches at noon to darken our sight:
Their popes and their pardons, the *purgatories* for souls:
Their mocking of the church and flinging of coals.

. . . .
I said that the mass and such trumpery as that
Popery, *purgatory*, pardons, were flat
Against God's word and primitive constitution,
Crept in through covetousness and superstition ...

And again we see that revenge is evil, for Perverse Doctrine goes
on:

34

                              I will batter thy head
        Though I hang therefore, I care not, I
        So I be revenged on a slave, ere I die.
        Sacrament of God! who hath heard such a knave?
                        (Dodsley, Vol. III, pp. 10, 17, 19, 24)

   In *The Conflict of Conscience* (1581) by Nathaniel Wood, a
minister of Norwich, the Pope is Satan's 'son' and 'darling dear'
who has

                              devised very well
        Many pretty toys to keep men's soul from hell,
        Live they never so evil here and wickedly,
        As masses, trentals, pardons, and scala coeli.
                        (Dodsley, Vol. VI, pp. 36–7)

(Trentals was a service of thirty masses, one each day, in order to
ease the soul of a deceased person through Purgatory.) Also in the
play a priest supposed to be speaking in the Scottish dialect
confides:

Far thaw ther frends frea Purgatory te help thea dea believe,
Yet af ther hope, gif need rewh [*sic*] ayre [*sic*], it wawd theam all
   deceive.
Sea wawd awr pilgimage, reliques, trentals, and pardons …

Grim the Collier of Croydon was not printed until 1662 but is
probably earlier than 1600. In its combination of Senecan–
Christian elements and anti-Catholicism it fits the last decade of
the sixteenth century. The ghost of Malbecco is brought before
the 'ever-dreaded judges of black hell' whom Pluto addresses:

        Grim Minos, Aeacus, and Rhadamanth,
        Lords of Cocytus, Styx, and Phlegethon,
        Princes of darkness, Pluto's ministers,
        Know that the greatness of his present cause
        Hath made ourselves in person sit a judge,
        To hear th'arraignment of Malbeccos's ghost.
        Stand forth, thou ghastly pattern of despair,
        And to this powerful synod tell thy tale …

St. Dunstan, 'the bald-pate friar', as Belphegor, a devil, describes
him, is satirized and Purgatory is mentioned jocularly by Robin
Goodfellow, who is also known as Akercock, another devil:

She gat me up a staff, and breaks my head.
But I'll no longer serve so curs'd a dame;
I'll run as far first as my legs will bear me.
What shall I do? to hell I dare not go,
Until my master's twelve months be expir'd,
And here to stay with Mistress Marian –
Better to be so long in purgatory.

(Dodsley, Vol. VIII, pp. 393, 428)

Anti-Catholicism and the attack on Purgatory continued when James I came to the throne. In *When you see me* by Samuel Rowley (1605 – Malone Society Reprint 1952) Purgatory once again is an anti-Catholic joke, put into the mouth of Henry VIII's jester Will Somers, who is here addressing Wolsey:

Good newes for you my Lord Cardinall, for one of the old wemen Waterbearers told me for certain that last Friday all the belles in Rome Rang backward, there was a thousand Derges sung, sixe hundred aue-maries said, euerie man washt his face in holy water, the peopel crossing and blessing themseues to send them a new Pope, for the old is gon to purgatory. (ll. 213 ff.)

In more serious vein the young Prince Edward asks Cranmer:

I doe beleeue both Heauen and Hell:
Doe you know any third place for the soules abode
Cald'd Purgatorie, as some would haue me thinke.

Cranmer answers by putting a direct question:

How thinkes your Grace, is there a place of Purgatorie or no?

And the Prince replies:

Truly I think none ...
But thinke ye Tutor that the compasse of that Heauen and hell,
Is able to containe those soules so numberlesse,
That euer breathed since the first breath was giuen,
Without a Tertium, or a third place?

Cranmer answers:

Who put these doubts within your Graees head
Are like their owne beleefe, slite, and vnregarde,
And as easily answered and confuted:
Quod est infinitum, non habet finem,

36

Coelum est opus Dei, opus Dei est infinitum:
Ergo Coelum est infinitum.

Yet another attack on Purgatory is made by the Queen:

Pray tell the King then, what Scripture haue yee,
To teach religion in an vnknowne language?
Instruct the ignorant to kneele to Saints,
By bare-foote pilgrimage to visite shrines,
For mony to release from Purgatorie,
The vildest villaine, theefe, or murderer,
All this the people must belieue you can,
Such is the dregs of Romes religion.

(ll. 2253 ff.)

By far the most violently anti-Catholic play was *The Devil's Charter* (1607 – Tudor Facsimile Texts) by Barnabe Barnes, which was played before King James. In this the villain is Pope Alexander VI,

A Pope by nature full of fraud, and pride;
Ambitious, avaricious, shameless, deuelish.

Alexander (like the Friar in *Bussy d'Ambois*) is a conjurer of devils, in addition to his satanic accomplishments. In spite of all however he claims to be 'Christ's Vicar General' chosen on earth and has the

power to bind and loose men's sins,
And souls, on earth, in hell, and purgatory.

Bernardo, who assists Alexander in the murder of Astor and Phillippo, blames the Pope thus:

Were it not that my conscience hath been fired,
With flames of purgatory by the Pope,
I never could endure such villainy.

And Baglioni, a creature of Cesare Borgia, who compounds poisons for the Pope, when he dies says:

in conscience I am guilty of mine own death.
Oh the pangs of hell and purgatory!

In the same year (1607) in the anonymous *The Puritan Widow* (2.1) Purgatory is used as a confidence trick although the play is not primarily anti-Catholic.

37

Other dramatists in whose works Purgatory is mentioned in a context which implies Protestant ridicule are Marlowe, Dekker and Webster. In *Doctor Faustus* when Faustus, invisible with the help of Mephistopheles, snatches the Pope's meat and wine a bishop says:

> Please it your holinesse, I thinke it be some Ghost crept out of Purgatory, and now is come vnto your holinesse for his pardon.
> POPE. It may be so:
> Go then command our Priests to sing a Dirge,
> To lay the fury of this same troublesome ghost.
>
> (3.2.79–84)

In the 'A' text the Pope then crosses himself three times, and in the 'B' text Faustus then says:

> How now? must euery bit be spiced with a Crosse?
> Nay then take that.

In 'A': Faustus then hits him a 'boxe of the eare'.
In 'B' the Pope goes on:

> O I am slaine, help me my Lords:
> O come and help to beare my body hence:
> Dam'd be this soule for euer, for this deed.

Only a Protestant audience, to whom Purgatory was 'a fond thing vainly invented', would treat this as a joke.

Similarly in *The White Devil*, Lucian's *Menippus* – a satire on the Underworld – is equated with Purgatory by Webster's Flamineo, who by so doing speaks like an Elizabethan Protestant instead of the Catholic he is:

> O Lucian, thy ridiculous purgatory! To find Alexander the Great cobbling shoes, Pompey tagging points, and Julius Caesar making hair buttons, Hannibal selling blacking, and Augustus crying garlic, Charlemagne selling lists by the dozen, and King Pepin crying apples in a cart drawn with one horse!
> (5.6.110–15)

Dekker's references to Purgatory are very interesting because he also alludes to St. Patrick, who was supposed to be the Keeper of Purgatory. In his Old *Fortunatus* (1599) Andelocia and Shadow are disguised as Irish costermongers and swear by

38

St. Patrick. When the masquerade is almost over Andelocia cries:

> Ha, ha, ha. So this is admirable, Shadow, here end my torments in St. Patrick's Purgatory. (4.2)

Similarly in *The Honest Whore* (Part 2, Act 1. Sc. 1) Carolo and Lodovico jest:

> LODOVICO. Why, then, should all your chimney-sweepers likewise be Irishmen?
> CAROLO. Faith that's soon answered, for St. Patrick, you know, keeps purgatory; he makes the fire, and his countrymen could do nothing, if they cannot sweep the chimneys.

In the same play Bryan is slightingly referred to as 'Little Saint Patrick' (Part 2, Act 3, Sc. 1). Thus as Purgatory was a target for ridicule it was inevitable that St. Patrick should also be attacked. It also seems possible that because he was synonymous with Ireland he shared the antagonism felt towards the Catholicism of the Irish. In *Misogynus* (1577) a ridiculous priest swears by St. Patrick; in *The Life of Sir John Oldcastle* the Irish murderer does so too; and in *The White Devil* there are several derogatory references to the 'wild Irish' (e.g. 4.2.95).

These then are the references to Purgatory, with a doctrinal connotation, which appear in Elizabethan drama outside Shakespeare. I may of course have missed some but from this body of evidence it seems clear that two courses were open to dramatists: they either as Protestants specifically attacked Purgatory as a Popish doctrine, or they treated it as a joke against the Catholics. In not a single play is there the slightest indication that Purgatory exists, nor is there a 'real' ghost from Purgatory. Hence it may be concluded that the censorship was completely effective in suppressing what it regarded as a heresy. It should be noted also that in *Horestes* and *When you see me* it was a Vice's or jester's joke, thus being in complete accord with its comic association with Tarlton. The hypothesis that the censorship was more lenient with works of fiction, such as the drama, cannot be substantiated, and I would add here that a similar theory – allowing playwrights more freedom to write political satire – was investigated by John Peter in his *Complaint and Satire in Early English Literature*. He concluded that 'this is surely dubious. So far as the printing of plays is concerned the responsibility for authorizing their appearance was vested in those very authorities who had suppressed the satiric books, the Archbishop of Canterbury and the Bishop of London.'[20]

As to the prose writings of the period I have made little investigation but without delving very deeply all the comments I encountered among lay writers agreed entirely with the ecclesiastics. For example, Reginald Scot, iconoclast though he was, wrote of Purgatory:

> Which place was not remembered by Moses ... which without doubt should not have been omitted, if any such place of purgatorie had beene then, as the pope hath lately devised for his private and speciall lucre.[21]

Thomas Nashe voices the same sentiments:

> What, is our religion all auarice and no good works? Because we may not build Monasteries, or haue Masses, Dirges, or Trentals sung for our soules are there no deeds of mercy that God hath enjoyned vs?[22]

Of particular interest is Cyril Tourneur, whose *The Atheist's Tragedy* is supposed by some commentators to have a 'good' ghost from Purgatory, for in his *The Worldes Folly* he uses Purgatory for the purposes of fiction and yet ends the piece by saying 'there cannot be such a thing'.

Shakespeare has only two specific references to Purgatory (leaving *Hamlet* aside) in his plays. In *Othello* it is a joke. Emilia says:

> but for the whole world, who would not make her husband a cuckold to make him a monarch? I should venture purgatory for't. (4.3.76–8)

But it is an even funnier joke if you hear it as an Elizabethan Protestant who regarded Venice as a place full of whores and cuckolded husbands. At the risk of spoiling the joke however it should be pointed out that adultery to a Roman Catholic is a mortal sin which could lead to eternal damnation.

The second reference consists of Romeo's words:

> There is no world without Verona's walls,
> But purgatory, torture, hell itself.
>
> (3.3.17–18)

Here again Purgatory is associated with mortal sin – the killing of a man in a duel – of which more will be said later, and this from

The

both a Protestant and Catholic standpoint is nonsense. For the moment however it is clear that the existence of Purgatory is not supported by the play – as we would expect, in view of the censor's attitude.

To sum up, there are strong grounds for believing that the censorship jealously guarded against the doctrine of Purgatory as expressed in recusant literature, that its attitude to the drama was just as stringent, and that very probably there was no exception to this rule in the licensing of books. To put the matter in more graphic form: it is impossible to find a single Elizabethan who could, in print, voice his belief in Purgatory. Only a Roman Catholic would have wished to do so, for to Protestants Purgatory was either a joke or a confidence trick, or both. But it should be added that not even a Roman Catholic of the time would have believed in a revenge ghost from Purgatory – Heywood, as we have seen, would certainly have not. Neither would Peter Thyraeus, a German Jesuit who wrote *Of Haunted Places* (1598) – to whom both Samuel Harsnett and Robert Burton make reference – for he believed apparitions 'to be devils, or the souls or damned men that seek revenge, or els souls out of Purgatory that seek ease';[23] revenge is associated with Hell, not Purgatory. Le Loyer also, in the part of his book that was never published in England, insists that the final test of an apparition is whether it utters anything contrary to Christian doctrine. Thus, as revenge is forbidden in the Bible, a revenge ghost could only be Satan or one of his devils – and on this point the Elizabethan censorship were in complete agreement.

It is clear that a revenge ghost in the drama would have to have come from Hell if it were to conform to Christian doctrine and so satisfy the censor. Thus it is quite inconceivable that there should be a 'good' revenge ghost which came, in addition, from the Catholic Purgatory because in Protestant eyes – Pasfield's eyes – a playwright would not only have blasphemed but have uttered heresy also. One can only conclude that such a ghost was 'allowed' because it was clearly evil to a theatre audience and this in turn suggests that the audience was mainly Protestant.

Dover Wilson claimed:

The ghost in *Hamlet* comes, not from a mythical Tartarus, but from the place of departed spirits in which post-medieval England, despite a veneer of Protestantism, still believed at the end of the sixteenth century.[24]

41

But as against this, far from Protestantism being merely a 'veneer':

> In the course of Elizabeth's long reign, the younger genera-
> tion, brought up on the Bible and Prayer book, and sharing
> the struggle for national existence against Spain, Pope, and
> Jesuits, became for the most part fervent Protestants.[25]

So wrote G.M. Trevelyan. That he was right and Dover Wilson
wrong can be seen in the increasingly anti-Catholic tone of the
drama. When we also consider that no dramatist can afford –
literally – to offend his audience, this too suggests that Shakespeare wrote for a mainly Protestant audience, as did his fellow
playwrights. Thus Shakespeare's audience had already made up its
mind about Purgatory before the Ghost was even conceived, and
even if there had been Catholics present they too would have
agreed that the Ghost was evil.

3

The Fellow in the Cellarage

IN SPITE OF the long history of *Hamlet* it was not until 1935, when Dover Wilson published *What Happens in Hamlet*, that the Ghost began to receive the attention it deserves. Only a handful of scholars, notably among them being T.A. Spalding and F.W. Moorman, had studied ghosts and the supernatural in Shakespeare's time.[1] In this chapter I wish to look closely at the Ghost that Shakespeare created, as we now have a clearer notion of how ghosts were treated by other dramatists and we know the code the censorship observed.

Dover Wilson argued that the Ghost was Catholic and that Shakespeare had Christianized 'the stock apparition of the Elizabethan theatre ... a classical puppet, borrowed from Seneca, a kind of Jack-in-the-box, popping up from Tartarus at appropriate moments'. On the first point – that the Ghost is Catholic – he was correct because it regrets not having had the Last Rites of the Roman Catholic Church:

> Unhouseled, disappointed, unaneled.
>
> (1.5.77)

These terms, as I.J. Semper shows, mean 'uncommunicated', 'unshriven', and 'unanointed', and are unmistakably the last sacraments 'although for metrical reasons [Shakespeare] does not follow the exact order of ministration – penance, viaticum, and extreme unction'.[2] Dover Wilson also pointed out that as the Ghost is

> Doomed for a certain term to walk the night,
> And for the day confined to fast in fires,
> Till the foul crimes done in my days of nature
> Are burnt and purged away
>
> (1.5.10–13)

it comes from Purgatory, as Dante described it. I.J. Semper adds that in the *Summa Theologica* we read:

43

The chief purpose of the punishment of purgatory is to cleanse us from the remains of sin; and consequently the pain of fire only is ascribed to purgatory, because fire cleanses and consumes,

and he also quotes from *The Golden Legend*:

They that be middle good, be they that have with them something to be burnt and purged.

Dover Wilson therefore claimed that such a ghost would have an immediate appeal to a contemporary audience because he believed in their 'veneer' of Protestantism, as we have already seen. And he went on to argue that problems of Elizabethan spiritualism were involved – Shakespeare had made good use of a topical theme. Hamlet and Horatio, he claimed, were Protestants since they were both students of Wittenberg, Luther's university, and were therefore sceptical about the Ghost until the Play Scene finally proved that it had spoken the truth – although immediately after meeting the Ghost Hamlet was convinced 'that he is a real ghost, and no demon masquerading in human form'. And as for the audience:

At the end of the first act, the Elizabethan audience could no more be certain of the honesty of the Ghost and of the truth of the story it had related, than the perplexed hero himself.[3]

I.J. Semper's view is substantially the same:

A study of the ghost scenes in *Hamlet* in the light of purgatorial doctrine corroborates the view … which has been summarized by Dr. John Dover Wilson in a single terse statement: 'The Ghost is Catholic: he comes from Purgatory'.

Roy W. Battenhouse however disagreed. He pointed out that

the Ghost as poetically presented has neither the mind nor the action of a Christian Purgatory ghost; that his character fits, rather, a spirit from pagan hell, a region considered purgatorial in classical but not Catholic doctrine.[4]

The Ghost, he said, does not come to ask help for his own soul: its message begins and ends with a command – revenge; the tale the Ghost unfolds lacks Christian perspective: facts are not presented in a frame of interpretation such as a soul in grace should have; it does not pass the four tests of goodness listed by Lavater; Hamlet

himself never mentions Purgatory and wavers between viewing
the Ghost as a bringer of 'airs from heaven or blasts from hell' –
the only alternatives he ever considers; and other characters, like
Horatio, do not accept the Ghost as a spirit from Purgatory.
Battenhouse therefore concluded that

> the Ghost, then, does not come from a Catholic Purgatory but
> from an afterworld exactly suited to fascinate the imagination
> and understanding of the humanist intellectual of the Renais-
> sance.

The most detailed, and in many respects the most convincing,
study of the ghost lore of the time has been made by Eleanor
Prosser, who has shown that the controversy about ghosts
stemmed from the Protestant reaction against the 'Catholic belief
in the efficacy of good works and thus of prayers for the dead.' In
the Protestant view the soul was either saved or damned at the
moment of death and so went either to Heaven or to Hell – there
was no Purgatory and no return. Thus all ghosts were demons.
The Catholic standpoint however did allow for a soul's return
from Purgatory, although such an occurrence was rare, but 'not
one instance has ever been noted of a Purgatorial spirit's
commanding revenge, either his own or God's ... [for] they
could not return to further any temporal end, much less any
purpose violating God's commandments'. She also discusses the
various tests that were advocated by the contemporary authorities, the Protestant Lavater and the Catholics Le Loyer and
Taillepied, from which she concludes that for neither Protestant
nor Catholic would the Ghost be established as 'unquestionably
demonic' by the end of the first scene, but every member of
Shakespeare's audience would be prepared to test it according to
the beliefs of his own faith. When the Ghost does appear to
Hamlet 'Shakespeare made the Ghost act like a devil because he
wanted his audience to notice that it acts like a devil'. But she
says:

> I am not suggesting that we are consciously aware of the
> Ghost's true nature or that we want Hamlet to ignore its terrible
> revelations ... We have been asked to test the Ghost, but have
> not been allowed an easy answer ... If we could unequivocably
> pronounce the Ghost a demon and its command a damnable
> temptation the tragedy would be destroyed.

Then after commenting on 'To be' she adds:

The Ghost, then, is not a mere demonic tempter, blinding Hamlet, tricking him into an obvious evil course. On the contrary, in one sense it opens Hamlet's eyes – shattering all conventional ethical assumptions, forcing him to define his own code, to determine for himself his own course.[5]

Now all these studies really depend upon a single unstated premise, and that is that Purgatory whether classical or Catholic was a fit subject for controversy and speculation in the contemporary drama, but, as we have seen, the censorship would not have allowed such freedom of discussion. Purgatory, for the correctors, simply did not exist, and it was heresy to claim that it did. If, as Dover Wilson claimed, the Ghost came from the Catholic Purgatory, Hamlet, the Protestant student of Wittenberg, has surely turned Catholic when he finally believes in the Ghost – and so has Horatio. It is difficult to believe that any Elizabethan corrector would have allowed such a play. And if Battenhouse is correct we have the option of having a Catholic Ghost from a pagan Underworld – in other words he postulates a degree of doctrinal confusion for which there is no evidence; Catholics believed in Purgatory and Protestants did not.

To clarify matters I think we must now recognize that Dover Wilson was wrong in claiming that Shakespeare was the first to Christianize the revenge ghost, for this had already happened in the earliest translations of Seneca, as we have seen. That the Ghost is Catholic, however, there is no doubt and its regret for not having received the Last Rites would not endear it to a Protestant censor because the sacrament of Extreme Unction disappeared from the revised Prayer Book, as imposed by Edward VI's parliament, in 1552, and had no place thereafter in the liturgical reformation which took place.[6] It follows therefore that performance of these rites as a sacrament would be a violation of Elizabeth's Prayer Book. Also a further point about the Catholicism of the Ghost is that De Voragine's *The Golden Legend*, to which Semper drew attention, was a Papist book banned by the censorship. It is mentioned derisively in *Grim the Collier of Croydon*, and also in *The Conflict of Conscience* and *New Custom*, all of which plays we have already encountered. Thus it would seem that Shakespeare has taken great pains to present the correctors with just the sort of material that would incur their wrath and that it did not can only be explained by its being so manifestly evil that no audience could fail to recognize it as such.

This will be amply borne out when we now turn to the play itself. *Hamlet* begins at midnight, the time traditionally associated with evil. Even today midnight retains its connotations – supernatural, mysterious, evil. In Shakespeare's time feelings were more intense because the Devil himself could appear, so people believed. Even when a writer like Nicholas Brereton in 1626 commented on the hours of the day the association with and fear of midnight is apparent: 'and he that trusteth in God will be safe from the Devil'.[7] For the dramatist then it was a convenient hour for dire doings. Tourneur's villain Vindice says:

> Well, if anything be damned
> It will be twelve o'clock at night; that twelve
> Will never 'scape.
> It is the Judas of the hours, wherein
> Honest salvation is betrayed to sin.
>
> (1.3.68–72)

So too Marlowe's Faustus, in terror as he awaits the coming of Mephistopheles at midnight, says:

> the clock will strike,
> The devil will come, and Faustus must be damn'd.
> (5.2.141–2)

And the Scholars tell us that:

> 'twixt the hours of twelve and one, methought
> I heard him shriek and call aloud for help:
> At which self time the house seemed all on fire,
> With dreadful horror of these damned fiends.
> (5.3.9–12)

Shakespeare of course makes use of the association elsewhere; e.g. in *Macbeth* the Witches are 'secret, black and midnight hags', and Banquo ominously marks the prelude to the murder of Duncan by answering Fleance's

> The moon is down; I have not heard the clock
> (2.1.2)

with

> she goes down at twelve.
> (2.1.3)

Then in *A Midsummer Night's Dream* it is when

47

The iron tongue of midnight hath told twelve
(5.1.372)

that

> The graves all gaping wide,
> Every one lets forth his sprite,
> In the church-way paths to glide.
(5.2.10–12)

And in *Othello* it is 'between twelve and one' that Iago arranges as the time when Roderigo is to kill Cassio. The list of associations then can easily be extended, for the ghosts that haunt Richard III appear at midnight and in *The Merry Wives of Windsor* Fenton's practical joke involves Herne the Hunter appearing ''twixt twelve and one'. And of course later in *Hamlet* Lucianus describes his poison as being of

> midnight weeds collected,
> With Hecate's ban thrice blasted, thrice infected.
(3.2.57–8)

Shakespeare's first audience would also have been aware of the foreign names of the sentries – Italian or Spanish and certainly Catholic. In 1876 C. Elliot Browne suggested that

> the names of Francisco and Bernardo, associated together in this play, had been previously associated in one of the greatest crimes of the sixteenth century. Bernardo Bandini and Francesco de' Pazzi were the assassins of Giuliano de' Medici in the cathedral of Florence. It is well worth noting that in the original Italian cast of *Every Man in his Humour*, to which Shakespeare is said to have contributed, and in which he certainly performed, the principal personage was Lorenzo de' Pazzi, – no doubt chosen as a distinctively Florentine name.[8]

As the play apparently dates from 1598 the comment is apposite. Then Horatio was a name familiar to theatre-goers from *The Spanish Tragedy* – and we should remember too that the Armada had sailed only a few years before. If then Shakespeare had wished to make his sentries and Horatio, Hamlet's closest friend, Protestants why did he choose such inappropriate names? It is clear that in the *Brudermord* the sentries are Catholics, for they exclaim 'Miserere Domine' and 'O holy Anthony of Padua'.[9] The name Horatio in the *Brudermord* is consonant with this setting.

For the keen play-goer there would be a further connection with *The Spanish Tragedy* because with Revenge in the opening scene appears the ghost of Don Andrea who is, or was, a 'martialist', a warrior, and would also, presumably, have been clad in armour. Similarly, 'Marcellus' would probably have sounded Catholic to the groundlings, for it is a saint's name, and to 'the wiser sort' who remembered their *Aeneid* the name, associated with Virgil's Underworld, would belong to the same Hell as Kyd's Don Horatio who encountered 'the ferryman of hell' and the 'infernal king'. It is noteworthy also that in the first fifty-odd lines Horatio's name is used no fewer than eight times, Barnardo's four and Marcellus's three.

As for the Ghost it is 'this thing', 'this dreaded sight', this 'apparition' and 'it'. It is a regal figure, clad in steel from head to foot with a baton in its hand. Only its bearded face is visible. We know who this is of course, because we have known the play from our school days, so that the producer of the play is allowed a certain latitude in presenting it. But the Ghost's method of entry was very important to Shakespeare's first audience. If the Ghost descended from on high it would have been regarded as a spirit from Heaven. If on the other hand the Ghost merely walked on from the wings how could the sentries have regarded it as a ghost? They are armed soldiers on the battlements of a castle, Francisco has already challenged Barnardo and then Horatio and Marcellus, but no one challenges the Ghost. Why not? The Ghost is a figure in armour and they are on guard. They do not challenge because Barnardo identifies 'him' as 'like the King that's dead' – this is a revenant. For Shakespeare's audience however where is the shock and the terror if 'this thing' merely stalks on to the stage – a soldier in armour whose face is very pale (perhaps whitened with flour)?[10] The description that is given later to Hamlet is that it appeared *before* them, not *behind* them, and then 'vanished' from their sight. Only thus could the Ghost seem 'ghostly' – an armed man with a pale face merely walking on and off stage would not do. Also, according to Marcellus, 'it faded'. How could a man in armour 'fade'? It seems therefore that the Ghost Shakespeare's first audience saw made its entrances, and its exists, through the trapdoor in the stage. And if that is so it must have been identified as demonic from the very first scene, for it came from 'Hell', and thus the associations with Don Andrea's ghost and with the Marcellus of Virgil's Underworld are borne out.

It would seem reasonable also to suppose that the onlookers, true to their Catholic names, would have 'crossed themselves for fear' as did the knights of Camelot when they saw the Lady of Shalott. If so their actions would have been viewed with scorn by Protestants in the audience – as they no doubt reacted to the Pope in *Faustus* crossing himself and being boxed on the ear:

> How now? Must every bit be spiced with a cross?
> Nay then, take that.
>
> (3.2.86–7)

Or when they saw Faustus using the sign of the cross in his conjurations:

> sigumque crucis quod nunc facio.[11]
>
> (1.3.21)

Horatio is badly shaken by his first sight of the Ghost. He recognizes the king and clearly recalls (but how?) the suit of armour he had worn when he slew 'the ambitious Norway' in single combat – a duel in fact as part of a wager. So Hamlet's father had been a 'betting man' and as the bet involved killing, clearly in a medieval Christian context he would have been in a state of mortal sin unless he had repented of the slaying. The religious implications will be dealt with more fully later.

We also learn that the son of Fortinbras has gathered a band of mercenaries and is about to invade Denmark in order to regain the territory that his father 'lost'. In consequence Denmark is arming in haste to cope with the threat. Horatio then goes on to compare the Ghost to the portents which preceded the assassination of Julius Caesar when

> The graves stood tenantless, and the sheeted dead
> Did squeak and gibber in the Roman streets
> ... and the moist star,
> Upon whose influence Neptune's empire stands,
> Was sick almost to doomsday with eclipse.
>
> (1.1.115–25)

In other words the portents resembled those of the Day of Judgment, paintings of which had been commonplace in the churches of the audience's grandparents and which were still used by the clergy in sermons to terrify their congregations. Unless the existence of Hell is accepted this passage becomes simply 'poetic'. But to an Elizabethan audience the Doom resembled our own fear of nuclear war – the Dies Irae may have changed in details, but the ultimate horror that may lie ahead of us is more than metaphorical. Similarly we too can share the terror that the dead should walk again. C.S. Lewis rightly stressed the importance of a child's reaction – 'naive and concrete and archaic' – and openly confessed to this kind of 'childishness'.[12] The Ghost's first function in the play is to frighten us and it always does so because while we love our parents and relatives we do not really want them on our doorstep after we have buried them. I think that unless we acknowledge the existence of these fears we deceive ourselves and also fail to recognize one of the elements that has made *Hamlet* so universally popular. The Ghost rises not only from the cellarage of an Elizabethan playhouse, the 'Hell' of the medieval stage, but further back from the primitive part of our minds that as children we share with the ancients. However much learning we accumulate about this play, unless we are frightened we do not share the terrors of the dark, of death, of the grave, and of what may lie beyond. Thus we can share Horatio's courage or rashness in trying to obstruct the Ghost and his addressing it.

He asks if it has foreknowledge that will affect the fate of Denmark – but the 'illusion' remains silent. He then asks, following an old superstition, if it is a miser haunting the scene of hoarded treasure. That the ghosts of misers were considered to be evil can be seen from Marlowe's *The Jew of Malta* in which the villainous Barabas says:

> Now I remember those old women's words,
> Who in my wealth would tell me winter's tales
> And speak of spirits and ghosts that glide by night
> Above the place where treasure hath been hid.
> And now methinks that I am one of those:
> For whilst I live, here lives my soul's sole hope,
> And when I die, here shall my spirit walk.

And in Marston's *The Insatiate Countess* we find:

> Curs'd creatures messengers of death, possess the world,
> Night – Ravens, screech owls, and voice-killing mandrakes
> The ghosts of misers, that imprison'd gold,
> Within the harmless bowels of the earth,
> Are night's companions: bawds to lust and murder.[13]

But it remains silent, the cock crows, Marcellus tries to strike it with his weapon and then it disappears. Barnardo finds that it vanishes at cockcrow significant. Horatio agrees:

>   it started like a guilty thing,
> Upon a fearful summons.
>
>   (1.1.148–9)

The disappearance of evil spirits at cockcrow is a belief as old as
Christian Europe, and Shakespeare has Marcellus emphasize its
symbolic significance:

>   I have heard
> The cock that is the trumpet to the morn
> Both with his lofty and shrill-sounding throat
> Awake the god of day, and at his warning
> Whether in sea or fire, in earth or air,
> Th' extravagant and erring spirit hies
> To his confine, and of the truth herein
> This present object made probation.
>
>   (1.1.149–57)

In the Middle Ages the cock was associated with Christ, as
can be seen in ballads such as *St. Stephen and King Herod* and
The Carnal and the Crane, in which at Herod's feast

> The capon crew Christus natus est
> Among the lordes all

and

> The cock soon freshly feathered was
> By the work of God's own hand,
> And then three fences crowed he,
> In the dish where he did stand.

Also in the Scottish ballad *The Wife of Usher's Well*, in which
a mother's dead sons return to spend a night under her roof:

> The cock doth craw, the day doth daw,
> The channerin' [fretting] worm doth chide;
> Gin we be missed out o' our place
> A sair pain we maun bide.

The same superstition appears also in a wider European context.
In *Gargantua and Pantagruel* by Rabelais we read:

> on the coming of the clear sun's light, all spectres, lamias,
> ghosts, werewolves, hobgolins and spirits of darkness vanish.[14]

And Mussorgsky included the crowing of the cock in his *A Night
on the Bare Mountain*.

The Fellow in the Cellarage

But, returning to Shakespeare we find in *King Lear*:

This is the foul fiend Flibbertigibbet: he begins at curfew and walks till the first cock. (3.4.118–19)

And in *A Midsummer Night's Dream*:

> yonder shines Aurora's harbinger;
> At whose approach, ghosts, wandering here and there,
> Troop home to churchyards: damned spirits all,
> That in cross-ways and floods have burial,
> Already to their wormy beds are gone;
> For fear lest day should look their shames upon,
> They wilfully themselves exile from light,
> And must for aye consort with black-brow'd night
> (3.3.380–7)

Milton also, in *L'Allegro*, shows that he knew of the superstition:

> Then lies him down the lubber fiend,
> And stretched out all the chimney's length
> Basks at the fire his hairy strength;
> And crop-full out of doors he flings,
> Ere the first cock his mattin rings.

The Christian symbolism of the cock is underlined as Marcellus goes on:

> Some say that even 'gainst that season comes
> Wherein our Saviour's birth is celebrated
> This bird of dawning singeth all night long,
> And then they say no spirit dare stir abroad,
> The nights are wholesome, then no planets strike,
> No fairy takes, nor witch hath power to charm,
> So hallowed, and so gracious is that time.

It is true that the fairies in *A Midsummer Night's Dream* are not treated as demons, but as I have pointed out elsewhere they were still regarded by many, including witches themselves, as satanic, and this seems to have been the case in Catholic times.[15] The link with Catholicism can be seen in *The Fairies' Farewell* by Bishop Corbet (1582–1625):

> Witness those rings and roundelay
> Of theirs, which yet remain,
> Were footed in Queen Mary's day,

53

On many a grassy plain;
But since of late Elizabeth,
And later, James came in,
They never danced on any heath
As when the time hath bin.

By which we note the Fairies
Were of the old profession;
Their songs were Ave Maries;
Their dances were procession:
But now, alas! they all are dead,
Or gone beyond the seas;
Or farther for religion fled,
Or else they take their ease.[16]

It is clear at any rate that Shakespeare wishes us to associate the Ghost with demonic agencies and witchcraft. The more knowledgeable also might well have anticipated the Ghost's eventual demand for revenge because witchcraft and revenge were closely linked by writers on witchcraft both in England and in France. Jean Bodin, for example, claimed that at the end of a sabat the Devil dismissed the coven by crying:

Revenge yourselves or die!

That this was a common belief in England also is evidenced in *Four Centuries of Witch-beliefs* by R. Trevor Davies.[17] And while the belief in fairies may have faded, belief in witchcraft had intensified. And we should also remember that by the time Q2 appeared in 1604 James's views on witchcraft had become widely known and this may have influenced Shakespeare's decision to write *Macbeth*.

By the end of this first scene I find it hard to believe that anyone in Shakespeare's first audience would have regarded the Ghost as other than satanic. Even an illiterate groundling would have reached this conclusion. For him the Devil was real and his works were real. As E.D. Pendry says, referring to *Doctor Faustus*, 'tales were told in the seventeenth century of performances ... when the actors were terrified, and chastened, to discover that the real Devil was present among them'.[18] Thus a black-bearded figure 'So majestical', clad in armour, encountered at midnight and rising out of and vanishing into the earth would be as close an approximation to Satan as any Elizabethan would wish.[19] Satan, after all, was the Prince of Darkness, the battle-scarred 'dread commander', as Milton depicts him, of the apostate angels. Barnabe Barnes's Pope Alexander conjures a devil dressed thus in armour who says he is

> Sent from the foggy lake of fearful Styx
> Am I commanded by that puissant monarch,
> Which rides triumphing in a chariot,
> On misty black clouds mixed with quenchless fire,
> Through uncouth corners in dark paths of death,
> To do what thou demandest.

A final point is that for a long time after *The Spanish Tragedy* and *Hamlet* had been written the ghosts in them were linked together in the popular mind. For example, in John Gee's *New Shreds of the Old Snare* (1624):

> The Jesuites being or having Actors of such dexteritie, I see no reason but that they should set up a company for themselves, which surely will put down The Fortune, Red-bull, Cock-pit, & Globe ... Representations and apparitions from the dead might be seen farr cheaper at other Play-houses. As for example the Ghost in *Hamlet*, Don Andreas Ghost in Hieronimo.

There is also *Hey for Honesty* by Thomas Randolph, who died in 1634:

> CHREMYLUS. ... 'tis some Erynnis that is broke loose from the Tragedy.
> BELP. By Jeronymo, her looks are as terrible as Don Andrea or the Ghost in Hamlet.

Both allusions are too late to apply to the *Ur-Hamlet*, but even if they did so, how can the Catholicism and evil nature of the ghost be distinguished from Shakespeare's Ghost? Neither of these writers could be described as groundlings yet they evidently reached the same conclusion as I have presumed that Shakespeare's groundlings did. Thus it seems safe to presume also that the better educated members of his audience – Protestants members – took a similar view. And furthermore, allusions such as these are impossible to explain according to the traditional Ghost or even an 'ambiguous' Ghost. If either theory is correct how has it come about that Gee and Randolph have both misinterpreted Shakespeare's intention, and yet reached the same conclusion? Or are we to assume that Randolph, for example, some time after 1620 saw the *Ur-Hamlet* somewhere?

Hamlet hears of the Ghost from Horatio, his 'fellow student' at Wittenberg, which has already been mentioned a few lines earlier. Dover Wilson believed that since this was Luther's university Hamlet and Horatio were Protestants. The association sounds plausible until we look a little more closely. Then we must consider that even the clergy in England had little connection with Lutheranism, for they were Calvinists who disliked the Lutheran approach to predestination. Strype records a letter written in the early years of Elizabeth's reign in which Lutherans are claimed to be not much better than Papists.[20] Also in Marlowe's *The Massacre at Paris* the Huguenots are referred to by the Guise as 'Lutherans' and 'Puritans', and he calls their clandestine meetings 'synagogues'. These terms evidently did not offend the corrector, for if he had thought that they could have applied to the established Church it would have been his duty at least to excise them. Thus also Hamlet's punning allusion to the Diet of Worms caused no offence. I cannot therefore see why an Elizabethan audience would associate Wittenberg with a form of Protestantism of which they did not approve.[21]

It seems much more likely that for them Wittenberg meant Faustus who in Marlowe's play is never once associated with Luther or Lutheranism; instead he is, if anything, a schismatic Catholic who uses holy water in his conjuration of Mephistopheles, and who ingratiates himself with Charles V, the Holy Roman Emperor, the very man who presided at the Diet of Worms, at which Luther was excommunicated. Just as Shakespeare seems to have made use of the name 'Horatio' to associate his Ghost with that of Don Andrea, and so at one stroke made the setting both satanic and Catholic, it seems at least possible that Shakespeare – or the author of the *Ur-Hamlet* – having read that Belleforest's Hamlet had been trained in black magic, naturally picked for him an educational establishment which was famed for such arts. The *Faustbook* was to hand to make the job easier for him, or the source could have been Marlowe's play. Certainly a theatre audience would be more likely to associate Hamlet's Wittenberg with Faustus than with Luther because of the very popularity of the play. It is also to be noted that the pagan background of the original story has become Catholic instead, which in Protestant eyes would only be a slight change. Also

Shakespeare may have derived the name 'Cornelius' from *Doctor Faustus*. Horatio then shares the same dubious university background as Hamlet and Faustus, and so too do Rosencrantz and Guildenstern.

There is yet another contemporary association with Wittenberg that may be relevant. Friedrich Taubmann had become the Professor of Poetry at Wittenberg but according to Enid Welsford:

> Anecdotes about him were collected, and like other famous jesters he was a magnet for stock jokes, some of them very gross in character. Taubmann bears a close resemblance to the Italian buffoons ... he was both a butt and a wit, and was equally renowned as an absurd glutton, a shameless beggar, a learned Latinist and a skilful improviser of poetry.[22]

Robert Armin, Shakespeare's clown, would have known about him and his reputation might well have been wider than this. Thus, as we shall see shortly, Taubmann's 'antic disposition' may also have influenced Shakespeare's choice of Wittenberg as the university of Hamlet and his friends. If you wished to contact the Devil or play the fool that was the place to go.

Horatio tells Hamlet that the Ghost is like his father and

> Armed at point exactly, cap-a-pe.

From Marston's *The Malcontent* we can see that he regarded the Ghost as demonic as he uses 'a-cap-a-pe' for Mendoza, who urges Malevole to murder the duke. And Nashe would have reacted similarly to a Ghost which appeared

> In the dead waste and middle of the night

and which claimed to be Hamlet's father:

> In the quiet silence of the night he [the Devil] will be sure to surprise us, when he vnfallibly knowes we shall be vnarmed to resist, and there will be full audience granted him to vndermine or perswad what he lists ... Neither in his owne nature dare he come nere vs, but in the name of sin, as Gods executioner. Those that catch birdes imitate their voyces, so will he imitate the voyces of Gods vengeance, to bring vs like birds into the net of eternal damnation.

And he goes on:

57

It will be demaunded why in the likeness of ones father or mother, or kinsfolks, he oftentimes presents himself vnto vs? No other reason can bee giuen of it, but this, that in those shapes which hee supposeth most familiar vnto vs, and that wee are inclined to with a naturall kind of loue, will sooner harken to him than otherwise.[23]

Horatio adds that the Ghost walked 'thrice before them. In Shakespeare and elsewhere, in *Faustus* for example, the number three has a satanic significance. One has only to think of Macbeth and the three Witches, the number three which occurs both in their spells and in that which Faustus makes, to realize that this was a way of 'abjuring the Trinity', as Mephistopheles puts it.

The sentries, says Marcellus, saw it upon 'the platform', a part of the castle where the watch was kept and which featured in scenes on the medieval stage when Hell itself was represented as a castle. Glynne Wickham draws attention to this and also provides a contemporary picture of 'Hell Castle' in an article on *Macbeth*.[24]

Horatio says the Ghost did not answer him and that it 'shrunk in haste away / And vanished' when the cock crew. As I pointed out above it could only have disappeared into 'Hell', the cellarage. He adds that the Ghost wore his visor up and that 'he' was very pale. Marston uses the term 'a heavy hell-like paleness'[25] and Lodge in *Wits Miserie* (1596) has a devil 'Hate-Virtue' who is 'a foule lubber, and looks as pale as the visard of ye ghost which cried ... Hamlet reuenge'.

As the result of his questioning of Horatio, Hamlet is perturbed and his words suggests that he suspects the Ghost is diabolic:

> If it assume my noble father's person,
> I'll speak to it though hell itself should gape
> And bid me hold my peace.
>
> (1.2.244–6)

'Gape' was indeed an appropriate word because we remember the 'hell-mouth' of stage tradition. And Hamlet's final remarks show his misgivings:

> My father's spirit (in arms !) all is not well,
> I doubt some foul play.
>
> (1.2.255–6)

Thus there is not a single item in this scene which points to a 'good' Ghost; all the evidence instead points to its malignity.

58

When we see Hamlet, Horatio and Marcellus on the battlements it is just after midnight and there is the sound of cannon fire as the court dance and get drunk. Hamlet disapproves and claims that the Danes are regarded as drunken pigs by other nations. But we must remember that in the Middle Ages drunkenness was associated with gluttony and so ranked as one of the Seven Deadly Sins. In *Faustus* Gluttony says:

> I come of a royal pedigree: my father was a gammon of bacon and my mother was a hogshead of claret wine. (2.2.143–4)

And in Tourneur's *The Revenger's Tragedy* Hippolito says:

> The worst of all the deadly sins is in him;
> That beggarly damnation, drunkenness.
>
> (4.2.187–8)

We should also remember that Hamlet accepts this view, although he does not mention it here, for he resolves to kill Claudius when he is 'drunk asleep' and so send his soul to Hell. But at this point of the play, while he seems to be adopting a moral attitude he is, instead, concerned with a man's reputation rather than with his soul. This is reminiscent of Cassio in *Othello*:

> Reputation, reputation, reputation! O! I have lost my reputation. I have lost the immortal part of myself, and what remains is bestial. My reputation, Iago, my reputation! (2.3.263–6)

In broad terms Hamlet's soliloquy, if we do not see it in a contemporary religious context, is about how a single failing in a man's character can, in terms of the popular judgment, blacken him. But Hamlet's words, from the standpoint of religion, show that he shares the same moral malaise as Cassio.

Hamlet says that some men are born with the 'stamp of one defect' and they are not really guilty because they cannot avoid something like a birthmark. The Elizabethans believed however that all mankind was born sinful – they inherited the sin of Adam. Faustus, translating from the Vulgate, says:

> If we say that we have no sin we deceive ourselves, and there is no truth in us. (1.1.42–3)

Hooker wrote:

It is true we are full of sin, both original and actual; whosoever denieth it is a double sinner and a liar. To deny sin, is most plainly and clearly to prove it; because he that saith he hath no sin, lieth, and by lying proveth that he hath sin.[26]

Hooker also makes it clear that corruption is more than loss of reputation:

Adam is in us as an original cause of our nature, and of that corruption of nature which causeth death; Christ as the cause original of restauration to life. The person of Adam is not in us, but his nature, and the corruption of his nature derived into all men by propagation; Christ having Adam's nature, as we have, but incorrupt, deriveth not nature but incorruption, and that immediately from his own Person, into all that belong unto him.[27]

To differ from this view was to fall into the Pelagian heresy, the belief in the natural virtues of man, and this was specifically condemned by Article IX of the Thirty-Nine Articles. On this matter the comment of Edgar Gibson is important:

The original object of this Article is shown very definitely by the words which in the Articles of 1553 followed the reference to the Pelagians: 'which also the Anabaptists do nowadays renew' ... These words, omitted at the revision of 1563 (possibly because the danger was less pressing), prove that it was designed at least primarily to meet the revival of the Pelagian error on the subject of original sin by the Anabaptists.[28]

Thus when Hamlet says that a man's virtues can be as pure as grace and 'as infinite as man may undergo' he is really accrediting to him the moral excellence that only Christ could attain, and he also appears to be uttering a heresy common some fifty-odd years before the play was written.

So also Hamlet talks of 'some vicious mole of nature in them' – not *on* them. This mole is an internal not an external blemish. The 'birthmark' is Satan, for 'mole' was perhaps, as Nevil Coghill pointed out, a soubriquet for Satan.[29] Its demonic connotation can be seen in *Bussy d'Ambois*:

> Show me a clergyman, that is in voice
> A lark of heaven, in heart a mole of earth
> That hath good living, and a wicked life.[30]

(3.2.40–3)

Richard Bernard (1568–1641) in his *Guide to Grand Jurymen with respect to Witches* (1627) claims a 'moale' was one of the forms in which Satan regularly appeared to witches.[31] Shakespeare himself refers to the 'moldwarp' as such a satanic metamorphosis in *1 Henry IV* (3.1.148). And Holinshed refers to the 'moldwarp, cursed of God's own mouth'.

Hamlet's observations then leave out Satan and original sin – just as Cassio's reputation has become more important to him than his immortal soul. L.C. Knights says: 'the world with which Hamlet has to deal is indeed evil, and the play shows convincingly what may be called the logic of corruption'.[32] Hamlet's moral logic in fact is the logic of the devil, the logic of despair, and he is not in a suitable frame of mind to cope with the Ghost:

> Be thou a spirit of health

(echoing 'healthy Spirit of thy grace' in the Book of Common Prayer – 'Prayer for the Clergy and People')

> or goblin damned.

> (1.4.40)

What he has so far heard of the Ghost should have left him in no doubt, and as it came up out of the ground his confusion would not have been shared by the audience, any more than a contemporary audience would have shared Macbeth's conclusion:

> This supernatural soliciting
> Cannot be ill; cannot be good ...

> (1.3.130–1)

Nor would they share Hamlet's reverence for the 'canonized bones' of his father, for canonization was a word which Catholics used of sainthood and hardly fitted the picture of a proud, imperious, warrior-king who had gambled his realm on a duel. Shakespeare also uses the biblical word 'sepulchre' to describe the tomb, an association of ideas which is also incongruous.

Both Horatio and Marcellus try to dissuade Hamlet from following the Ghost, but he does not set his life 'at a pin's fee', and he goes even further:

> And for my soul, what can it do to that
> Being a thing immortal as itself.

> (1.4.66–7)

L.C. Knights comments thus:

'Desperation', moreover, like 'desperate' a few lines later ('He waxes desperate with imagination') is a far stronger word than, say, 'recklessness' (it is related to 'despair') and I think the speech as a whole gives an unambiguous clue: the Ghost is tempting Hamlet to gaze with fascinated horror at an abyss of evil.[33]

In Elizabethan eyes Hamlet and Faustus are brothers under the skin, for they both turn from God and so turn towards Satan. Mephistopheles shows us the tricks of the trade:

> For when we hear one rack the name of God,
> Abjure the Scriptures and his Saviour Christ,
> We fly in hope to get his glorious soul;
> Nor will we come unless he use such means,
> Whereby he is in danger to be damned.
>
> (1.3.47–51)

If we do not place Hamlet in a religious context we distort the play because we see him acting courageously instead of foolishly, but if we accept for the duration of the play the existence of eternal damnation then we must take a different view. M.C. Bradbrook of *Faustus* says:

> The idea of despair in the theological sense (that is, a conviction of damnation such as the one from which John Bunyan suffered) runs through the play. It is the means by which the devils, from the very beginning, secure Faustus' soul.[34]

And Helen Gardner:

> The final sin of Faustus is despair ... Donne gives presumption and despair as one of the couples which the Schoolmen have called sins against the Holy Ghost 'because naturally they shut out those meanes by which the Holy Ghost might work upon us ... for presumption takes away the feare of God, and desperation the love of God.' They are the two faces of the sin of Pride.[35]

It is because Horatio is aware of this 'desperation' in Hamlet that he pleads with him to avoid being lured to the 'dreadful summit of the cliff', for devils were supposed to do just that[36] – as in *King Lear*:

> As I stood here below methought his eyes
> Were two full moons; he had a thousand noses,

Horns whelk'd and wav'd like the enridged sea:
It was some fiend.

(4.6.70–3)

But Hamlet is adamant:

My fate cries out,
And makes each petty artery in this body
As hardy as the Nemean lion's nerve.

(1.4.82–3)

(The Nemean lion was associated with Hercules whose rage and madness were part of the tradition of the stage.) And so he decides to follow the Ghost.

At this point Partridge in *Tom Jones* may represent the typical reaction of a Shakespearean audience, although the author had, of course, no such intention.

Ay, ay; 'go along with you!' ay, to be sure! who's fool then! Will you? Lud have mercy upon such foolhardiness? ... 'Follow you!' I'd follow the devil as soon, – nay, perhaps it is the devil, – for they say he can put on what likeness he pleases.

And, to anticipate a little, his final comments on the scene are:

'Nay, sir,' answered Partridge, 'if you are not afraid of the devil, I can't help it ... Then, turning his eyes again upon Hamlet, 'Ay, you may draw your sword; what signifies a sword against the power of the devil?'

The Partridge goes on:

'Bless me! what's become of the spirit? As I am a living soul, I thought I saw him sink into the earth.' 'Indeed you saw right,' answered Jones. 'Well, well,' cries Partridge, 'I know it is only a play; and besides, if there was anything in all this, Madam Miller would not laugh so; for as to you, sir, you would not be afraid, I believe, if the devil were here in person.'[37]

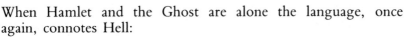

When Hamlet and the Ghost are alone the language, once again, connotes Hell:

> My hour is almost come,
> When I to sulph'rous and tormenting flames
> Must render up myself.
>
> (1.5.3–6)

Virgil's Underworld was not sulphurous and neither was Dante's – the most likely association is the book of Revelation where plenty of brimstone is promised on the Last Day. So too perhaps Milton's Hell:

> As one great furnace flamed ...
> ... a fiery deluge, fed,
> With ever-burning sulphur unconsumed.
>
> (*Paradise Lost*, Bk. I, ll. 62–9)

Thus far I have avoided reference to the experts on ghosts of the period, but it is worth mentioning that Le Loyer claimed that sulphur was an indication that an apparition was from Hell.[38]

John Fletcher in *The Woman Hater* (1607) burlesqued Hamlet at this point. Hamlet says:

> Speak, I am bound to hear.
>
> (1.5.6)

Fletcher has:

> LAZARELLO. Let me not fall from my selfe; speake I am bound to heare.
> COUNT. So art thou to reuenge, when thou shalt heare the fish head is gone, and we know not whither.

If we ask ourselves why Fletcher wrote thus, the most obvious answer is that he, like Partridge, saw Hamlet being drawn into the toils of the Devil – who had the power to terrify an audience but was also a figure of fun.

The Ghost continues, claiming that it comes from Purgatory – which for Fletcher and the majority, presumably, of Shakespeare's audience, would be part of the joke. Furthermore, the 'prison-house' from which it claims to have come meant 'Hell' to the Elizabethans. In the original form of Article III of the Thirty-Nine Articles occurs the following:

> As Christ died, and was buried for us: so also it is to be believed that He went down into hell. For the body lay in the sepulchre until the resurrection: but His ghost, departing from Him was with the ghosts that were in *prison or hell*, and did preach to the same, as the place of St. Peter doth testify.[39]

64

And Milton wrote:

> here their prison ordained
> In utter darkness, and their portion set.
>
> (*Paradise Lost*, Bk. I, ll. 71–2)

But 'prison' as a synonym for Hell goes further back into medieval times. Glynne Wickham records the usage in the Towneley Cycle – 'pryson' and 'prison, pit and dungeon are the words used variously in the Chester cycle to describe hell'.[40] (In addition the Ghost's words 'Would harrow up thy soul' belong to that sort of context because the Harrowing of Hell was a feature of the cyclic plays.) No such synonym was in general currency to describe Purgatory even though it was considered by Catholic theologians to be part of Hell, but not 'the hell of the damned'.[41] If we turn to *The Shakespeare Allusion Book*, 'I.M.S.' who wrote *On Worthy Master Shakespeare and his Poems* (1632) did not accept the Ghost's claim to come from Purgatory; instead, he refers to Hell as a 'dungeon', as Milton did:

> A mind reflecting ages past, whose cleere
> And equall surface can make things appeare
> Distant a Thousand yeares, . . .
> Rowle back the heavens, blow ope the iron gates
> Of death and Lethe, where (confused) lye
> Great heapes of ruinous mortalitie . . .
> In that deep duskie dungeon to discerne
> A royall Ghost from churles.[42]

He also mentions Lethe, which like the rest of Virgil's Underworld was part of Hell, and we may anticipate the Ghost's reference to Lethe a little later.

The Ghost continues: it cannot tell of the horrors it suffers, for it would cause Hamlet's hair to stand on end like the bristles on a 'porpentine'. This line appears to be echoed in *The Merry Divel of Edmonton* (1607):

> O what a trembling horror strikes my head!
> My stiffened hayre stands upright on my head,
> As doe the bristles of a porcupine.

An editorial footnote reads: 'Fabell makes this exclamation at the approach of the evil spirit Coreb, with whom he has covenanted for his soul.'[43]

The Ghost further tells Hamlet that Claudius is guilty of adultery and incest at which T.S. Eliot considered Hamlet's disgust 'disproportionate'. C.E.M. Joad too, in characteristic vein, asked, 'why shouldn't one marry one's dead husband's brother? It is neither forbidden in law nor reprobated in morals. Perhaps it was forbidden in Elizabethan English law – I don't know.'[44] Joad was correct in his supposition, for in 1563 the Protestant Church, following previous Catholic practice, forbade such a union.[45] Besides, would the Ghost not have seemed prissy, instead of morally indignant, if it had been seen to deplore a trivial breach of the law? Eliot's comments have led to much confused thinking. How could he ignore the fact that in the Ghost's view Claudius was guilty of '*damned* incest'? When we realize of course that the Ghost is satanic we must concede that it knows what it is talking about, for damnation is its business.

The Ghost's reference to, and Shakespeare's choice of, Hebona as a poison is interesting. It may be from Ovid, but as the Ghost is Catholic a source which is both papist and demonic, such as occurs in *The Jew of Malta*, may be preferred:

> let it work like Borgia's wine,
> Whereof his sire the Pope was poisoned.
> In few, the blood of Hydra, Lerna's bane,
> The juice of hebon, and Cocytus' breath,
> And all the poisons of the Stygian pool.

(In view of Harold Jenkins's annotation this association seems somewhat facile, but at least it does not strain probability.)[46]

The Catholicism of the Ghost is again emphasized when it bewails not having received the Last Rites – a sure method of arousing the antagonism of the audience. Similarly, the disappearance of the Ghost when the 'matin' is near has the same effect, for 'mattin' had disappeared as a part of Church ritual by 1552, when 'mattins' became merged with 'Morning Prayers' in the Book of Common Prayer.

Hamlet's soliloquy which follows upon the disappearance of the Ghost is blasphemous, as I have already claimed. The 'host of heaven' to whom he appeals were, as Richmond Noble points out, 'the gods of the heathen'.[47] And Hamlet also disobeys the injunction 'Swear not at all; neither by the heaven, for it is the footstool of His feet' (Matt. 5: 34–5). Thus Hamlet acts like a Vice at this point, according to the description by Philip Stubbes: 'if you will learn to play the Vice, to swear, tear and blaspheme both heaven and earth'.[48] Hamlet indeed goes further and 'couples hell'.

Hamlet answers Marcellus's call, according to a gloss that has become traditional, as if he were a falconer. This point will be returned to shortly, but according to any interpretation it can be said that Hamlet's action in the dim light of dawn is in keeping with the unbalanced state he exhibits. The news, he tells Horatio, is 'wonderful', but he will not be pressed into revealing what has happened. He evades their questions, and says inconsequentially:

> There's ne'er a villian dwelling in all Denmark
> But he's an arrant knave.
>
> (1.5.123–4)

Horatio, who by now must be worried about Hamlet's agitated state says:

> There needs no ghost, my lord, come from the grave,
> To tell us this.
>
> (1.5.125–6)

Hamlet's desire is to be rid of them and his words are 'wild and whirling'. He will, he says finally, 'go pray'. But in fact Hamlet does not pray, he doesn't even try, as Claudius did. Neither did Hieronimo. Hamlet has an awareness of evil but he does not turn to God in his distress, as an Elizabethan had been taught to do. Instead he accuses St. Patrick of committing an offence. It is a joke, of course, for St. Patrick who kept the door of Purgatory could only be a comic figure to a Protestant audience.

Then Hamlet demands that his friends keep the night's proceedings secret, which both swear 'in faith' twice to do. But this is not enough for Hamlet, and what follows is a threefold oath on Hamlet's sword, the Ghost acting as a prompter. Dover Wilson drew attention to a passage in Reginald Scot's *Discoverie of Witchcraft* which throws light on what is happening:

> The threefold oath finds ... a parallel in Scot who speaks of 'promises and oths interchangeable made betweene the con-iuror and the spirit', oaths which were sworn three times and for the violation of which eternal penalties were exacted.[49]

And Dover Wilson concluded that 'Marcellus to his dying day will believe that he has sworn an oath thrice in the hearing of a powerful fiend, and will hold his tongue'. This seems to be a deal of trouble to take only for Marcellus's benefit. Why, after all, do we have a 'spirit of health', an 'honest ghost' pretending to be a devil? When did God pretend to be Satan? What we see is the sealing of a revenge pact which is so phrased that eyewitness accounts of Horatio and Marcellus are permanently suppressed so that Hamlet has not the slightest shred of evidence that he can openly present against Claudius, and this makes it certain that Hamlet can never publicly challenge him – his only course of action must be private, in fact murder.

To return to the oath 'in faith' that Horatio and Marcellus swear and which does not satisfy Hamlet, it is noteworthy that Faustus did not like 'faith' to be mentioned either:

> Scare can I name salvation, faith, or heaven,
> But fearful echoes thunders [*sic*] in mine ears.
>
> (2.2.19–20)

Taking an oath on Hamlet's sword, on the hilt of which 'Jesu' might have been inscribed, as Douce points out,[50] was in essence an old Catholic custom which would not have found any favour with Protestants because they abhorred crosses. So in *1 Henry IV* we find:

> And swore the devil his true liegeman on the cross of a Welsh hook. (2.4.376–8)

So too Lorenzo in *The Spanish Tragedy* frightening the wits out of Pedringano:

> Swear on this cross that what thou sayest is true;
> And that thou wilt conceal what thou hast told.
> PEDRINGANO. I swear to both by him that made us all.
> LORENZO. In hope thine oath is true, here's thy reward,
> But if I prove thee perjur'd and unjust,
> This very sword whereon thou took'st oath,
> Shall be the worker of thy tragedy

As for the change of location each time the oath is taken, this was, presumably, another method of abjuring the Trinity and of affirming that Satan is 'hic et ubique'.[51]

That the diabolic pact made a dramatic impact can be seen from Wye Saltonstall's *Picturae Loquentes* in which the situation is burlesqued and the rascally chamberlain is 'as nimble as Hamlet's ghost heere and everywhere'.[52] Leslie Hotson shows that 'Hamlet with . . . "hic and ubique" is jestingly recalling the old Vice when he calls the ubiquitous Ghost "boy" "this fellow" "old mole", and "truepenny"'.[53] Then there is Jonson's Vice, Iniquity, in *The Devil is an Asse* who is

> Here, there, and everywhere, as the Cat with the Mice,

which reinforces Hotson's belief that Hamlet speaks to the Ghost as if he were playing the Vice to the Ghost's Devil. George Rylands had a similar idea:

> Hamlet's cries to the Ghost suggest the way in which the 'Vice' or Clown in the old Morality plays provoked the Devil. It seems to bewilder Marcellus, to relieve the Prince's pent-up, hysterical emotion, to prepare for the 'antic disposition', and to keep alive the possibility that the Ghost may be diabolic.

Most recently Harold Jenkins has shown his agreement:

> The familiarity with which Hamlet addresses it may recall the manner in which the stage Vice traditionally addresses the Devil.

But first let us look more closely at what Hotson had to say. 'Truepenny', he showed, is defined in Littleton's Latin dictionary as 'veterator vafer' or 'crafty old knave' – 'and who could be craftier or more knavish than Satan?' Nashe uses the term to describe Martin Marprelate, the tone being ironic:

> ... the good olde truepennie Marprelate.[54]

The 'mole' Hotson also correctly identified as Satan, as we have already seen, and it might be added that Samuel Harsnett recognized the demonic association of the mole because he speaks of rascally Roman Catholic priests who 'play the Bats and the Moales'.[55] But 'mole' as a synonym for the Devil himself seems a rather rare usage and may have been in particular a Vice's soubriquet for Satan – as we may see from Jack Juggler 'the vyce' of the play of that name:

> I woll cungere the moul and god before.

The 'fellow in the cellarage' fits the context because, as we have seen, the cellar beneath the stage represented Hell, 'the dongyon where the deuyll dwelleth'.[56] So too 'boy' seems to have been another nickname for Satan – James Russell Lowell in an essay on witchcraft records that at the end of a coven:

> At last the Devil vanisheth, and all are carried to their several homes in a short space. At their parting they say, 'A Boy! merry meet, merry part'.[57]

The evidence which he quotes appears to have been taken in 1664. The exclamation 'Ah ha' which precedes 'boy' at 1.5.150 seems to have been part of the 'expository formula', as Spivack called it, of

the Vice – the First Folio (F1) form is to be preferred here. Thus
we have:

> 1 A ha! let the catte wynke!
> 2 A ha! mayster, that is good chere.
> 3 Aha! Wanton is my name
> 4 A ha! Now Lust and Lyking is my name!
> 5 A ha here is sporte for a Lorde.
> 6 A! a! now I have it! I have it, in-deed!
>   My name is Ambidexter: I signifie one
>   That with both hands finely can play.[58]

Feste in *Twelfth Night* confirms this view:

> I am gone, sir,
> And anon, sir,
> I'll be with you again,
> In a trice,
> Like to the old Vice,
> Your need to sustain:
> Who with dagger of lath,
> In his rage and his wrath,
> *Cries, Ah, ha!* to the devil: [most editors, following Rowe]
> Like a mad lad,
> Pare thy nails, dad;
> Adieu, goodman devil.
>
> (4.3.134–45)

We may also add that 'pioner' is similar in meaning to 'collier', an
epithet which Sir Toby Belch uses for the Devil.

The identification of Hamlet as Vice is a fruitful one and it turns
what seems incoherent into a dramatic formula well known to all,
including the correctors. Harsnett, for example, wrote:

> It was a pretty part in the old Churche-playes, when the
> nimble Vice would skip vp nimbly like a Iack an Apes into the
> necke, and ride the deuil a course, and belabour him with his
> wooden dagger, til he made him roare, whereat the people
> would laugh to see the deuil so vice-haunted.[59]

The Ghost as Hamlet's 'dad' also fits the symbolism. Spivack
wrote that,

> although the Vices of the later moralities occasionally refer to
> the Devil as their father or godfather, their relationship to him
> is doctrinal and hierarchic rather than genetic. He is their father

70

only in the loose sense that he is the universal source of evil, and they are, figuratively, his children because by their domination over man they serve the Devil's purpose, which is to bring the human soul to hell.[60]

It is possible then to see Hamlet's role as including both the genetic and doctrinal aspects which Spivack distinguishes.

It may seem incongruous that humour is entwined with deadly seriousness here. The distraction of Hamlet – the 'mad lad' – is not funny any longer. But we must remember that what we regard as the cruel treatment of Malvolio was evidently comic to the Elizabethans. Perhaps also the laughter of the audience was in part relief from the gravity of the scene. In the Middle Ages the Devil had always been a comic figure on the stage but that did not lessen his reality or therefore the fear that he engendered. We can see this same curious mixture of the comic and the demonic in *The Malcontent*:

> Illo, ho, ho, ho! arte there, old true penny? Where hast thou spent thy selfe this morning? I see flattery in thine eyes, and damnation i' thy soule. Ha ye huge Rascal!

There appears to be an echo of *Hamlet* here. If so it is strange that 'Illo, ho, ho, ho', which is nearly the call Hamlet makes in reply to that of Marcellus and is generally glossed as a falconer's call, is attached to 'truepenny', the soubriquet for Satan. Is it possible that Hamlet in fact echoes what was and had been for centuries the opening formula of the Devil – 'Ho, ho, ho!' – in the Mysteries and Moralities, just as Robin Goodfellow came to do, as Sir Edmund Chambers pointed out in his edition of *A Midsummer Night's Dream*?[61] Hamlet calls the Ghost 'bird' it is true but such a description would have fitted a Satan dressed in feathers, as he apparently was in the craft plays. At any rate a Hamlet calling like a falconer in the dimness of dawn is not arguably a sane Hamlet.

The element of burlesque is reflected in Samuel Rowlands' *The Night Raven* (1620):

> I will not call Hamlet Revenge my greeves,
> But I will call Hang-man Revenge on theeves.

Yet again in Dekker's *Lanthorne and Candlelight* (1609) the demonic note is dominant. Speaking of gypsies enclosing a murdered man in a circle he goes on:

> But if any mad Hamlet hearing this smell villanie, & rush in by

71

violence to see what the tawny divels are doing, they excuse the fact & c.

If Shakespeare's *Hamlet* had disappeared, as did the *Ur-Hamlet*, and only the allusions as recorded in the *Allusion Book* had survived, we would have little difficulty in concluding that the Ghost was evil and Catholic and had comic overtones. It would be a 'foul lubber' with a pale face such as Lodge associated with the ghost of the *Ur-Hamlet*. It would also resemble the ghost in the *Brudermord* which is certainly demonic – we know from the Prologue that Night wishes to 'give joy to hell' and enlists the help of the Furies in her plan of revenge – and there would be touches of satire such as the sentry who feels like a man in Purgatory when the Ghost boxes him in the ear, the Pope having allowed the incestuous marriage, and the reference to the nunnery, 'where two pairs of slippers lie at the bedside'. We would also understand why some Elizabethans paired the Ghost with that in *The Spanish Tragedy*. We might also apply Stoll's argument to reinforce our conclusion:

> Many critics wholly literary in their interests ... are shocked and indignant at the old *Hamlet* (and *The Spanish Tragedy*) being spoken of in the same breath with Shakespeare's, and at the heroes at all resembling each other; and they more than intimate that such comparisons argue an insensibility in the speaker. They rush to the conclusion that he discerns little difference between them in quality, as well as kind. They do not realize that Shakespeare, writing for an audience, and a company, not for them, had not a free hand, if really, he desired it; that since the audience remembered the old *Hamlet*, and other plays like it now on the stage, he, writing apparently only another *Hamlet*, must constantly remember the earlier too.

And Stoll also said:

> The story must in general be the same story, though better told, or both company and public would be disappointed; and the principal improvement expected was no doubt in style and metre.[62]

Of course it may be argued that this is all nonsense because Shakespeare's Ghost is 'honest' – it tells the truth about the murder – and it must therefore be good, but against this it must be said that if this is the essential criterion of the Ghost's goodness then the *Brudermord* ghost and the ghost of the *Ur-Hamlet* are good too, because both of them tell the 'truth'.

In addition we may refer to Eleanor Prosser who shows clearly that the Ghost's having told the truth did not mean that its purpose was honest, and quotes Le Loyer:

> [The Devil] often exhorts man to do the commandments of God; often speaks the truth; preaches virtue; dresses his ministers as ministers of justice, making night pass for day, death for life, despair for hope, apostasy for faith . . . In brief, the Devil intermingles the good with the evil, and the true with the false.[63]

But, to return to the allusions. Are they really representative of the reactions of Shakespeare's audience? What difference, if any, would a knowledge of the experts on ghost lore have made? Ludwig Lavater's *Of Ghostes and Spirites Walking by Nyght* (1572) gave the Protestant view. Pierre Le Loyer's *IIII Livres des spectres* (1586), as we have seen, was translated only in part and was not licensed until January 1605. Father Noel Taillepied's *Traité de l'apparition des esprits* (1588) was never translated into English, did not figure in the recusant controversy, and was not even mentioned by Robert Burton although he knew of Lavater and Le Loyer. Thus the influence of these experts on Shakespeare's early audiences must have been, at best, slight. Even if this were not so it must be recognized that the 'wiser sort' would have had no advantage over the groundlings because their criteria were the same. A revenge ghost was clearly demonic according to the Catechetical teaching of either faith, and the midnight hour, in accordance with the folklore of centuries, was the time when the Devil was most likely to appear. If we add that a theatre audience also saw the Ghost emerge from the 'Hell' that was the cellarage we have no grounds for claiming that they regarded it as ambiguous.

The ambiguous Ghost is a product of our lack of religious belief. In a religious setting a revenge ghost must be evil. Hamlet certainly believes in a revenge ghost from Purgatory but in the eyes of Shakespeare's audience he was a fool to think so – and for Protestants in particular he was a Catholic whose obnoxious, nonsensical, heretical belief helped to lead him to damnation. Hamlet's 'error' was good Protestant propaganda, which pro-bably had Pasfield's blessing. It also went down well at the box office, for while it is doubtful whether the ghost books influenced the audience it is more than likely that in Shakespeare's audience

73

there were fervent Protestants such as G.M. Trevelyan described, who had laughed at Tarlton's *Newes out of Purgatorie* and/or *The Cobler of Caunterburie*, and who could no more abide St. Patrick and the Last Rites of the Catholic Church than Bryan, Dekker's 'little St. Patrick', could 'abide a fart'. The Protestant position was that there were no good Catholics, and Satan in the guise of a dead Catholic must have been not only apt but comic also. The joke is on Hamlet, and on us too if we, like him, cannot recognize the Devil when we see him.

Some awareness of the sectarian bias in the play is evident in Warburton, whom Steevens quotes:

> Shakespeare apparently through ignorance, makes Roman Catholicks of these Pagan Danes; and he gives a description of Purgatory; but mixes it with the Pagan fable of Lethe's wharf. Whether he did it to insinuate to the zealous Protestants of his time, that the Pagan and Popish purgatory stood upon the same footing of credibility, or whether it was by the same kind of licentious inadvertence that Michael Angelo brought Charon's bark in to his picture of the Last Judgement, is not easy to decide.[64]

So I submit that besides the necessity to see *Hamlet* in a religious setting we have to recognize its Protestant bias. The Catholicism in *Hamlet* is distorted by it, and probably so too is Catholicism in the whole Elizabethan drama. The 'ambivalence which Shakespeare perceives in revenge' to which Harold Jenkins alludes[65] and with which several others would agree is rather the moral confusion of the Catholic as seen by the Elizabethan Protestant who was epitomized by the corrector. For Pasfield there was nothing ambiguous or ambivalent about revenge or Purgatory.

4

Antic Disposition

IN THE LITERATURE of the seventeenth century Paul S. Conklin concluded that

> Hamlet was seen, first of all, most decidedly as a malcontent; and at times as 'madd', either as a lover or as possessed with a madness that is quite primitive and realistic, with comic overtones.

And, focussing particularly on the first twenty years of the seventeenth century, Conklin adds:

> His madness was a phenomenon of special interest; in fact the malcontent was supposed to be suffering from a malady which hovered between melancholy and downright insanity.[1]

The controversy about Hamlet's sanity seems to have been started in 1778 by a Dr. Akinside and when Hudson reviewed the position in 1872 medical opinion seems to have crystallized:

> Now the reality of his madness is what literary critics have been strangely and unwisely reluctant to admit; partly because they did not understand the exceeding versatility and multiformity of that disease.[2]

In our own time, with the advances in psychiatry, diagnosis has been more specific. In 1962, for example, W.I.D. Scott claimed that Hamlet was suffering from manic-depressive psychosis.[3] On the other hand in 1967 we find Eleanor Prosser concluding that

> Hamlet is unquestionably morbid at times, emotionally un-balanced at times, and even out of control for brief moments. But his erratic behaviour cannot be compassionately dismissed as the symptom of a mental illness for which he is not responsible.[4]

The 'antic disposition' has in fact a long confused history, a study of which leads to the predominant impression that it is a phrase that is uniquely associated with Hamlet – no one before, or

75

after, Hamlet assumed one voluntarily or developed one 'natural-ly'. But before proceeding further we must realize that if an Elizabethan agreed with Dr. Scott that Hamlet was 'madd' he would have expected the Devil to be involved. If on the other hand we accept Eleanor Prosser's contention that 'antic' meaning 'grotesque, ludicrous' was the 'usual epithet for Death',[5] there again we must at least have regard to an Elizabethan word-usage that we no longer share. In either case then there would appear to be no exact modern equivalent to the 'antic disposition'; whatever standpoint we assume, the connotations will be dif-ferent. To adopt the Elizabethan point of view however is to enter a quite alien world of ideas and attitudes. For example we have to realize that madness inspired as much mirth as it did fear – the custom of paying a penny to visit the sights in Bedlam was discontinued only in 1770. And we must accept that the standard treatment of the insane was confinement in a dark place, fetters and whipping, and the pharmacopeia of the leading expert in 'mental and nervous affections' included 'the skull of a stag and of a healthy man who had been executed' and 'the backbone anointed with a very choice balsam of earthworms or bats' – this was the best that the 'Harley Street' of 1606 could do.[6] As E.M.W. Tillyard said, 'it must be confessed that to us the Elizabethan is a very queer age'.[7]

If we turn to C.T. Onion's *A Shakespeare Glossary*, 'antic' as an adjective meant 'fantastic, grotesque, ludicrous'; 'antic' as a noun is 'grotesque entertainment' or 'a burlesque performer, buffoon, merry-andrew'; and 'antic' as a very is 'to make like buffoons'. Harold Jenkins quotes a gloss dated 1604: '*anticke*, disguised' and goes on: 'The word is particularly used of an actor with a false head or grotesque mask.'[8] Etymologically 'antic' according to the *OED* seems to have been derived from the Italian 'antico' perhaps from its application to fantastic carvings found in the ruins of ancient Rome. Perhaps too it carried overtones of the comic *persona* of the Roman actor. At any rate we find 'antic' applied to the comic grimaces of the jester Will Somers:

> At last out comes William with his wit, as the foole of the play does, with an antick looke to please the beholders.[9]

Or we may look at Lodge's description of a 'jeaster':

> This fellow in person is comely, in apparel courtly, but in behaviour a very ape, and no man; his studye is to coin bitter

jeastes, or to show antique motions, or to sing baudie sonnets and ballads: give him a little wine in his head, he is continually flearing and making of mouths ... It is a special marke of him at table, he sits and makes faces.[10]

It could also refer to a comic dance:

... and Archee Armstrong the King's Fool, on the back of the other fools, to tilt one at another, till they fell together by the ears; sometimes Anticke Dances.[11] [The king referred to is James I.]

We may then appreciate why a grinning, dancing skeleton was called an antic – the figure of Death in the Danse Macabre whose companion is often depicted as a jester. Douce records that printers in the sixteenth century used such engravings as decorations for the alphabet and shows a letter *A* illustrated in this manner. Death the antic and Death's fool went together.[12] Thus far then it would seem that 'antic' did not mean 'mad' in the sense of 'insane'.

But if we look further afield we find that it could, and did. For example in Middleton's *The Changeling*:

Thou wild, unshapen antic; I am no fool,
You bedlam.

(4.3.129–30)

And in Dekker's *The Honest Whore*:

There are of mad men, as there are of tame,
All humoured not alike: we have here some,
So apish and fantastic, play with a feather,
And though 'twould grieve a soul to see God's image
So blemished and defaced yet do they act
Such antic and such pretty lunacies
That spite of sorrow they will make you smile.

(Part 1, Act 5, Sc. 2)

'Antic' was a word which Shakespeare knew well, to his cost, for Greene in his diatribe had written of actors: 'these antics garnished in our colours' and scorned Shakespeare as 'an upstart crow, beautified with our feathers'. And we may turn to M.C. Bradbrook for an explanation of the language:

Country 'anticks' were used to present grotesque derisory mimes against objects of social contempt, reducing their

77

victims to animal level. Queen Elizabeth was disgusted when Cambridge tried to entertain her with an anti-papal show of this kind, although at her first Twelfth Night cardinals, bishops and abbots appeared in the likeness of crows, asses and wolves. Such grotesque beast-shows were found in plays ... and dumb shows of scorn ... In real life, such rituals of public humiliation as riding through the city, dressed in 'papers' setting out the victim's crime (a punishment for perjury), could precede the worse humiliation of the pillory or the stocks. Shakespeare, as 'the upstart crow', is wearing a feather costume of black, which was what the Devil wore in the old craft plays (he 'pomped in feathers'); he has become part of Greene's private beast fable, at once an 'antick' in a disgraceful show, and also the victim of it.[13]

'Antic' then we may certainly accept as 'ludicrous' or 'grotesque' but we may add that it described the behaviour of a clown or jester or of a real madman whose behaviour was considered humorous. If also we take 'disposition' separately we find from Onions that it meant 'natural constitution or temperament' so that if we ask ourselves who, to the Elizabethans, would, other than Hamlet, have possessed an 'antic disposition' we might answer that it would be a 'natural fool'. We may then turn to Robert Armin for further information:

> Naturall fooles are prone to selfe conceipt:
> Fooles artificiall, with their wits lay wayte
> To make themselues fooles, liking the disguise,
> To feede their owne mindes, and the gazers eyes.[14]

The 'natural fool' therefore was mad, and the 'artificial fool', the professional entertainer, acted as though he were mad. Armin, speaking of a visit to Oxford, says:

> I promised them to proue mad; and I thinke I am so, else I would not meddle with folly so deepely, but similis similem.[15]

Indeed, a doubt about the sanity of a fool seems to have enhanced his reputation. For the author of *Tarlton's Jests* said:

> Well, howsoeuer, either naturall or artificiall, or both, he was a mad merry companion, desired and loved of all.

In the courts and households of Westerns Europe in the Middle Ages the fools became collectors' items and the real madness of a fool was no barrier to his employment. Enid Welsford gives an absorbing account of the subject and what follows is taken from her book *The Fool*.[16] In Italy, for example, Matello, who died in 1499, 'could not have been wholly imbecile', and 'Buffoon Symone' (c.1500) was probably 'simple'. In Germany Conrad Pocher had a successful career although he began it by hanging a man – homicidal mania was no barrier to advancement. Claus Narr mentioned in the Dresden archives in 1461 and 1518 was a half-wit who also 'displayed uncanny powers of insight and prophecy'. In France, Triboulet, the famous court fool, was a simpleton; Thony, fool to the Duke of Orleans, was an imbecile; and other French fools are described as being slightly deranged or insane. In England, Wolsey's fool, Patch (c.1529), was a natural; Jack Oates blinded a rival; and another, Leonard, was mad without doubt.

There were of course 'artificial' fools too, some of them eminent, such as Chicot, a gentlemen trained to the profession of arms who was killed at the siege of Rouen in 1592. Although he was officially 'bouffon du roi' he gave Henry IV political advice. And in England Henry VIII's jester Will Somers and Elizabeth's Dick Tarlton were famous, the latter being also a skilled swordsman. The distinction between the 'natural' and the 'artificial' fool in fact goes back to at least the twelfth century – the court fool, that is. But the fool also became part of dramatic tradition, for the domestic fool or jester influenced the development of the Vice, according to Sir Edmund Chambers, who noted that he was always a 'riotous buffoon'. Enid Welsford agreed with him. Professor Cushman on the other hand believed that the Vice was derived from the Morality play, and Bernard Spivack supported this view.[17] Others trace him back to the Miracles and the comic devils that became so popular.

What is important for our purpose is to recognize that the medieval Church made a contribution to the complex symbol that was the fool – besides being comic the Vice was also evil and his satanic aura remained even though the Devil who had been an indispensable part of the Miracles faded out and made a personal appearance in only nine of about sixty Moralities. And the Vice also became associated with anti-Catholic satire in the reign of Henry VIII. For example in John Bale's *Three Laws* (c.1531) there is the stage direction:

> The aparellynge of the six vyces, or frutes of Infydelyte. Lete Idolatry be decked lyke an olde wytche, Sodomy lyke a monke of all sectes, Ambycyon lyke a byshop, Couetousnesse like a

pharyse or spyritall lawer, false doctrine, lyke a popysh
doctour, and hypocresy lyke a graye fryre.[18]

Then in the reign of Edward VI there is *Lusty Juventus* in which the
Vice is part of the anti-Catholic satire and his 'father' the Devil
appears:

> DEVIL. O my child, how dost thou fare?
> HYPOCRISY (THE VICE). Sancti amen. who have we here?
>   By the mass, I will buy none of they ware;
>   Thou art the chapman for the devil.
> DEVIL. What, my son, canst thou not tell,
>   Who, is here, and what I am?
>   I am thine own father Satan.

And later the Vice says:

> And [I have] brought up such superstition,
> Under the name of holiness and religion,
> That deceived almost all.
> As holy cardinals, holy popes,
> Holy vestments, holy copes,
> Holy hermits and friars . . .

The list continues and includes 'holy oil', 'holy saints' and 'holy
crosses'. It would therefore seem reasonable to suppose the audience's reaction to *Hamlet* – in which Satan plays 'father' to Hamlet
and complains that he did not receive 'holy oil' ('unaneled') and in
which Hamlet swears by the 'holy saint' Patrick – would have
been similar.

The Vice also made his appearance in revenge tragedy. Thus in
Horestes (1567) we find the Vice urging rebellion, then pretending
to Horestes that he is 'courrage' sent to help him from heaven, and
Horestes exclaims:

> My thinkes, I feel courrage prouokes my wil forward againe
> For to reuenge my fathers death and infamey so great
> Oh, how my hart doth boyle in dede, with fiery perching heate!
> Corrrage, now welcome, by the godes: I find thou art in dede
> A messenger of heauenly gostes; come let vs now procede
> And take in hand to bringe to pas reuengyd forto be
> Of those which haue my father slaine . . .

Later the Vice reveals himself as Revenge and Horestes instructs
him to dispose of Clytemnestra. While there has been critical
argument about the play as a whole the role of the Vice as demonic

tempter and agent seems clear. To an Elizabethan audience it would be preposterous that Heaven would urge a man to murder his own mother. As we have seen 'just revenge' was the twisted thinking of the villain or the crazed murderer. A human avenger had no connection with God and neither had the Vice. And we should also remember that the author of the play put a joke about Purgatory in the Vice's mouth thereby adding a touch of anti-Catholic satire.

Whatever the true genealogy of the Vice it is generally accepted that he became the ancestor of the Elizabethan stage clown – there appear to be no dissentient voices. But concurrent with this evolution of the artificial fool in the drama there remained in the real world the natural fool, the idiot, the madman, representing a range of mental impairment which included what we would now term mental deficiency to psychosis. Enid Welsford recalls that in Roman times real lunatics wore hoods with asses' ears and the practice continued into the Middle ages, and she adds that 'there is indeed considerable variety in fool-clothes and we hear of fox-tails, cockscombs, long petticoats and feathers as suitable wear for lunatics'. She goes on: 'The fact that the fool's dress was sometimes imposed on offenders as a peculiary degrading form of punishment is only explicable on the assumption that it was no mere carnival costume, but a badge of madness and servitude.'[19]

This can be seen in the Morality play called *Robert Cicyll* which was presented at Chester in 1529, although it probably dates from the preceding century. In this play, Enid Welsford informs us,

> King Robert of Sicily ... was punished for spiritual pride by being transformed into a fool and forced to play the part of court-jester in his own palace:

> > He was evyr so harde bestadd,
> > That mete nor drynke noon he had,
> > But his babulle was in hi hande ...
> > When that the howndes had etyn their fyll,
> > Then mygt he ete at hys wylle
> > At lower degre he myght not bee,
> > Then become a fole as thynketh me.[20]

The tale was, incidentally, presented by Lodge as a play, and also *réchauffé* as a poem by Longfellow.

A similar story was that of *The Lyfe of Robert the Deuyll* printed in London in 1599, a prose version of the original which dates from 1496. It is of particualr interest because it is so close to the

probable genesis of Shakespeare's *Hamlet*. According to this tale
the Duchess of Normandy (wife of the father of William the
Conquerer), barren after twelve years of marriage, promises that
if she conceives she will give her child 'both soule and bodye' to
the Devil. Robert is born and grows up to be a killer, a rapist and a
robber. Eventually he goes to Rome where he confesses to the
Pope, who sends him to a hermit. He in turn commands that as
penance Robert 'must counterfeyt a fole in all manere', and he
'taere hys clothes and grewe his shyrte'. Robert also could not eat
food unless a dog ate the same morsel. This amused the Emperor
who said:

> sythe I was borne
> Saw I neuer a more foole naturall
> Nor such an ydeot sawe I neuer beforne.

And the Court were 'gladde to see hym playe the foole'. In the
end, his penance completed, he performs mightily against
the Saracens.[21]

There are other examples of such 'transformation' in the
dramatic tradition of the fool. In *Wyt and Science* (c.1530)
'Ignorance' puts a fool's cap and coat on 'Wyt'; and after 'Idleness'
has blackened his face he looks in a glass which 'Reason' gives him
and says:

> Hah! Goges sowle! what have we here? A dyvell?
> Goges sowle, a foole, a foole, by the mas!
>
> . . . .
>
> Ingrorance [*sic*] cote, hoode, eares, – ye by the masse
> kokescome and all . . .
> > the stark foole I playe
> before all people.[22]

Thus too in *The Marriage of Witt and Wisdome* (1579) we find:

> Here shall Wantonis sing this song . . . and hauing sung him a
> sleep vpon her lappe, let him snort; then let her set a fooles
> bable on his hed, and colling his face: and Idleness shall steal
> away his purse from him, and goe his wayes.[23]

But, to focus particularly on the dress of the natural fool, we
must remember that what he wore in real life set the pattern for
the costume of the artificial fool. There were no institutions other
than Bedlam in England for the mentally handicapped and the
insane, and thus a person wearing a fool's insignia had been

'certified', so to speak. Thus Robert the Devil above is shown in a contemporary illustration as barefoot and clad in a petticoat with a coxcomb on his head and so represents a tradition of stigmatizing lunatics which began in the early Middle Ages and continued into Shakespeare's time. Minsheu's dictionary (1627) records that 'natural idiots and fools have and still do accustome themselves to wear in their cappes cockes feathers, or a hat with a necke and head of a cock on the top'.

To 'play the fool' then Will Somers imitated the 'certified lunatic'. Leslie Hotson, commenting on an engraving of him, says, 'On his head he wears a cap, with the feather which some-times replaced the bell or "cock's comb" of red cloth'. And he also quotes from *The Passions of the Mind* (1604) by Thomas Wright: 'It will become them as well as a peacock's feather in a fooles cap.'[24] Again, in *Kemps Nine Daies Wonder* (1600), his own account of his dance to Norwich, an illustration shows him with a plume of feathers in his hat.

F.P. Wilson records that

> when Lovell in *Henry VIII* speaks of 'fool and feather', and the Princess in *Love's Labour's Lost* asks 'What plume of feathers is he that indited this letter?' the collocation was already so well established as to have become proverbial; and for many generations 'he has a feather in his cap' was a periphrasis for a fool.[25]

In Italy we find the same symbolism. Leslie Hotson refers to

> Florio's apt dictionary definition of the bird called by the Italians *guffo*: 'An Owle called a Horne cout [coot] with feathers on each side of his head ... also a simple foole or gross – pated gull, a ninnie patch'.[26]

Then too Arlecchino, the ancestor of Harlequin, wore headgear usually decorated with an animal's tail or a bunch of feathers. A print in the *Recueil Fossard* (sixteenth century) shows 'Harlequin' with a horned cap and a single feather protruding from the back of it, the combined symbolism perhaps illustrating the fusion of his demonic origin with his comic role.[27] Callot, it may be added, has a painting of clowns wearing feathered head-dresses.

If we go to Germany we find that Douce has a woodcut of a German jester wearing a hood with ass's ears and with a single peacock's feather in it. And Ben Jonson in his *Masque of the*

Fortunate Isles (1626) describes Eulenspiegel, the legend of whom goes back to the fourteenth century:

> With feathers upright
> In his horned cap[28]

So too the Hamlet of the *Brudermord* refers to 'the black hats [of the players] full of feathers on their heads, and with about as many feathers below as above'.

What the English Vice wore is a mystery. Chambers said: 'Whether he ever had a cockscomb, a bauble, or an eared hood is not apparent'.[29] But Enid Welsford believed

> there is evidence that the Vices were sometimes dressed as fools, and a 'vice's coat', of motley and cap and bells, was provided for the real jester Will Somers when he appeared in the train of the Lord of Misrule in the reign of Edward VI.[30]

Thus as we have already learned from Hotson that Will Somers sometimes wore feathers in his hat it is reasonable to suppose that Vices sometimes did too. And we may note in particular that the combination of horns and feathers worn by Arlecchino and Eulenspiegel would have caused an English reader or member of a theatre audience to have identified them as Vices.

As for the petticoat which Robert the Devil wore, Hotson records:

> The petticoat, we find, was inescapably part of the Elizabethan mental picture of an idiot. For even when they thought of an ancient Roman pretending to be an idiot, they would clothe him in their mind's eye with their own fool's familiar long coat. In proof of this, we have Shakespeare (both in *Henry V* and in the *Rape of Lucrece*) describing what the classical Junius Brutus put on when he simulated idiocy to avert suspicion when plotting the death of Tarquin the tyrant.[31]

For Chambers this long coat and lathen sword which the Vice carried linked him with the domestic fool who also carried a gilded wooden sword,[32] and Hotson's findings were similar:

> Domestic fools and little boys often showed another piece of equipment in addition to the long coat. This was the dagger, worn at the back, suspended from the girdle. It was usually wooden (sometimes gilded) like the dagger of lath wielded by the Knavish Fool or Vice of the Morality plays.[33]

Douce contributes:

> In some old plays the fool's dagger is mentioned, perhaps the same instrument as was carried by the Vice or buffoon of the Moralities; and it may be as well to observe in this place that the domestic fool is sometimes, it is presumed improperly, called the Vice.[34]

Shakespeare seems to have favoured the wooden dagger rather than the sword, for in *Twelfth Night* we find 'dagger of lath' at 4.2.136, and in *1 Henry IV* at 2.4.151, 'wooden dagger' in *Henry V* at 4.4.77, and 'Vice's dagger' in *2 Henry IV* at 3.2.343. There is only one reference to a 'sword of lath', in *2 Henry VI* at 4.2.2.

But by Shakespeare's time the distinction between the Vice and the jester was blurred. For example Hotson points out that

> in *The Divell is an Asse* Ben Johnson introduces an old-time Vice named 'Iniquity', who recalls that about the year 1560 'every great man had his Vice [meaning his domestic jester] stand by him, in his long coat, shaking his wooden dagger'.[35]

Then in *Bussy d'Ambois*:

> A merry fellow, 'faith; it seems my lord
> Will have him for his jester: and, believe it,
> Such men are now no fools; 'tis a knight's place.
> If I, to save my Lord some crowns, should urge him
> T'abate his bounty, I should not be heard;
> I would to heaven I were an arrant ass,
> For then I should be sure to have the ears
> Of these great men, where now their jesters have them.
> 'Tis good to please him, yet I'll take no notice
> Of his preferment, but in policy
> Will still be grave and serious, lest he think
> I fear his wooden dagger.
>
> (1.1.197–208)

And in *Alphonsus, Emperor of Germany*:

> MENTZ. I am the Jester.
> EDWARD. O excellent! is your Holiness the Vice?
> Fortune has fitted you, i' faith my Lord;
> You'll play the Ambidexter cunningly.[36]

John Florio in his *A World of Wordes, or Dictionarie in Italian and English* (1598) glosses 'Zane' as 'a simple vice, clowne, foole, or simple fellow in a plaie or comedie'.[37] Cotgrave in his dictionary (1611) defines the French 'mime' as a 'Vice, foole, jeaster, scoffer, dauncer in a Play'. And we may turn to Enid Welsford who records that Richard Tarlton, 'the most famous jester to Queen Elizabeth', was 'sometimes called a Vice'.[38] Spivack observed:

> In his own time and after, the Vice is often identified explicitly as the fool of the play, or his behaviour is described in such a way that the association is unmistakable. Thus Philip Stubbes in his *Anatomy of Abuses* (1583) asks, 'For who will call him a wiseman, that plaieth the part of a foole and a vice?' In his *Art of English Poesie* (1589) Puttenham refers to 'Carols and rounds and such light and lascivious poems, which are commonly and commodiously uttered by those buffons [*sic*] or Vices in playes then by any other person.'[39]

So also in Massinger's *The Duke of Milan* (1623):

> No smile, not a buffoon to be seen
> Or common jester.
>
> (Act 1, Sc. 1)

Most importantly the fool–jester–Vice association is found in Shakespeare. Prince Hal uses all these terms to describe Falstaff. Dover Wilson's comment is therefore apposite:

> as heir to the Vice, Falstaff inherits by reversion the functions and attributes of the Lord of Misrule, the Fool, the Buffoon, and the Jester, antic figures the origins of which are lost in the dark backward and abyss of folk-custom.[40]

Then too Hamlet describes Claudius as 'a vice of kings' (3.4.98) and as 'A king of shreds and patches' (3.4.103), of which latter phrase Harold Jenkins says: 'Some eds. suppose the phrase to have been suggested by the parti-coloured dress of the Vice'.[41] Dover Wilson indeed glosses it as 'referring to the motley of the "Vice" or clown'.[42] But if we again turn to Harold Jenkins for his reading of 'pajock' at 3.2.278 we find that he glosses it as 'a contemptuous diminutive of *patch*, clown'.[43]

Hamlet's first appearance – to Ophelia – after meeting the Ghost has been much argued about:

> Lord Hamlet, with his doublet all unbrac'd,
> No hat upon his head, his stockings foul'd,
> Ungarter'd and down-gyved to his ankle,
> Pale as his shirt, his knees knocking each other,

> And with a look so piteous in purpot
> As if he had been loosed out of hell
> To speak of horrors.

Hamlet indeed looks like a ghost to Ophelia – he is pale, as the Ghost is, and his stockings are like fetters such as were believed to be worn by the damned in Hell (the 'prison-house'), a tradition which goes back at least to Virgil's Tartarus in the *Aeneid* and which Dickens followed in presenting Marley's Ghost. He also waves his head up and down 'thrice' – the diabolic number again – and sighed piteously. Dover Wilson quotes Quincy Adams who refers to Scoloker's lines:

> Puts off his clothes, his shirt he only wears
> Much like mad Hamlet

and concludes that 'Hamlet's madness, as it impressed the audience of the Globe, was conspicuously a madness "in clothes"'. But Adams meant real madness:

> This slovenliness in costume has usually been interpreted as the pose of the forlorn lover. It is true that literary artists of the seventeenth century sometimes represented a disappointed lover as adopting a melancholy pose accompanied by a certain carelessness in dress. But Hamlet's appearance cannot be explained on this score.[44]

I agree. We may compare Hamlet's 'madness in clothes' with 'a special clown's get-up' worn by Tarlton, 'who came like a rogue in a foule shirt without a band, and in a blew coat with one sleeve, his stockings out at the heeles, and his head full of straw and feathers'.[45]

This leads on to the question of Hamlet's dress in the play and whether it could be identified as being that of a Vice or jester. As tradition would seem to support the idea of plain black clothes we may note that Guérin, the jester of Margaret of Navarre, wore a cassock of black satin, and Chicot who died in 1592, wore black taffeta.[46] As for Hamlet's sword, Chambers considered that Touchstone's sword was perhaps 'inherited from the "Vice" of the later moralities'.[47] (Perhaps we should also remember that Tarlton was a skilled swordsman.) Chambers also believed that Shakespeare was 'aware of the abundant fool-literature, continental and English', and pointed out that Feste quotes Rabelais 'in whose work ... the fool Triboulet figures'.[48] Thus there is nothing incongruous in seeing Hamlet as a Vice wearing a sword or in supposing that Shakespeare knew Chicot had used his in earnest at the siege of Rouen.

Then again, while this is to anticipate, when Hamlet feels that he is good enough to 'turn professional' as an actor his reference to 'a forest of feathers' is almost certainly to the costume of fool, jester, clown, Vice, buffoon, idiot, lunatic – call him what you will. The phrase in fact is echoed in a comic context in Chapman's *Monsieur d'Olive* (3.2.152–5). So too in *The Malcontent* (1604) the following dialogue takes place:

> CONDELL. I beseech you, sir, be covered.
> SLY. No, in good faith, for mine ease: look you, my hat's the handle to this fan: God's so, what a beast was I, I did not leave my feather at home! Well, but I'll take an order with you. *Puts his feather in his pocket.*
> BURBADGE. Why do you conceal your feather, sir?
> SLY. Why? Do you think I'll have jests broken upon me in the play to be laughed at? This play hath beaten all your gallants out of the feathers: Blackfriars hath almost spoiled Blackfriars for feathers.
> SINKLO. God's so, I thought 'twas for somewhat our gentlewomen at home counselled me to wear my feather to the play.

Dover Wilson, following Steevens, believed that Sly might have been the original performer of Osric and that 'not only Sly but Sinklo, and probably the other members of the company, are represented as wearing ridiculous feathers'. Yet while Dover Wilson believed that this has 'obvious reference' to the 'forest of feathers' he still glossed the phrase thus: 'Plumes were worn by tragic actors and contemporary references to the fact are frequent.'[49] But no editor has produced any convincing evidence to support the contention.

But what of the 'razed shoes' decorated with 'two Provincial roses'? Is Hamlet raving or could a clown have worn such footwear? We may observe that 'razed' shoes – shoes slashed for decoration – had been popular in the later part of Henry VIII's reign but had faded out by 1560. So we may guess that the clown's costume may have belonged to that era. But the rosettes on the shoes are a puzzle because the fashion of wearing rosettes on shoes did not appear in England until the 1590s, and even then the rosettes are small.[50] As Harold Jenkins indicates, the 'Provincial roses' referred to the cabbage rose, the rose of Provence, and 'what persists, through many shifts of identity, as the essential feature of a "provincial rose", and one of particular relevance to Hamlet's shoe-roses, is the profusion of its layers of petals'.[51] So the rosettes are large if they are contemporary with *Hamlet* but in spite of their apparently French origin there are no allusions to them in sixteenth-century France as a decoration for shoes; nor do they appear to be connected with any other continental country. But if we look at what Brachiano says in *The White Devil* we find:

> Why, 'tis the devil
> I know him by a great rose he wears on's shoe,
> To hide his cloven foot.
>
> (5.3.106–8)

And in Jonson's *The Devil is an Asse* Fitzdottrell says:

> 'fore hell, my heart was at my mouth,
> Till I have view'd his shoes well; for those roses
> Were big enough to hide a cloven hoof.
>
> (1.3.7–9)

Thus it seems possible that a clown's costume which included feathers on the head and slashed shoes with big rosettes would belong to a comic devil – to a Vice in fact. And we may date the costume c.1560 which agrees with the period when the Vice was in his heyday.[52]

That this hypothesis may be correct may be seen from Hamlet's

Ah ha! Come, some music: come, the recorders.

For as we have seen 'Ah ha! was an exclamation which was characteristic of the Vice, and recorders were played by clowns in the jig which followed a tragedy. Woodcuts of Tarlton and Kempe show them thus equipped, as is Rafe Simnel, Henry VIII's fool, on the title-page of *Friar Bacon and Friar Bungay*.

While more will be said about Hamlet's costume when we look at the Play Scene we may pause briefly to consider how several eminent critics have seen Hamlet's role. First there is A.J.A. Waldock who thought of the 'antic disposition' as producing effective theatre, but in explaining it 'Shakespeare has not proferred his assistance'. He believed that 'a partial failure to assimilate ... original material' might have been a contributory factor, and he goes on:

We can easily see the purpose which Hamlet's madness serves in the economy of the play. He realizes himself in and through it. And what a shield for his satiric comment! From its shelter, with the security of a jester, he launches his barbs. But the motivation of it is another question.[53]

For Dover Wilson:

The 'antic disposition' was assumed on a sudden impulse ... it was obviously prompted by his hysteria at the moment; and it would be accepted as a convenient disguise while he was maturing his plans. To consider it more curiously than this is to treat Hamlet as history not drama ... Shakespeare saw that it possessed immense dramatic possibilities ... 'Mad Hamlet' is indeed the fool of the play that takes its name from him. By acting the natural, he usurps the natural's privileges, and Touchstone-like uses his madness 'like a stalking-horse, and under the presentation of that he shoots his wit'. Far too little has been made of this aspect of the play.[54]

Gilbert Murray said:

It is very remarkable that Shakespeare, who did such wonders in his idealized and half-mystic treatment of the real Fool, should also have made his greatest tragic hero out of a Fool transfigured.[55]

And Harry Levin:

Hamlet, like Robert the Devil in the legend, becomes a court jester ... Hamlet, at the court where he cannot be king, must perforce be fool, an artificial fool pretending to be a natural. His assumption of foolishness is the archetypal feature of his story, as it has come down from primitive legend. In fact his name derives from the Old Norse Amlo i, which means 'a fool, a ninny, an idiot' – and, more especially, a Jutish trickster who feigns stupidity.[56]

Thus all four see Hamlet as acting the part of fool/jester. But, as we have seen, George Rylands, Leslie Hotson and most recently Harold Jenkins have found echoes of the Vice in Hamlet's dialogue with the Ghost. I therefore suggest that as we have good grounds for believing that the Ghost is diabolic and that jester and Vice were synonyms for Shakespeare's audience we may accept that all these commentators are in fact in agreement. Hamlet does become a fool, the Devil's fool, his Vice / jester. But the irony is that he never realizes it – he has become a natural who thinks he is acting the artificial. This is Levin's 'formula' but in reverse. Hamlet has become 'le fol', the madman, transformed by the poison of revenge, a natural in his own court like Robert of Sicily; like Lodge's 'jeaster' a man who coins 'bitter jeastes' who is 'continually flearing', who shows 'antique motions' like walking about reading a book or playing hide and seek with Polonius's body. He is more than this for us of course and probably too for the Elizabethans but for them the symbol of the fool is something we can no longer share. As Enid Welsford says:

> It is impossible to study Shakespeare's use of the fool in tragedy without realizing afresh how deep and how wide-spreading were the roots of his art, and how much even the greatest poet owes to the environment which supplies him with suggestive poetic symbols. The king and the fool still walked the world in Shakespeare's day; but even in the world they were regarded with a certain superstitious awe, which was no doubt ultimately related to the old notions of possession and inspiration.[57]

Thus while we have seen the development of the court fool into the Vice, and then into the Elizabethan stage clown, there was always the real madman, the real idiot, the 'poor fool' who did not even have a Bedlam to go to:

> What if your Fiery spirits had bin bound
> To *Antick Habits*; or your heads bin crown'd
> With *Peacock Plumes*; had yee bin forc'd to feed
> Your Saviour's dear-bought Flock in a *fools weed*;
> He that was scorn'd, revil'd, endur'd the Curse
> Of a base death, in your behalfs; nay worse,
> Swallow'd the cup of wrath charg'd up to th' brim,
> Durst ye not stoope to play the fooles for him?
> (Francis Quarles, 1592–1644)

But how mad did Hamlet seem in soliloquy to Shakespeare's audience? Consider for example his attitude to Fortinbras and his army:

> Led by a delicate and tender prince,
> Whose spirit with divine ambition puffed
> Makes mouths at the invisible event,
> Exposing what is mortal and unsure
> To all that fortune, death and danger dare,
> Even for an egg-shell.
>
> (4.4.48–53)

'Delicate and tender' was the title given to Babylon in the Genevan version of the Bible,[58] while 'puffed' was commonly associated with 'pride' by the Elizabethans. In Nowell's *Catechism* for instance we find: 'the mind of man ... is puffed with pride, and loth to be under other's commandment'.[59] But the context was not exclusively ecclesiastical, for the collocation is also common in the drama. For example, in *Antonio and Mellida* Feliche says:

> this same smoke, called pride ...
> Entices princes to devour heaven,
> Swallow omnipotence, out-stare dread fate ...
> Heaves up their heart with swelling, puffed conceit,
> Till their souls burst with venom'd Arrogance.

And ambition was universally condemned because it was the sin of Satan himself – 'by that sin fell the angels'. James I wrote, referring to the Devil: 'so ambitious is hee and greedy of honour'. Thus a Fortinbras possessed of such 'ambition' was also possessed of the Devil who

> trusted to have equalled the Most High,
> If he opposed; and with ambitious aim
> Against the throne and monarchy of God
> Raised impious war in Heaven and battle proud,
> With vain attempt.

This attitude and word usage persisted at least until the time of Coleridge who wrote:

> I do not approve the so frequent use of this word relatively to Milton. Indeed the fondness for ingrafting a good sense on the word 'ambition', is not a Christian impulse in general.

Thus when even Byron scorned 'vile ambition' we must accept that Hamlet's attitude is warped, to say the least.[60]

So too the following lines:

> Rightly to be great
> Is not to stir without great argument,

> But greatly to find quarrel in a straw
> When honour's at the stake.

$$(4.4.53-6)$$

are often quoted out of context and lose their essential meaning –
that this is the Devil's honour. L.C. Knights however is not
misled:

> Professor Dover Wilson paraphrases the last sentence: 'Fighting
> for trifles is mere pugnacity, not greatness; but it is greatness to
> fight instantly and for a trifle when honour is at stake.' Right
> enough, but this is arguing in a circle, for it leaves honour as no
> more than the prompting to fight instantly and for a trifle ...
> Honour here is not a defining word, but a mere justifying blur.[61]

It might be added that one of the symptoms of Ophelia's
madness is that she 'spurns enviously at straws' and hears 'There's
tricks i' th' world' which sounds like echoes of 'find quarrel in a
straw' above and 'for a fantasy and a trick of fame'.

The truly Elizabethan view of what Hamlet has so distorted can
be seen in a passage from Marston's *Histrio-mastix*:

> What should make
> Men so enamour'd on this Strumpet war
> To dote upon her form? When (in herself)
> She's made of nothing but infectious plagues,
> Witness the present chaos of our Scene
> Where every street is chain'd with links of spoil,
> Here proud Ambition rides; there Fury flies,
> Here horror, and there ruthless Murder stalks,
> Led on by Ruin, and in Steel and fire,
> That now on tops of houses; now in vaults,
> Now in the sacred Temples; here, and there
> Runs wild.

What we see Hamlet doing is adopting a kind of inverted
morality – 'good' has become what is evil, 'foul' is 'fair'. 'Divine
ambition' was the sin of Satan and thus in the same category as
'just revenge', both being denials of the goodness, and the
supremacy, of God.

Similarly Hamlet claims that 'conscience doth make cowards of
us all'. This has been quoted so often out of context that it has in
effect come to mean that guilt makes us fearful of consequences
whereas Hamlet repudiates the workings of his conscience and
thus agrees with the villainous Richard III.

> Let not our babbling dreams affright our souls;
> Conscience is but a word that cowards use,
> Devis'd at first to keep the strong in awe:
> Our strong arms be our conscience, swords our law.
>
> (5.3.309–13)

Hamlet also says later:

>   is't not perfect conscience
> To quit him with this arm? And is't not to be damned,
> To let this canker of our nature come
> In further evil?
>
> (5.2.67–70)

Both Hamlet and Richard III are justifying unlawful killing, and Hamlet reaches a point where he can dismiss his murderous scheme to dispose of Rosencrantz and Guildenstern with 'they are not near my conscience'.

In his 'To be' soliloquy Hamlet also claims that if conscience did not make him a coward he could have taken his own life – a brave man would have committed suicide. This again is nonsense for it contradicts Christian teaching – Job for example shows the need to endure the tribulations of life. And again we see from Nowell's *Catechism* that the Elizabethan child was taught that

> Christ hath set himself for an exemplar for us to follow, to frame our life according thereunto and ... we ought henceforth to put on the image of the heavenly man, quietly and patiently bearing, after his example, all sorrows and wrongs, and following and expressing his other divine virtues so far as mortal man be able.[62]

We may see how this teaching bore fruit by looking again at the drama. In Massinger's *The Maid of Honour* we find Adorni saying:

> What will become of me now is apparent.
> Whether a poniard or a halter be
> The nearest way to hell (for I must thither,
> After I've killed myself) is somewhat doubtful.
> This Roman resolution of self-murder
> Will not hold water at the high tribunal,
> When it comes to be argued; my good genius
> Prompts me to this consideration. He
> That kills himself to avoid misery, fears it,
> And, at the best, shews but a bastard valour.
> This life's fort committed to my trust,

> Which I must not yield up till it be forced:
> Nor will I. He's not valiant that dares die,
> But he that boldly bears calamity.
>
> (Act 4, Sc. 3)

As L.C. Knights remarks in *An Approach to Hamlet* (p. 79): 'What Hamlet needs is not less of conscience but more'. And he quotes one of the murderers of the Duke of Clarence in *Richard III*,

> who declared of conscience, 'it makes a man a coward ... 'Tis a blushing shamefast spirit, that mutinies in a man's bosom; it fills a man full of obstacles: it is turned out of towns and cities for a dangerous thing; and every man that means to live well endeavours to trust to himself and to live without it'.

It is also valuable to note that Charles Lamb, speaking for all of us, remarked:

> I confess myself utterly unable to appreciate that celebrated soliloquy in *Hamlet* beginning, 'To be, or not to be,' or to tell whether it be good, bad or indifferent; it has been so handled and pawed about by declamatory boys and men, and torn so inhumanly from its living place and principle of continuity in the play, till it has become to me a perfectly dead member.[63]

But a glance at the possible associations of parts of the soliloquy may be worthwhile. Georg Brandes, for instance, quoted a close parallel to 'To die, to sleep ...' from Florio's translation of Montaigne's summary of the Apology of Socrates:

> If it [i.e. death] be a consummation of ones being, it is also an amendment and entrance into a long and quiet life. Wee finde nothing so sweete in life, as a quiet rest and gentle sleepe, and without dreames.[64]

The association is all the more plausible because the context also is suicide, and therefore unChristian, just as the taking of arms against a sea of troubles may have been a reference to a pagan Celtic custom mentioned in Fleming's translation of Aelian's *Histories* (1576). Moreover, Hamlet regarding death as sleep beset with troubled dreams is not just a striking image, because this attitude to death was not regarded as Christian by the Church, as can be seen in the draft Forty-Two Articles:

> They which say, that the souls of such as depart hence, do sleep, being without all sense, feeling, or perceiving, until the day of judgment, or affirm that the souls die with the bodies, and at

the last day shall be raised up with the same; do utterly dissent from the right belief, declared to us in holy scripture.

The Church had clearly indicated what happened to the soul after death – it went either to Heaven or to Hell and that was what was to be believed. Hamlet has lost his moral bearings but the corrector, we may be assured, had not, and so allowed this speech because he did not think that Shakespeare's audience would be misled by it.

Thus also Shakespeare's word 'shuffle' suggests shirking the burden of life, and the association of 'coil' with rope (I have in mind Dover Wilson's note in his edition of *Hamlet*, p. xxxiv) connotes suicide by hanging. It seems that 'a poniard or a halter' as above was the classic means of committing suicide which Satan and his minions offered to their intended victims, as we may see in *Doctor Faustus*:

> My heart's so hardened I cannot repent!
> Scarce can I name salvation, faith or heaven,
> But fearful echoes thunders [*sic*] in mine ears,
> 'Faustus, thou art damned': then swords and knives,
> Poison, guns, halters and envenomed steel
> Are laid before me to dispatch myself:
> And long ere this I should have done the deed,
> Had not sweet pleasure conquer'd deep despair.
>
> (2.2.18–25)

Also the description of death by suicide as a 'consummation' may be a blasphemous reference to Christ's last words, 'Consummatum est' – Faustus's oath ends with the words:

> *Consummatum est*: this bill is ended,
> And Faustus hath bequeathed his soul to Lucifer.
>
> (2.1.74–5)

With such associations I find it difficult to believe that 'To be ...' could refer to anything other than suicide. Two recent editors – T.J.B. Spenser and Irving Ribner – take the same view.[65] After all, Cassius, who was no philosopher, said:

> I had as lief not be as live to be
> In awe of such a thing as I myself.
>
> (*Julius Caesar*, 1.2.95–6)

To a groundling – and why should we neglect him? – the meaning surely was plain enough. The whole soliloquy presents us with the problem of existence, of life itself, entailing as it does suffering and mystery. 'Why did I not die at birth?' says Job. Aristotle – and Faustus – wrestled with 'on kai me on' (ὄν καὶ μὴ ὄν). Boethius claimed, as L.C. Knights pointed out, that evil men do not in fact exist – his answer to the problem of evil.[66]

For the Christian, including the Christian groundling, acceptance of the goodness of God was the answer – Man could not stand alone. The slings and arrows to which Hamlet refers may have come from the book of Job: 'The arrow cannot make him flee; for him slingstones are turned to stubble' (Job 41:28–9). Eleanor Prosser also sees an association of ideas between 'The undiscover'd country' and the book of Job, and Harold Jenkins also refers to Job 10:21.[67] But there are no certain sources for the images in the passage, and there is no clear line of thought. Instead there is confusion – neither acting nor refraining from action offers a solution to his problems. Not even death is a solution. But what never occurs to him is to act as a Christian should, and as an Elizabethan had been taught since childhood to do, that is turn to God and pray for guidance. Even Claudius tries. Today we probably wouldn't either and this may well enable us to empathize with him, but in Elizabethan eyes Hamlet is in a state of despair – not merely 'depression' (which in the modern sense has also a psychiatric connotation) but theological despair.

'To bee or not to bee' fascinated Pepys and the fascination remains. When the speech is so compelling it is difficult to maintain that in layman's terms Hamlet is mad, for he speaks for all of us. It is only when we reflect that he is on the verge of stabbing himself that we can think in modern terms of a manic-depressive psychosis, or in Elizabethan terms of a despair so deep that he is close to damning his soul for all eternity. Hamlet is in a state where he feels no one, not even God, loves him. We have all been there. Little wonder then that we identify with Hamlet, and the very imprecision of the imagery may make the identification easier. It does not seem helpful to regard Hamlet as uttering philosophical profundities when in dramatic terms Shakespeare's first audience waited to see whether Hamlet would sink his dagger into Claudius or himself. In either case his soul would have been damned to eternity. And to a contemporary audience whose acquaintance with Christian ideas was almost certainly greater than with philosophic speculation, instruction such as this in Nowell's *Catechism* would perhaps have been apposite:

M. Is man able in this fear and these hard distresses to deliver himself by his own strength?

S. Nothing less. For it is only God which strengtheneth man despairing of his own estate, raiseth him up in affliction, restoreth him in utter misery, and by whose guidance the sinner conceiveth the hope, mind, and will.[68]

We also, I think, have to realize that in the language of despair words come to mean their opposites. For example, just as Hamlet 'devoutly' wishes the consummation of death, so Faustus is counselled by Mephistopheles to 'pray devoutly to the prince of hell', and also Faustus asks pardon for his 'presumption' – but from Lucifer, not God. Today, Catholic children are more likely than others to react in the Elizabethan manner to words like 'despair' and 'presumption', as these extracts from a modern Catechism show:

Despair. To be without hope of salvation.
Presumption. Expecting salvation without taking the necessary means to obtain it.

And:

Sins opposed to the virtue of hope are:
1. Despair, or want of confidence in God.
2. Presumption. An expectation that God will save us even though we do not make use of the necessary means of salvation.

As for 'disobedience' we have only to remember the opening lines of *Paradise Lost*:

Of Man's first disobedience, and the fruit
Of that forbidden tree, whose mortal taste
Brought death into the world, and all our woe ...

to realize that certain words had a fixed religious meaning and that Elizabethan children had been conditioned to them from a very early age. Thus they would be the more aware as adults of words, like those of the Black Mass, that were perverted parodies of Christian doctrine – 'just revenge', 'divine ambition', 'coward conscience', and death as a 'consummation devoutly to be wished' and as 'sleep'.

The book of Job was one of Shakespeare's favourite books in the Old Testament,[69] and parts of it were included in the lectionary of the Book of Common Prayer. And it is virtually certain that when Shakespeare and his contemporaries thought of despair the name of Job came to mind, for he was an object lesson in overcoming it. Falstaff for example knew that life was a 'weaver's shuttle', and even today the patience of Job is proverbial. Robert Burton's comments illustrate the importance of Job in counselling against despair:

> [They] talk familiarly with Devils, hear and see Chimeras, prodigious, uncouth shapes, Bears, Owls, Anticks, black dogs, fiends, hideous out-cries, fearful noises, shrieks, lamentable complaints, they are possessed, and through impatience they roar and howl, curse, blaspheme, deny God, call his power in question, abjure religion, and are still ready to offer violence unto themselves, by hanging, drowning &c.... To such persons I oppose God's mercy, and his justice; the judgments of God are mysterious, not unjust ... To put confidence, and have an assured hope in him, as Job had, Though he kill me, I will trust in him.[70]

The advice of the Old Man to Faustus follows the same line, and we must remember that this was a popular play, a box-office success, and not a sermon delivered in church to a bored congregation:

> O gentle Faustus, leave this damned art,
> This magic, that will charm thy soul to hell,
> And quite bereave thee of salvation ...
> FAUSTUS. Where art thou Faustus, wretch, what hast thou done?
> Damned art thou Faustus, damned; despair and die.
> Hell claims his right, and with a roaring voice,
> Says, 'Faustus come, thine hour is almost come',
> And Faustus now will come to do thee right.
> OLD MAN. O stay, good Faustus, stay thy desperate steps!
> I see an angel hover o'er thy head,
> And with a vial full of precious grace,
> Offers to pour the same into thy soul;
> Then call for mercy, and avoid despair.
>
> (5.1.35 ff.)

Hamlet's reference to the 'pale cast of thought' is also part of his 'satanic' vocabulary, for man's reason was a unique gift bestowed on him by God:

Thou art a man, endued with reason and understanding, wherein God hath engraven his lively image. In other creatures there is some likeness in him, some footsteps of his divine nature; but in man he hath stamped his image. Some things are like God in that they are; But this is not the image of God. His image is only in that we understand. Seeing then that thou art of so noble a nature and that thou bearest in thine understanding the image of God, so govern thyself as is fit for a creature of understanding. But not like the brute beasts which want understanding.[71]

Coleridge of course also accepted this religious formulation: 'Man is distinguished from the brute animals in proportion as thought prevails over sense.'[72] Indeed Hamlet himself accepts it elsewhere:

> a beast that wants discourse of reason
>   Would have mourned longer

and:

> What a piece of work is man ... in apprehension, how like a god.

Yet in this soliloquy he rejects the very faculty which places him nearer than all other creatures to God.

The entire soliloquy is, in Elizabethan terms, 'desperate'. Hamlet for all his flashes of wit and gaiety is sinking deeper into 'despair', which is for most of us today, unless we are Catholics, a rather remote conception. Despair of this kind could not hold a theatre audience today, but the despair of Faustus and of Hieronimo enthralled the Elizabethan audience. Shakespeare strikes the note early, for when we first meet Hamlet he is already contemplating suicide:

> O, that this too too sullied flesh would melt,
> Thaw and resolve itself into a dew,
> Or that the Everlasting had not fixed
> His cannon 'gainst self-slaughter

> (1.2.129–32)

Philip Edwards says: 'Hamlet when we first meet him is in a state of despair. He longs for death, and would take his own life if suicide were not forbidden by divine decree.'[73] To add to the complexities Hamlet's melancholy must also be considered. It has been claimed that his mental state could be described in contemporary terms as 'melancholy adust'. Thus Burton quoting Avicenna: 'those men ... are usually sad and solitary, and that continually, and in excess, more than ordinary suspicious, more fearful, and have long, sore, and most corrupt imaginations'.[74] Whatever the contemporary diagnosis it is clear that Hamlet himself is aware of his melancholy:

> The spirit that I have seen
> May be a devil, and the devil hath power
> T'assume a pleasing shape, yea, and perhaps
> Out of my weakness and my melancholy,
> As he is very potent with such spirits,
> Abuses me to damn me.
>
> (2.2.602–7)

Dover Wilson believed that Shakespeare drew on Timothy Bright's *Treatise on Melancholy*. Kenneth Muir agrees.[75] Bright wrote:

> The perturbations of melancholy are for the most parte, sadde and fearfull, and such as rise of them, as distrust, doubt, diffidence, or dispaire, sometimes furious, and sometimes merry in apparaunce through a kinde of Sardonian, and false laughter.[76]

But Dover Wilson did not pursue the topic of diabolic intervention in the life of a melancholic. On that score Bright wrote:

> Of this kinde [of temptations] are certaine blasphemies suggested of the Devill, and laying of violent handes of them selves, or upon others neither moved therto by hate or malice: or any occasion of revenge: of the same sort is the dispaire and distrust of gods mercy, and grace.[77]

Burton took the same line in his *Anatomy of Melancholy*:

> The melancholy humour is the Devil's bath; and as in Saul, those evil spirits get in, as it were, and take possession of us.

And so he agrees with Hamlet.

Once again we are faced with the strange phenomenon of Hamlet making what seems to be a poetic statement of what is universally valid, when in fact, in the context of Shakespeare's age, he is talking nonsense, even blasphemous nonsense. But the very decay of our own religious beliefs brings us closer to Hamlet – suicide is no longer sinful in most people's eyes, nor does it lead

101

to eternal damnation. Our view of the soliloquy is also distorted because we know in advance that Hamlet does not in fact use his 'bare bodkin' on himself. If he had done we would of course have had a different play, but we would also have questioned his wisdom and even his sanity, for we reject any philosophy which would cause death by our own hands. And we would certainly have ceased to identify with Hamlet.

At the end of this soliloquy an Elizabethan would see Hamlet advancing further along the Devil's road, which leads only to Hell:

> There is a path upon your left-hand side,
> That leadeth from a guilty conscience
> Unto a forest of distrust and fear,
> A darksome place and dangerous to pass:
> There shall you meet with melancholy thoughts,
> Whose baleful humours if you but uphold,
> It will conduct you to despair and death.
>
> (*The Spanish Tragedy*, Act 3, Sc. 2)

As Hamlet's conscience is no longer in working order, as it were, he is heading for destruction. The association of the 'sea of troubles' with conscience may have been a familiar one to the Elizabethans, for in 'Prayers for a quiet Conscience' the *Primer* of 1553 has:

> The wicked is like a raging sea which is never quiet, neither is there any peace to the ungodly; but such as love the law, O Lord, they have plenty of peace, they have quiet minds and contented consciences.[78]

Thus, to sum up, when we examine Hamlet's attitude to ambition, to conscience and to suicide we must see them in a religious context as the Elizabethans did, and that means in effect recognizing that Satan is at the root of his troubles. It is not enough to take the view of the psychiatrist:

> It is evident to the Elizabethans that melancholy comprehended a wide range of mental attitudes, from a normal and praiseworthy gravity of bearing, through mild eccentricity, to established neurosis and to the wildest psychotic derangement.[79]

In Harold Jenkins's view,

> in modern criticism there has been much discussion of Hamlet as a melancholic type. But although this is often illuminating

102

... the formalistic approach unduly restricts the characterization.

In symbolic terms which they were familiar with Hamlet has let himself become the tool of the Devil and a modern approach which does not appreciate this misunderstands the diabolic role of the Ghost in the play. Timothy Bright, however up to date he was as a physician, did not deny Satan's exploitation of the melancholic, so that even an illiterate groundling would have shared the religious view of Nashe:

> The Devil when with any other sickness or malady the faculties of our reason are enfeebled and distempered, will be most busy to disturb and torment us.[80]

In Elizabethan eyes Hamlet

> More needs ... the divine than the physician.
> *(Macbeth,* 5.2.81)

5

The Play Scene

ALTHOUGH SOME DIGRESSION is involved it is convenient to begin an enquiry into the Play Scene at the point where the troupe of actors arrives (Act 2, Sc. 2). First it is important to realize that references to Seneca and Plautus and to 'Hercules and his load' may refer mainly to a period that corresponds roughly to that of the generation before Shakespeare's. *Ralph Roister Doister* (1550) was based on Plautus, and 'Hercules and his load' goes back to Jasper Heywood's translation of Seneca's *Hercules Furens* (1561). About that time the Children's companies did 'carry it away', for between 1558 and 1576 they gave 46 performances at Court as against the adults' 32. These plays were also written in blank verse, the invention of the Earl of Surrey who used it in his translation of the *Aeneid* (Book 2) in 1557 – which is of course 'Aeneas' tale to Dido'. Hamlet's reference to 'blank verse' at 2.2.329 also fits the context.

So much attention has been focused on the Poetomachia that the reference to the 'little eyases' has been regarded as contemporary, but there is little to support such a theory. If the Children had been so successful I find it difficult to believe that Shakespeare would have admitted that his rivals had scored over him and that Burbage would have continued to lease the Blackfriars to them. There seems to be no way of gauging the relative successes of the rival companies at that time even though there was evidently a renewal of interest in the Children's companies. But appearances at Court do not show that the Children were more popular – the Children gave 7 as against 57 adult performances between 1594 and 1603, and only 18 as against 281 between 1603 and 1616. And while the Children were to enjoy the patronage of the new queen, and become in 1603 the Children of the Revels, they did not succeed in maintaining their popularity. Another point in favour of the earlier date is the reference to 'the common stages', for in Shakespeare's time they played at the Blackfriars, which was a 'private' theatre, whereas in the 1560s they had played at Lincoln's Inn at a time when inns, such as the Boar's Head and the Saracen's

Head, provided the 'public' stages before the permanent theatres appeared. It is possible of course that 'Hercules and his load' could refer to the Globe Theatre, but if it does this may indicate that *Hamlet* was written before the Blackfriars was leased to the Children.

As for the 'late innovation' which has been taken by some as a topical allusion to the Essex rebellion and by others to the exclusion of the players from London in 1596, it is not possible to be certain. But if we must have allusions why not the Northern Rebellion of 1569–70? However, within the context of the play surely the rebellion of Fortinbras will do? We are perhaps on safer ground when we try to identify the 'Pyrrhus speech' as an attempt to echo the style of the earlier plays. Coleridge said of it:

> This admirable substitution of the epic for the dramatic, giving such a reality to the impassioned dramatic diction of Shakespeare's own dialogue, and authorized too, by the actual style of the tragedies before his time (Porrex and Ferrex, Titus Andronicus &c) – is well worthy of note. The fancy, that a burlesque was intended, sinks below criticism: the lines, as epic narrative, are superb.[1]

That *Hamlet* was deliberately given an old-fashioned look, and sound, can be seen also from two points which connect them with Richard Edwards who wrote *Damon and Pithias* (c.1571) for the Children of the Chapel (see 'Damon dear' at 3.2.281) and *The Paradise of Dainty Devices* (1575) (see 'While the grass grows' at 3.2.345). These allusions have been so assigned by editors even though it must be admitted the latter is probably proverbial. Then there is the gravedigger's song 'In youth when I did love' written by Lord Vaux and printed in *Tottel's Miscellany* in 1557; 'Jephtha' was first registered in 1567, and of course the references to the Herod and Termagant of the Miracle plays are distinctly old-fashioned. Shakespeare's audience were, it would seem, being encouraged to indulge in nostalgia. The Admiral's men seemed to have had a similar object, for they produced *Dido and Aeneas* in 1598 and *Jephtha* in 1601. Their leading actor Alleyn was nicknamed 'Roscius' and it has been claimed that Shakespeare was really guying his company when ostensibly Hamlet was giving advice to the players. If so it is also possible, since Hamlet addresses Polonius as 'old Jephtha', that the actor who played him mimicked Alleyn.

But in the context of *Hamlet* what we see is the 'hellish

105

Pyrrhus', the son of Achilles, avenging the death of his father –
and his acting meets with the approval of Hamlet ("'Tis well').
Thus the moral coordinates of the translations are retained –
revenge is associated with Hell. Hamlet then, in the hearing of
Rosencrantz and Guildenstern, arranges for 'a speech of some
dozen or sixteen lines' to be inserted in a performance of the
'Murder of Gonzago'. They, it is safe to assume, would have
reported this to Claudius either before, or after, the Play Scene.

Hamlet in the soliloquy that follows likens himself to 'John-a-
dreams', who, according to Armin, was a real natural.[2] (John in
fact was a generic name for a clown – on the Continent a clown
was 'English John', and 'Zanni', the Venetian form of 'Giovanni',
gave rise to our word 'Zany'.) Following as this does Hamlet's
warning to the First Player not to mock Polonius this may give us
a clue to the garb of the First Player – who may have worn the
outfit of a jester. He has been acting the tragedian, but why then
the sudden transition to burlesque if this were not his stock in
trade? Leslie Hotson points out that

> In Jonson's *Staple of Newes* Gossip Tattle declared 'The Foole is
> the finest man i' the company, they say, and has all the wit.'
> King and Fool came to be reckoned the leading dramatic roles,
> and the ironical Donald Lupton, writing on 'Playhouses' in
> 1632, agreed that in the player's troupe 'most commonly the
> wisest man is the fool.'[3]

At this juncture it is I think pertinent to ask what costume the
First Player wore when he made his first appearance on stage. It
seems to have been J. Isaacs who first suggested that the Players
were 'a stock commedia dell'arte company'.[4] This is almost
certainly correct because the 'chopine' (2.2.432) worn by a 'lady'
in the company was, according to the *OED*, associated with
Venice c.1600, and was still characteristically Venetian in 1645, for
we find John Evelyn commenting that 'the ladies of Venice are still
stepping out in their "choppines".'[5] Yet another connection with
Italy appears in Hamlet's "twas caviare to the general"[6] a few lines
later (2.2.441–2), for according to Douce:

> Dr. Ramsey, physician to King Charles the Second, wrote a
> curious treatise on the worms of the human body, in which he
> says, 'Caviale also is a fond dish of the Italians, made of the roes
> of sturgion, and altogether as unwholsome, if not much worse;
> invented by idle brains, and fancied by none but such as are

106

ignorant what it is; wherefore I would have them consider the Italian proverb,

> Chi mangia di Caviale,
> Mangia moschi, merdi, & sale.

Which may be Englished thus,

> He that eats Caviales,
> Eats salt, dung, and flies.

For it is only (as was said) the roes of sturgion powdred, pickled, and finely denominated *Caviale*, to be a bait for such woodcocks and dotrils that account every exotic fansie a real good.[7]

Jenkins shows that caviare looked like black soap to two contemporary writers in 1616 and 1618. The association with Italy no doubt came about through trading interests in the Black Sea in which the Venetians played a prominent part. The murder of Gonzago was also probably a reference to a real murder – a Luigi Gonzaga murdered the Duke of Urbino in 1538, and it seems to be generally accepted that Shakespeare's knowledge is founded on an Italian original.

If these links with Italy are valid and justify our identifying the Players as a Commedia dell'arte troupe we may go on to conjecture that the First Player was indeed a comic actor – Arlecchino or, to give him his more familar name, Harlequin. Nashe mentions him in 1590, Day in 1606, and Heywood in 1612 talks of 'the Doctors, Zawnyes, Pantaloons, Harlakeenes in which the French, but especially the Italians, have excelled' (*OED*). Indeed one Tristano Martinelli, known as Arlechinus or Dominus Arlechinorum, corresponded with French and Italian princes, and most notably Henry IV of France in 1599. He also corresponded with a Cardinal Gonzaga. Arlecchino however appeared in England in the seventies of the sixteenth century as a stock figure, and Chambers associated him with the Bergomask dance which was known to Shakespeare because the 'rude mechanicals' in *A Midsummer Night's Dream*[8] offer to perform one.

In short, the appearance of the Players in Italian costume would have added colour and variety and topicality to the first performance. It would also have enriched the 'fooling' in the play and ensured too that the religion of the Players could be presumed to be Catholic, for no Protestant in a play would have been represented as mocking a prince of the blood royal however provoked he might have been – only Catholics would have acted in such a rebellious manner. And Italians could and did poison each other as in the Gonzaga play – they were Machiavels at heart, poisoners like the Borgias, libertines like the Venetians.

That the First Player was indeed dressed as a jester may be inferred from the *Brudermord*, for he then becomes 'the master of the comedians' and also Hamlet says to him, 'When you were at Wittenberg you acted good comedies'. There are also references to the feathers they wore in their hats. More will be said about this shortly. The important point is that Hamlet in Shakespeare's play – and the Shakespearean audience – would see a 'Vice' acting as the avenger of his 'father'. We cannot assume that all of Shakespeare's audience knew their *Aeneid* and so were aware that Pyrrhus was the son of Achilles, but the Vice symbolism would be clear to everyone. And, it may be added, if Hamlet removed the jester's headgear from the First Player when he warned him not to mock Polonius and then donned it when he compared himself to John-a-dreams he would in fact be adopting the costume which fits the role he himself has chosen to play in Satan's scenario – the Vice Revenge. He also uses the satanic dialogue:

> Prompted to my revenge by heaven and hell.
>
> (2.2.588)

He reproaches himself for being a coward, not for not killing himself on this occasion, but for not murdering Claudius.

Hamlet's advice to the Players has been so often quoted as being Shakespeare's own attitude to acting that its relevance to the play tends to be ignored. But, it must be asked: why is Hamlet giving this advice? and who needs it? The First Player is a competent actor – his performance astonishes Polonius, and Hamlet is impressed by its verisimilitude:

> all his visage wanned,
> Tears in his eyes, distraction in his aspect,
> A broken voice, and his whole function suiting
> With forms to his conceit.
>
> (2.2.557–60)

Surely he is preaching to the converted. Moreover, his

> O, it offends me to the soul, to hear a robustious periwig-pated
> fellow tear a passion to tatters, to very rags, to split the ears of

108

the groundlings, who for the most part are capable of nothing
but inexplicable dumb-shows and noise (3.2.8–12)

is not calculated to do other than rouse the hostility of Shakespeare's own groundlings, who no doubt showed their dis-
approval.

Shakespeare's attack on clowns has been thought to include
Kempe, but it might also have been directed towards the
Admiral's company – if Alleyn is guyed why not the rest? Allusive
as the remarks may be, the point is that when Hamlet himself
plays the clown he disobeys his own strictures, as we shall see
shortly. At this juncture however we must see that Hamlet has
offended the Players, and in particular their leader, and he has even
threatened to whip any offenders. So much for his concern for his
'old friend'. Hamlet already has enough enemies but now he
makes more. He should have known better, indeed he warned
Polonius to be careful how he handled them:

> for they are the abstracts and brief chronicles of the time; after
> your death you were better have a bad epitaph than their ill
> report while you live. (2.2.525–30)

Before the Play Scene begins we must also look at the attitude
of Claudius. He had been very cautious and non-commital about
Polonius's view that thwarted love was the cause of Hamlet's
derangement, and Gertrude's belief that the death of Hamlet's
father and the 'o'er hasty marriage' was the source of the trouble.
Thus when he eavesdropped on Hamlet's meeting with Ophelia
and heard Hamlet say:

> I am very proud, revengeful, ambitious
>
> (3.1.125)

and

> I say we will have no mo marriage – those that are married
> already, all but one, shall live, the rest shall keep as they are
> (3.1.150–2)

whatever he had thought of Hamlet's mental condition before, the
words 'revengeful' and 'ambitious' together with his final threat
could only make him fear that Hamlet might kill him in order to
gain the crown. He certainly does not suspect that Hamlet has
discovered the truth about his father's murder. Indeed at this point
in the play the first audience could not be sure that Claudius was

really guilty, for they only had Satan's word for it. Thus Claudius concludes:

> Love! his affections do not that way tend,
> Nor what he spake, though it lacked form a little,
> Was not like madness – there's something in his soul,
> O'er which his melancholy sits on brood,
> And I do doubt the hatch and the disclose
> Will be some danger.
>
> (3.1.165–70)

So when he comes to the play in the evening Claudius is wary, very wary, for he thinks he has an ambitious nephew who may threaten his throne and even his life.

When the Play Scene begins Hamlet 'must be idle' – he will put on his 'antic disposition'. We must remember that sloth or idleness was regarded as one of the Seven Deadly Sins. Even in our own day the following appears in a Catholic Catechism: 'The sins that commonly lead to the breaking of the sixth and ninth Commandments are gluttony, drunkenness, and intemperance, and also idleness, bad company, and the neglect of prayer.' Because of this attitude Idleness appeared as a Vice, for example in *Wyt and Science* and in *The Mariage of Witt and Wisdome*. The medieval name for it was 'accidie', a state of restlessness and inability to work or pray to which monks were prone. 'Idle' also meant foolish, silly or crazy, so we are about to see Hamlet play the fool, jester or clown, but clearly his brand of idleness, like his melancholy, has no exact modern equivalent.

The Play Scene in *Hamlet* is a fascinating problem. Coleridge, aware of its similarity to the older drama, called it an 'interlude'. Dover Wilson's *What Happens in Hamlet* is mainly concerned with it. For the producer of the play however there is no real problem because the force of tradition is so strong that the Dumb Show and the dialogue between the Player King and the Player Queen can be excised, apparently, without damaging the scene. For so long have we been accustomed to believing that Hamlet's plan is successful – that he proves Claudius guilty – that only part of the scene seems really necessary. Now, if we grant that Shakespeare was a supremely skilful dramatist, and one does not have to be a Bardolater to admit that, it remains to be explained why he took such pains over a scene when so much of it is not required.

The main part of the problem is the Dumb Show in which a king is poisoned, his queen laments his death, and is finally wooed with gifts by the poisoner – yet Claudius does not react to it. Two representations of the murder seem to be required before Claudius's guilt overpowers him and he rushes away. But, it is argued, Claudius is a hardened villain, and that it takes a double blow, as it were, to knock him out is not unreasonable. Dover Wilson however believed that Claudius, Gertrude and Polonius are so absorbed in conversation that they do not see the Dumb Show, but when Claudius sees the second enactment of the Gonzago murder and hears Hamlet's 'talk of the poisoning' as well as that of Lucianus, not only is his conscience caught but he realizes that Hamlet 'knows all'. And the Court, for their part, see in the Gonzago murder the ambitious Lucianus / Hamlet murder the king whom they can only identify as a Claudius. The Dumb Show, therefore, in Dover Wilson's view, adds suspense to the scene, for Hamlet is afraid that the Players, who have put it on against his wishes, will give the game away before the 'dozen or sixteen lines' which he wrote specially have been spoken.

In Dover Wilson's favour it may be said that he was the very first commentator to see the significance of the Court's reaction – as exemplified by Rosencrantz and Guildenstern – and so clear up a point that had puzzled Bradley:

> The state of affairs at Court at this time, though I have not seen it noticed by critics, seems to me puzzling. It is quite clear ... that everyone sees in the play-scene a gross and menacing insult to the King. Yet no-one shows any sign of perceiving in it also an accusation of murder. Surely that is strange.[9]

To the Court, Hamlet is undoubtedly Lucianus the Poisoner, an ambitious nephew – and perhaps with thwarted ambition – who is threatening to assassinate Claudius. It may be added that Hamlet's 'confession' to Rosencrantz and Guildenstern immediately afterwards that he lacks 'advancement' confirms their view. Hamlet in fact, as far as the Court is concerned, has not exposed a murder but has threatened to commit one. It seems then that Hamlet is willing to represent himself as seeking revenge because of his ambition while concealing his real motive for revenge. Surely this is odd? Hamlet cannot publicly accuse Claudius as a result of the

Gonzago play for he has convinced no one in the Court that Claudius is guilty of murder; instead he has shown everyone that he is mad and a potential assassin, and Claudius now has a lawful pretext for banishing Hamlet. Dover Wilson did not discuss that.

Granville Barker did not agree with Dover Wilson's interpretation of the Play Scene. He believed that Claudius did not see the Dumb Show and that it took two representations of the murder to destroy his composure. But if Claudius does become aware by the end of the scene that Hamlet has discovered the truth about his father's death – according to both Dover Wilson and Granville Barker – why does he allow Hamlet to go to see his mother, knowing that he will tell her, and why does he also allow Polonius to eavesdrop on them? By so doing Claudius puts the crown in jeopardy – for neither Gertrude nor Polonius knew about the murder – and banishing Hamlet after he had 'told all' would have solved nothing. And why, later, can this same Claudius, tricked by his nephew, plot with Laertes against a Hamlet who, in Claudius's own words, is 'most generous and free from all contriving' (4.7.134)? Besides, there is never mention in the text that Claudius suspects, or acknowledges, that Hamlet knows of the murder. So something is wrong somewhere. Even without further analysis it is surely evident that we have made a mistake or that Shakespeare's hand has slipped. Granville Barker did not discuss these points.

John Wain however has his doubts about the scene:

> In any case, the whole ruse of staging the play has failed. If Hamlet could have controlled his terrible inner agitation sufficiently to sit quiet and watch the King's face, other people would have done the same, and the business of undermining Claudius would have begun without Hamlet's having to show his hand ... Altogether, Hamlet's behaviour during the whole episode is such as to draw attention to himself and therefore away from Claudius and in addition to arouse Claudius's suspicions. Hamlet is no plotter. Deeply meditative, he cannot gear his meditations to action; he acts only in rash bounding sorties.[10]

Adverse criticism of this kind is relatively recent, but it is a healthy sign – a sign of a departure from the identification with Hamlet that has so bedevilled commentators. Hamlet believes that his plot is wholly successful, but clearly he did not plot the scene as it was actually played. He did not even plan the Dumb Show, so that what he originally intended was a play in which the Poisoner, Lucianus, spoke the lines he had written for him. But this Lucianus could not have been the king's nephew because how then could Claudius identify with him? As John Wain says:

> Since there is no evidence in the play itself that the poisoner is in fact the king's nephew, the detail is evidently invented by Hamlet – or, more precisely, forced out of him by the pressure of his hatred for Claudius, the usurper who sits so temptingly close by on the throne that should be Hamlet's, side by side with Hamlet's mother who has forgotten his father. Under these circumstances it amounts to a threat.[11]

Moreover, the characters were not intended to be a king and queen, but a duke and duchess:

> This play is the image of a murder done in Vienna. Gonzago is the duke's name, his wife Baptista. (3.2.237–8)

That the scene may have been originally played this way may be deduced from Q1 where a duke and duchess do in fact appear, although the Dumb Show – the Player's interpolation – has a king and queen. But it looks more like a printer's error.

Dover Wilson also saw 'nephew to the king' as 'unpremeditated' and that 'Hamlet is ... identifying himself with the assassin, and he ... uses the play to threaten his uncle in a fashion which no one who sees it can mistake'. Dover Wilson also went on to suggest that 'the identification should be made plain by dressing Lucianus in a black doublet like Hamlet's', but withdrew his remarks because 'it infers previous instructions as to costume by Hamlet'.[12] But it need not, for the Players are bent on revenge on Hamlet, and what better way than to make their Lucianus look like Hamlet? They present a play in fact where 'Hamlet' threatens Claudius, but by guying Hamlet – their Lucianus is grotesque – they also dissociate themselves from any serious intent and thus prevent Claudius's wrath from falling on them. Their Lucianus / Hamlet then with his 'damnable faces' (or 'antic grimaces'?) is the 'croaking raven' that bellows for revenge. The Players indeed not only consider that Hamlet has insulted them, but that he is mad and wants to kill Claudius – what else can they think of Hamlet's 'dozen or sixteen lines' which must be Lucianus's speech before he poisons the king?

The Players obviously disobey Hamlet – the First Player, their leader, who acted the Pyrrhus speech so well has included a Dumb

Show which Hamlet had told them he detested, and has hammed the part of Lucianus, but there are no complaints about the acting of the Player King and Queen.

While 'the croaking raven' has been suggested as having come from an old play – and a very poor one – the allusion seems far-fetched. Why should audiences remember *The True Tragedy*? And why should they remember it when Hamlet does not quote from it but apparently *misquotes* from it?

> The screeking Raven sits croking for reuenge.

The raven was an ominous symbol in Elizabethan times – in *Macbeth*:

> The raven himself is hoarse
> That croaks the fatal entrance of Duncan.

In Drayton's *The Barrons Warres* we find:

> The ominous raven with a dismal cheer,
> Through his hoarse beak of following horror tells.

In *Othello* we find:

> As doth the raven o'er the infected house,
> Boding to all.

And in Nashe's *Terrors of the Night*:

> [The raven is a] continuall messenger ... of dole and mis-fortune.[13]

Also in *The Witch of Edmonton* we find Mother Sawyer pleading with her familiar to reappear:

>   prithee come,
> Revenge to me is sweeter than life;
> Thou art my raven, on whose coal-black wings
> Revenge comes flying to me.
>
> (Act 5, Sc. 1)

Obviously the symbolism has wider implications than a mere allusion to an old play. For not only had the raven an ominous connotation, it was also interchangeable in symbolic significance with the jackdaw and the crow. E.M.W. Tillyard in discussing Greene's scornful remarks on Shakespeare and his ilk as 'antics garnished in our colours' and Shakespeare in particular as 'an upstart crow beautified with our feathers' says:

Greene certainly refers to the fable ... of the jackdaw or raven or crow which, being undistinguished, begs plumes from the other birds and then boasts of his finery. The other birds in anger reclaim their feathers, and the crow is left naked.[14]

Hamlet/Lucianus then as an 'unpstart crow' would be a symbol of ambition that has outstripped itself – like Satan himself, who, as we have seen earlier, wore a stage costume of black feathers. Moreover, as revenge was associated with witches we find witches metamorphosed into ravens as in Jonson's *The Sad Shepherd*, and Middleton associates them with Hecate. K.M. Briggs also records the appearance of a demon which takes the form of a raven.[15] And Jonson again associates ravens with witches in *The Masque of Queenes*.

What the Players do is therefore dangerous for them – they risk being whipped by Hamlet. They also risk offending Claudius. So they put on the Dumb Show not only to annoy Hamlet, but to see what they can get away with. But Claudius does not react, and so all is clear to proceed. Hamlet, on the other hand, does react:

> Marry, this is miching mallecho, it means mischief
> (3.2.135)

and

> The players cannot keep cousel, they'll tell all.
> (3.2.139–40)

Then follows the long dialogue between the Player King and Queen full of trite moralising, reminiscent of the Morality plays. The reference to 'An anchor's cheere' probably recalled the monasticism of the Catholic Church. It is also noteworthy that 'desperation' (3.2.217) is used in its correct theological sense. There is also the possible religious connotation of Hamlet's 'That's wormwood, wormwood' (3.2.180), for Proverbs 5:3–4 refers to a harlot whose end is 'bitter as wormwood sharp as a two-edged sword'. Perhaps also there is a contextual link with the Apocalypse:

> And the name of the star is called Wormwood: and the third part of the waters became wormwood; and many men died of the waters, because they were made bitter. (Revelation 8:11)

and:

for she saith in her heart, I sit a queen, and am no widow, and shall see no sorrow. (Revelation 18:7)

As the dialogue ends Hamlet taunts his mother by enquiring politely if she liked the play, and Claudius asks Hamlet if there is 'no offence' in the 'argument', to which Hamlet replies:

> ... they do but jest, poison in jest.
>
> (3.2.233)

And yet again Claudius's only reaction is to enquire the name of the play. Hamlet however is frustrated – Claudius has seen the Dumb Show, which represents the murder as the Ghost described it, heard the conversation of the Player King and Queen with its reference to second marriages, heard 'talk of the poisoning' but has not revealed his guilt. Then, at this crucial moment, in walks Lucianus ....

Hamlet is thunderstruck; all the influences that he has hoped have been working on Claudius have also been acting on him and seeing his double, as it were – the First Player dressed in black as he himself is – about to poison 'Claudius' his anger wells up and he identifies himself with the murderer – 'nephew to the king' – and the 'croaking raven' that 'doth bellow for revenge'. Then Lucianus, declaiming some of Hamlet's 'dozen or sixteen lines', pours poison

> of midnight weeds collected,
> With Hecate's ban thrice blasted, thrice infected
>
> (3.2.257–8)

into the king's ears.

Hamlet then says:

> A' poisons him i' th' garden for's estate, his name's Gonzago, the story is extant, and written in very choice Italian, you shall see anon how the murderer gets the love of Gonzago's wife.
> (3.2.261–4)

At this Claudius rises, calls for 'light' and stalks out.

It is so easy for us, knowing beforehand that Claudius is guilty and believing that the Ghost – according to tradition – is good, to interpret Claudius's actions as indicative of guilt. But if we were Shakespeare's very first audience how could we be sure? Hamlet has in effect threatened before the entire Court to assassinate Claudius, and Claudius is very angry – 'marvellous distempered

... with choler', as Guildenstern puts it. Claudius has apparently reacted to a threat, but not to a representation of the murder as the Ghost described it.

Dover Wilson's theory does not allow for this and his solution is wrong because if Claudius does not see the Dumb Show and sees only Hamlet / Lucianus kill 'him' he can be reacting solely to an assassination threat from his nephew, and that does not prove that he has murdered Hamlet's father.

We know that when the Play Scene begins Claudius suspects that Hamlet is 'proud, revengeful, ambitious' and Hamlet's quibble

I eat the air, promise-crammed – you cannot feed capons so

reinforces his suspicions, for Hamlet is saying that as the chameleon lives on 'air' he, the 'heir', is being fed on promises, and even stupid creatures like capons – castrated cockerels – would not be satisfied with that. And then Hamlet's jibe at Polonius who as Julius Caesar had been 'killed i' the Capitol' follows the same theme. Then too Claudius sees the Dumb Show in which a king is assassinated and he must scrutinize Hamlet closely when he talks with Ophelia. Then what he sees is an astonished, angry Hamlet who bursts out:

The players cannot keep counsel, they'll tell all.

So Claudius, hardened murderer that he is, does not show his feelings and does not speak again until the dialogue between the Player King and Queen is over. In the meantime he has been subjected to a homily on second marriages but he wonders what else Hamlet has in store for him:

Have you heard the argument? is there no offence in't?

But only when Hamlet as Lucianus threatens to assassinate him does he realize, he thinks, what Hamlet's intentions are. He and Gertrude have been openly insulted and he personally has been threatened by a nephew who is 'ambitious' to deprive him of his crown. The report that we may presume Rosencrantz and Guildenstern made to him would confirm his conclusion.

HAMLET. Sir, I lack advancement.
ROSENCRANTZ. How can that be, when you have the voice of the king himself for your succession in Denmark?
HAMLET. Ay, sir, but 'While the grass grows' – the proverb is somewhat musty.

(3.2.341–5)

The Elizabethan Hamlet

So Claudius's suspicion that Hamlet is 'ambitious' is confirmed. But how can he suspect that Hamlet has discovered how his father was murdered? The answer is, of course, that he cannot, for Hamlet has done nothing to show that he has fathomed Claudius's secret – he has not spoken out against the coronation of Claudius, nor has he attempted to confide in Gertrude or Ophelia. What is more Hamlet cannot have proof of any kind or he would have already used it. Besides, he was in Wittenberg when it happened. Thus Claudius allows Polonius to eavesdrop on Hamlet's conversation with Gertrude. If he had suspected Hamlet of knowing of the murder he could not possibly have done so. We must give the Devil his due – Claudius never panics.

The mechanism of the Play Scene is really then quite simple if we are Elizabethans – the Players, whom Hamlet has antagonized, revenge themselves on him by turning the Gonzago play into an assassination threat to Claudius and an insult to his queen, and they do so by dressing up the First Player to look like Hamlet and turning the duke and duchess of the original into a king and queen. Their presentation of the Dumb Show – to which Claudius does not react – frustrates Hamlet's design to 'catch the conscience of the king', and finally, goaded on by his hatred for Claudius, he identifies himself with Lucianus and thus openly threatens, it seems to all, including Claudius, assassination. Claudius, for his part, does not reveal his guilt in this scene and Shakespeare's first audience had to wait until later to hear Claudius's confession.

If we now turn to Hamlet's 'antic disposition' in this scene it is surely clear that his intended role was that of court jester. First, like Feste, he is a 'corrupter of words' – puns and quibbles come readily to his lips. He also uses double meanings – 'to kill a calf' was to declaim a speech and also a comic trick played by a clown in which a dummy calf's head stuck through a curtain exchanged wisecracks with him and which he eventually 'cut off'. A 'calf' was also a cant term for an idiot. Then, 'using the license of an allowed fool, he quibbles grossly on sexual matters', as J.H. Walter says.[16] 'Country matters' is still broad enough for most ears even today. He protests to Ophelia that he is her 'jig-maker' (which George Rylands paraphrased as 'I am a born jester (ironic))'. He talks of the 'hobby horse' which was a feature of the Morris dance and the May-games, and also associated with the antics of the Lord of Misrule. And he also congratulates himself on his performance as worthy of a professional clown dressed in feathers.

A miscellaneous point may be mentioned here because while Hamlet thinks he is good enough to be a professional clown he looks upon players generally with scorn, for he refers to them as a 'cry' (3.2.277), a term used for a pack of hounds. The *OED* records the usage as contemptuous, but Dover Wilson and Chambers, to name only two, make no mention of this. Why not? I suspect this is another 'Hamletism' – a word whose connotation is not contemporary but supplied by an editor and/or a faulty tradition. For all Hamlet's effusive welcome he insults them.

After Hamlet's brief conversation with Polonius Hamlet is at last alone, with no need to put on his 'antic disposition'. So now we see a Hamlet who believes in 'the very witching time of night' and Hell itself 'which breathes out / Contagion to the world'. Now he could drink 'hot blood'. Eleanor Prosser points out that this practice was connected with the Black Mass and refers to Faustus's vows to 'build an altar to Beelzebub' and offer 'lukewarm blood of newborn babes', and she also records several examples of Elizabethan stage villains who talk of drinking their victims' blood.[17] Hamlet is in a mood to kill but tries to fight down the anger he feels towards his mother – he does not wish to become another Nero. But with Hamlet in a murderous frame of mind Shakespeare's first audience must have expected that anything might happen – that he might lose control completely.

We know then that Hamlet tries to act like a 'natural' in this scene, but if to act the madman is proof of his sanity we must explain away somehow his belief that he has trapped Claudius into revealing his guilt and his astonishing 'admission' to Rosencrantz and Guildenstern that he 'lacks advancement'. Horatio, it is true, appears to accept that the Ghost is 'honest' but he is a partner to a diabolic pact sworn in the presence of Satan and is no more capable of rational judgment than Hamlet. But Hamlet, while concealing his real motive for revenge, only makes matters worse for himself by claiming that he is ambitious – he gives Claudius not only the motive but the pretext to get rid of him. And now at the end of the scene we see a Hamlet possessed of a homicidal fury which he can barely control.

If then we try to classify him as a natural or an artificial fool in the Play Scene what can we say? He thinks he is merely playing the fool or vice or jester, but in fact he is becoming a Vice with a capital *V*, and he has persuaded himself that the Ghost – Satan himself – is honest. If that is not madness why then does Edgar in

119

King Lear who also wishes to feign madness, take a similar view of the Devil?

> The prince of darkness, is a gentleman.
>
> (3.4.147)

Feste, on the other hand, who is a real artificial, castigates Malvolio as 'thou dishonest Satan'. Hamlet in his encounter with the Ghost referred to 'we fools of nature'. Is he then like Lear to be regarded as a 'natural fool of fortune', or like Touchstone – 'nature's natural'? I do not find it difficult to conclude that the Ghost has made a fool of him, in the full Elizabethan sense that he has become the Devil's Vice – the Vice Revenge.

Hamlet was so incensed by clowns who interrupted when 'some necessary question of the play be then to be considered' is guilty of just that offence, and the 'most pitiful ambition in the fool that uses it' is what he admits to Rosencrantz and Guildenstern. If he had not interjected 'nephew to the king' or he had not claimed to be ambitious all might have been well. But it may be pertinent to ask if he really was ambitious and whether the Elizabethan audience would have so regarded him. Their opinions might have been divided – some who thought him mad might have absolved him of the charge of ambition, perhaps following the opinion of Erasmus:

> Erasmus vindicates fools from this melancholy catalogue, because they have most part moist brains, and light hearts, they are free from ambition, envy, shame and fear, they are neither troubled in conscience nor macerated with cares, to which our whole life is most subject.[18]

Thus it may be that feigning madness, as in the original version of the story, was a way of allaying suspicion because presumably a lunatic could not succeed to the throne. In Elizabethan times it was possible to 'beg a fool', i.e. to take over the property of a person who was mad. Hotson refers to such a case in 1613.[19] But Hamlet as a potential assassin does not fit into this more benign form of lunacy – he wants to kill his king.

Whatever sane motive can be ascribed to Hamlet's feigning madness – Samuel Johnson could not find one – there can be no doubt that Claudius regards Hamlet as a potential assassin, and Rosencrantz and Guildenstern agree that the king is in danger. That being so, while they are sycophants, their attitude to the sanctity of a king was that instilled in Elizabeth's subjects by the

Catechism and the Homilies which had to be read out to church congregations. Thus in Nowell's *Catechism* when an explanation of the Fifth Commandment is given:

> For if it be for every private man a heinous offence to offend his private parents, and parricide to kill them; what shall we say of them that have conspired and borne wicked armour against the commonweal, against their country, the most ancient, sacred, and common mother of us all, which ought to be dearer unto us than ourselves, and for whom no honest man will stick to die to do it good, and against the prince, the father of the country itself, and parent of the commonweal; yea and to imagine the over-throw, death and destruction of them whom it is high-treason once to forsake or shrink from? So outrageous a thing can in no wise be expressed with fit name.[20]

When Shakespeare was a child he would have been instructed thus, and E.M.W. Tillyard points out that, 'when Shakespeare was ten, he would have heard a part of a homily on order and civil obedience nine Sundays or holy-days in the year'. In the year 1574 the homily *Against Disobedience and Wilful Rebellion* insisted that even the oppression of evil rulers had to be borne with patience and all disobedient persons were threatened with damnation 'forasmuch as they resist not man but God'. The fear was that if rebellion was allowed against a bad prince it could not be pre-vented against a good. 'Moreover it is not blind chance but God who sends a bad prince, and he does it to punish a people's sins. To revolt is to add new sin not yet expiated.' And the Homily goes on to emphasize that the ambition of the Papacy and the ignorance of simple folk are the chief causes of rebellion. What is more, the homilist gives rebellion a biblical background with its reference to the Garden of Eden and Satan 'the first and greatest rebel'.

Tillyard also quotes from the *Mirour for Magistrates*:

> For indeed officers be God's deputies and it is God's office which they bear; and it is he which ordaineth thereto such as himself listeth: good when he favoureth the people and evil when he will punish them. And therefore whosoever rebelleth against any ruler either good or bad rebelleth agaist God and shall be sure of a wretched end, for God cannot but maintain his deputy.[21]

I think then it is significant that the reference to the sanctity of the

121

king, villain though Claudius is, should precede the Prayer Scene, for Shakespeare, to me at least, is underlining a religious and a civil prohibition known and accepted by all in real life. In the theatre the same strictures would apply – regicide could not be tolerated by God or man and for Hamlet to assassinate Claudius would not only incur civil punishment but damnation as well.

This brief conversation between Claudius and Rosencrantz and Guildenstern therefore is also a prelude to Claudius's soliloquy where yet again the audience are made sharply aware of their religious background. But they did not, presumably, share the 'Most holy and religious fear' (3.3.8) of Rosencrantz and Guildenstern which had allowed them to accept an incestuous monarch – only Catholics could act like that, they thought. Nor would an audience – nor the corrector – have missed as we do the oaths which Hamlet utters 'by'r lady' at 2.2.430 and 3.2.131. What Protestant swore by the Virgin? Yet Dover Wilson would have us believe that Hamlet is a Protestant. But he completely omits any comment on these oaths which contradict his theory. According to Onions the older Shakespearean editors used the form 'by'r Lady' which makes the point more clearly. Denmark is Catholic in the play, the Players being Venetian are Catholic, and so is Hamlet. He believes in Purgatory, so why should we be surprised when he swears by the Virgin Mary?

The idea of a Catholic Hamlet may well seem repellent. It all depends on how much we identify with him and of course how strong our religious prejudices are. Whatever we think now, Elizabethan Protestants would probably have identified less, and so would not have made the mistake of looking at what happens in the Play Scene through Hamlet's eyes. Hamlet's plan is a failure, not a success. Bradley, as we saw, felt there was something wrong with this scene; Charles Lamb was obviously puzzled by 'nephew to the king' because he turned this into 'Lucianus a near relative to the duke'.[22] Hamlet begins the scene determined to play the fool for all he's worth and ends it in a homicidal rage. In Elizabethan terms he is like the 'old Vice' and like his predecessor, the Vice Revenge in *Horestes*, he wants to see murder done. As I have shown, the symbol of the Vice was plastic and, as the following lines indicate, even as early as 1560 a Vice could ad lib like any clown or jester, just as Hamlet does so disastrously in this scene:

> But Vices in stage plaies,
> When theyr matter is gon,

The Play Scene

> They laugh out the reste
> To the lookers on.
> And so wantinge matter,
> 'You brynge in my coate,' &c.[23]

From this point on we are to see the evil, implicit still in the symbolism, possess Hamlet.

6

Aftermath

THE SETTING of the Prayer Scene is crucial to its interpretation. We must consider that Claudius's concern is with religion and with prayer and not merely with metaphors which have a religious tinge. The *Brudermord* puts 'Erico' before an altar in a temple; in Shakespeare's version however we find later that the body of Polonius is to be placed in 'the chapel' (4.1.37 and 4.2.8). This also would be an appropriate place for this scene to be enacted. If then the inner stage were to represent a chapel, since Denmark is Catholic like its late king, the chapel might contain a small altar placed before a statue of the Virgin and Child. Such a Madonna made of silver is illustrated in *The Story of Art* by Sir Ernst Gombrich, who adds that 'works of this kind were not intended for public worship. Rather were they to be placed in a palace chapel for private prayer.'[1] Such a setting seems appropriate, for as Eleanor Prosser puts it 'Heaven is doing a very good job'.[2] For even without punishment administered below Claudius is tortured by guilt even before the Play Scene:

> How smart a lash that speech doth give my conscience.
> The harlot's cheek, beautied with plast'ring art,
> Is not more ugly to the thing that helps it,
> Than is my deed to my most painted word:
> O heavy burden!
>
> (3.1.50–4)

Like Cain he is 'persecuted' with the 'worm of conscience':

> And the devil that then told thee that it was a light sin, or no sin at all, now aggravates on the other side, and telleth thee that it is a most irremissible offence, as he did by Cain and Judas, to bring them to despair.[3]

The Elizabethans were brought up to believe that in the end there was no escape from the wrath of God – without penitence there was only damnation. Claudius is not only a fratricide like Cain whose crime had 'the primal eldest curse upon't' (3.3.37) and upon

124

whom all human revenge was forbidden lest they bring down upon themselves 'sevenfold vengeance' of the divine variety, but he is a regicide as well and that in itself was sufficient reason, as we have just seen, for incurring damnation,

> The deep damnation of his taking off

as Macbeth says of Duncan (1.7.20).

For Claudius, as for Faustus, the means of bring him to heaven were 'contrition, prayer, repentance' but in Claudius's case his contrition is at best imperfect, he cannot pray sincerely, and he cannot repent. Impenitence, as L.A. Cormican puts it, was considered the greatest sin of all.[4] Hell awaited Claudius even if Hamlet had never lifted a hand to him. Even Claudius's appeal to the angels (3.3.69) would have been brushed aside by Shakespeare's audience because the current Protestant teaching was 'it appeareth nowhere in the word of God that God would have us pray to angels, or to godly men deceased'.[5] And finally, as J.H. Walter, referring to the Homily of Repentance points out, Claudius 'would be repenting without Christ, and that is Cain's and Judas' repentance'.[6]

In the whole soliloquy there is no mention of Hamlet – the conflict is between Claudius and his conscience. But even in the abbreviated form to which the soliloquy is reduced in Q1 the religious implications are emphasized:

> It is an act gainst the vniuersal power,
> Most wretched man, stoope, bend to thy prayer,
> Aske grace of heauen to keepe thee from despaire.

Is it then merely fanciful to see Claudius on his knees before a statue of the Madonna and Child?

> Bow stubborn knees, and heart, with strings of steel,
> Be soft as sinews of the new-born babe –
> All may be well.

> (3.3.70–2)

He refers to *the* new-born babe, not *a* new-born babe.

When Hamlet enters to find Claudius praying he may be wearing the 'Arlecchino' or 'Harlequin' cap with horns and feather that belonged to the First Player. After all, only minutes earlier he was 'playing the fool' in the Play Scene and it does not seem unreasonable to have him garbed thus. If he did it would remind the audience when he draws his sword of the First Player declaiming his 'Pyrrhus' speech and they, as the first audience, would have been tense with expectation that Hamlet as Vice might emulate the Vice / Pyrrhus and murder the king – that from being a John-a-dreams he would emerge into full Vicehood, as it were. Jenkins stresses the importance of the comparison:

> Pyrrhus . . . whatever you choose to make of him, in some sort images Hamlet. The account of how his sword 'seem'd i' th' air to stick' while he 'stood, and . . . did nothing' describes what a later scene will show.[7]

As I have said earlier a groundling who did not know his *Aeneid* could still see the parallel situation in these terms.

At the risk of being foolish and rushing in where angels fear to tread I would venture to say that to a modern audience who know the play it is almost inevitable that they regard Hamlet's bark as being worse than his bite. As Bradley put it:

> Shakespeare has taken care to give this perfect opportunity so repulsive a character that we can hardly bring ourselves to wish that the hero should accept it.[8]

This means in fact that what Hamlet is doing is rationalizing – 'a process of attributing morally acceptable motives to unacceptable desires or actions', in Eleanor Prosser's words, but a process she does not accept because, as she points out, what purpose would be served by concealing a good motive from himself?[9] And why also, she asks, should Shakespeare conceal it from the audience? If we attempt an answer in the form that Hamlet does not allow for the goodness that is within him and that he is trying to stifle his real misgivings – barking but not biting – a glance at Shakespeare's stage-practice may help to settle the matter. Kenneth Muir, writing about the problem of Iago's soliloquies, maintains that 'there are no soliloquies in Shakespeare's plays – or indeed, in any Elizabethan plays – which do not express the genuine feelings or beliefs of the characters speaking them'.[10] Hamlet then must be held to mean exactly what he says – he intends to kill Claudius's soul as well as his body but he cannot achieve his aim when Claudius, he thinks, is purging his soul by praying. Now there is nothing modern about that – we do not see on television or read in the newspapers of murderers who have such motives, and because we do not we are all the more ready to write off Hamlet's words as mere bluster, and so shut our eyes to Shakespeare's own stage practice and also to that of his contemporaries. Besides, in medieval times, and particularly in medieval Italy,

> there is nothing wherein they take greater delectation, pleasure and contentment, than to execute a vengeance; inasmuch as, whensoever they can haue their enemie at their pleasure, to be reuenged vpon him they murder him after some strange and barbarous fashion, and in murdering him they put him in remembrance of the offence done vnto them, with many reproachfull words and iniurues to torment the soule and the bodie together; and sometimes wash their hands and their mouthes with his blood, and force him with hope of his life to giue himselfe to the diuell; and so they seeke in slaying the bodie to damne the soule, if they could.[11]

The circumstances in which this strange aim could be achieved were dictated by religious belief – the belief of medieval Catholics like the Borgias. For example to die when dead drunk and thus be unable to repent – as in *The Revenger's Tragedy* – was a sure method of sending a man's soul to Hell:

> VINDICE. Shall we kill him now he's drunk?
> LUSSURIOSO. Ay, best of all.
> VINDICE. Why then he will ne'er live to be sober.
> LUSSURIOSO. No matter, let him reel to hell.
>
> (5.1.46–50)

Other sins were also 'deadly'. Marlowe presented the Seven Deadly Sins as a pageant in *Faustus* and they are still taught to Catholic children.[12] Hamlet's 'in his rage' relates to the sin of Wrath, 'At game' refers to the sin of Avarice, and Protestants in Elizabethan times accepted the connection and taught it as an adjunct to the Eighth Commandment. 'Incestuous pleasure' of course speaks for itself but again in modern eyes Claudius is not guilty of incest. So we have to accept that Hamlet is talking sense, warped as it is, and not merely 'barking' or raving. Eleanor Prosser has found twenty-three examples in Elizabethan plays in which 'even the mere desire to damn another soul for eternity was unquestionably viewed by the audience as morally reprehensible and emotionally horrifying'.[13]

The essential point is that Hamlet is talking a religious language which was presumably understood by the theatre audience, and it should be added that the mere utterance of sentiments was sufficient to attract the attention of Satan according to contemporary beliefs. For example, Faustus is told by Mephistopheles:

> For when we hear one rack the name of God,
> Abjure the scriptures and his saviour Christ,
> We fly in hope to get his glorious soul;
> Nor will we come unless he use such means
> Whereby he is in danger to be damn'd.
>
> (1.3.47–51)

If also we look at *The Witch of Edmonton* we find Mother Sawyer, the witch, exclaiming:

> Would some power, good or bad,
> Instruct me which way I might be revenged
> Upon this churl, I'd go out of myself,
> And give this fury leave to dwell within
> This ruined cottage ready to fall with age,
> Abjure all goodness, be at hate with prayer,
> And study curses, imprecations,
> Blasphemous speeches, oaths, detested oaths,
> Or anything that's ill: so I might work Revenge ...
> *Enter a Black Dog [Satan]*
> DOG. Ho! have I found thee cursing? now thou art Mine own.
>
> (Act 2, Sc.1)

This is not unlike Othello's oath of vengeance, after which Iago says:

> I am your own forever.

If we now add that Hamlet's vow of vengeance is probably taken within sight of an altar we may see that it, like Othello's swearing a 'sacred vow' of vengeance 'by yond marble heaven', is blasphemous and his apparent lack of action is not merely

> To do the right deed for the wrong reason

but to go deeper into the 'devil's labyrinth', as Granville Barker put it. Eleanor Prosser's view is similar:

> Any interpretation of *Hamlet* must stand or fall on the play itself, but other plays by both Shakespeare and his contemporaries would seem to confirm the view that Hamlet has set

foot on a path that can lead only to barbarism, destruction, and Hell.[14]

Harold Jenkins's attitude is:

> First, theatrically, the convention facilitates at the centre of the play a spectacularly ironic scene: the revenger, with his passion at its climax following proof of his enemy's guilt, is presented with his victim defenceless and alone; and yet it is revenge itself that provides an incontestable reason why this seemingly perfect opportunity is one impossible to take. But second, thematically, the convention enables revenge to be shown in its most repulsive aspect: for the appropriateness of Hamlet's utterance here is not to his lack of resolution, nor to the scruples of conscience ... but to that savage mood which he has just exhibited to us, that mood in which he could 'drink hot blood' with the contagion of hell upon him.[15]

'Hamlet without the Prince' has become a cant phrase, but Hamlet without the Devil is more apt, because instead of religious belief we are left with empty rhetoric full of sound and fury, but signifying nothing. If we do not share the Elizabethans' belief in the Devil we must inevitably misinterpret this scene.

That the Devil is not far away is evident from Hamlet's threefold utterance 'Mother, mother, mother!' Gertrude hears him and dismisses Polonius who advises her to tell him that his 'pranks' have gone too far, and when Polonius has concealed himself we see that Gertrude regards Hamlet's words as 'idle', which is reminiscent of his plan to be 'idle' during the Gonzago play. In Gertrude's eyes he is still the court jester, the 'jig maker' of the Play Scene, but she is also afraid of him, as we are soon to see. It is therefore appropriate that he should continue to wear his Harlequin head-dress. Hamlet assures her 'by the rood' that he has not forgotten her – this was a Catholic oath traceable far back into medieval times, as the *OED* shows, but not appropriate to Elizabethan Protestants who disliked crosses as being popery – as witness the removal of the rood loft from the church in Stratford.

When Hamlet seizes Gertrude by the arm she is terrified for she thinks he is in a homicidal fury, and she calls for help. Polonius of course answers and Hamlet, as if he were betting on the thrust, cries 'dead for a ducat, dead'. Thus it would seem that Hamlet here 'at game' commits murder and so places himself in one of the situations in which he had hoped to find Claudius in order to kill him and also damn his soul. But instead by combining gambling and murder he damns himself. Hamlet's language too is appropriate to an Italianate revenger, for the gambling stake is a ducat, a coin of Venetian origin in the Middle Ages and still in use there in the time of Thomas Coryat (1612), and which we see of course in *The Merchant of Venice*. A writer on coins contributes the following:

> Although the coins of Venice never lacked some sacred Christian symbol the Venetians consistently put cash before religion. (They had a popular saying: 'We are Venetians first and Christians afterward.')[16]

Reference to the ducat is also made at 4.4.20 by the captain of Fortinbras's 'lawless resolutes' or mercenaries who may then have been regarded by Shakespeare and his audience as condottieri. The ducat was, then, a 'Catholic' coin.

Ironically Hamlet calls Polonius a 'fool' when he himself is a fool to have killed him, and he then proceeds to castigate Gertrude for her sins, ignoring the perilous state in which he has placed his own soul. His mother is no better than a harlot and her vows are 'false as dicers' oaths', and she has made 'sweet religion' a mere string of words (ignoring the fact that for Hamlet 'sweet religion' is a means of securing his victim's damnation), and the very moon, as on Judgment Day, is perturbed. The association of 'the doom' with Gertrude is perhaps to encourage us to see her as the Whore of Babylon.

Hamlet tells Gertrude that he will set up 'a glass' where she may see the 'inmost part' of her and later she says:

> Thou turn'st my eyes into my very soul,
> And there I see such black and grained spots
> As will not leave their tinct.

The image may have been a conventional one used by preachers, for in Nowell's *Catechism* we find:

> Finally, when beholding by the law, as it were in a glass, the spots and uncleanness of their souls, they learn thereby that they are not able to attain perfect righteousness by their works:

by this means they are trained to humility, and so the law prepareth them and sendeth them to seek righteousness in Christ.[17]

Again turning to Nowell, it is clear that Hamlet himself has ignored the law of God, for he has only 'revenge' written in his 'tables':

M. How cometh it to pass that God would have these commandments written in tables?
S. I will tell you. The image of God in man is, since the fall of Adam by original sin and evil custom, so darkened, and natural judgment so corrupted, that man doth not sufficiently understand what difference is between honest and dishonest, right and wrong.

So, it may well be asked, what is Hamlet up to here? Who does he think he is? Eleanor Prosser comments:

Many Christian commentators who see Hamlet as the divinely appointed minister of God's punishment view his shending of Gertrude as priest-like, as an attempt to shock her into self-knowledge and repentance. Hamlet cannot be thus absolved. A priest does not talk to a sinner as Hamlet talks to Gertrude. There is no compassion, no mercy in his tone, no suggestion that he is but waiting to hear the voluntary words of confession that will indicate his charges have struck home.[18]

To anticipate a little, he perhaps sees himself as someone licensed to hear confession, and the language he employs – 'grace', 'unction', 'habit', 'frock' – suggests a priest, curate or friar, and the adjective 'Catholic' should be used to prefix all three. His role is all the more incongruous, as, whatever he thinks he is, he is a murderer. But what did the audience think? They have seen a Vice/clown/jester playing the role of a curate – and that may remind us of Feste masquerading as 'Sir Topas' ('Sir' being a conventional courtesy prefix before the name of a Catholic priest in those times, i.e. pre-Elizabethan times), when he visits Malvolio in the dark room. Burlesque of religious ceremonial was apparently popular and part of the stock-in-trade of French and Italian court fools. One Matello, for example, who was in the service of Isabella d'Este, gave particular pleasure by imitating friars.[19] And such burlesque of Catholic ceremonial would have been enhanced if the audience were Protestant.

131

That the Vice/jester symbolism is relevant here can be seen from Hamlet's contemptuous sneer at Claudius – 'a vice of kings' and 'a cutpurse of the empire'. In fact however it is Hamlet who is the Vice and his 'cousin' Claudius is the cutpurse (the Vice and his cousin cutpurse was a cant phrase). It is a case of the pot calling the kettle black. Also, as 'father' of the Vice, Satan disguised as the Ghost makes his appearance in a dressing gown – of sable fur perhaps? He comes from 'Hell' beneath the stage and should look suitably satanic. The Ghost shows no concern about the killing of Polonius; instead he reprimands Hamlet for his 'almost blunted purpose', a strange image to associate with Hamlet whose keen sword has pierced the body of Polonius. Instead the Ghost shows concern for Gertrude's 'fighting soul', and the state of mortal sin in which Hamlet's soul has been placed is not even mentioned. As a contrast and as evidence of the reaction of an Elizabethan audience who were fully aware of the religious issues involved we may refer to the Old Man in *Doctor Faustus* who counsels:

> Though thou hast now offended like man,
> Do not persever in it like a devil;
> Yet, yet, thou hast an amiable soul,
> If sin by custom grow not into nature:
> Then, Faustus, will repentance come too late,
> Then thou art banished from the sight of heaven;
> No mortal can express the pains of hell.
>
> (5.1.38–44)

Hamlet reacts just as the Ghost had promised would happen if he told him the secrets of his 'prison house', for this would

> Make thy two eyes like stars start from their spheres,
> Thy knotted and combined locks to part,
> And each particular hair to stand a end,
> Like quills upon the fretful porpentine.
>
> (1.5.16–20)

For we find Gertrude's words echo him:

> Forth at your eyes your spirits wildly peep,
> And as the sleeping soldiers in th' alarm,
> Your bedded hairs like life in excrements
> Starts up and stand on end.
>
> (3.4.119–22)

132

Hamlet, by emphasizing that the Ghost is 'pale' (3.4.125), indicates clearly that it is a hellish apparition. We hear also the inverted language of evil in 'preaching to stones' which makes a mockery of Luke 19:40 where Christ answers the Pharisees who wish him to rebuke the disciples for crying 'Blessed is the King who comes in the name of the Lord!' with 'I tell you, if these were silent, the very stones would cry out'. Hamlet also refers to the 'habit' his father wears which suggests that it may have had a hood attached like a monk's or friar's and thus also there may be an imaginative link with the Devil that cozened Gertrude at 'hoodman-blind' (3.4.77). The Ghost then exits through the 'portal' which can only be the gate of Hell through which he made his entrance – the trapdoor in the floor of the stage.

The effect on Gertrude is that she is convinced that Hamlet is mad, for the Ghost is not visible to her. That the Ghost is hallucinatory is not possible in terms of contemporary dramatic practice, for a 'true' hallucination would have involved 'bending the eye on vacancy'. The effect on Hamlet, far from restraining his verbal attack on Gertrude, causes him to intensify it and the Vice–cutpurse association makes an oblique appearance in:

> For in the fatness of these pursy times
> Virtue of vice must pardon beg.
>
> (3.4.153–4)

Hamlet says he repents but in fact he sees himself as the instrument of divine justice – a delusion common to revengers, like Othello who believed his 'cause' was just and 'heavenly'. No doubt Hamlet feels justified in further castigating Gertrude for the same reason. But as has been frequently said he seems to take a lickerish relish in the sexual details which also revolt him. The Elizabethans had never heard of the Oedipus complex but probably knew that Nero had killed his own mother:

> let not ever
> The soul of Nero enter this firm bosom,
> Let me be cruel, not unnatural.
> I will speak daggers to her, but use none.
>
> (3.2.396–9)

and it seems more likely therefore that they saw a Hamlet so disgusted by Gertrude's incest that he might kill his mother – his nausea in their eyes was a motive for murder. Moreover, Gertrude has disobeyed God's law as written in the Decalogue which bade

133

her be chaste and obedient instead of lewd and disobedient as
Satan, the arch-rebel, required:

> Rebellious hell,
> If thou canst mutine in a matron's bones,
> To flaming youth let virtue be as wax
> And meet in her own fire.
>
> (3.4.82–5)

Jenkins points out other examples in Shakespeare of the 'identification of sexual desire with the rebellion of man's lower nature'.[20]

There are two further points which do not seem to have
attracted much attention. First there are the curious lines

> And when you are desirous to be blessed
> I'll blessing beg of you.
>
> (3.4.171–2)

It would appear to mean that when Gertrude repents Hamlet will
beg a blessing from her. But in fact Hamlet himself needs to
confess himself to Heaven and to beg the blessing of God – he
treats his mother like the Virgin Mary, or 'Our Blessed Lady', as
Catholics refer to her. Thus we may have a continuation of
Catholic ideas which would have invited scorn from a Protestant
audience. This may seem speculative to our eyes which are no
longer sensitive to Catholic ritual, but it may be conceded that
Gertrude is in no position to bless anybody and least of all Hamlet
who now has blood on his hands. And for another ironic
treatment of 'blessing' we find Laertes saying to Ophelia at his
leave-taking:

> but here my father comes.
> A double blessing is a double grace.
>
> (1.3.53–4)

The other point which seems to have escaped notice, so far as I
am aware, is the possible pun on 'queen' – 'quean' being a harlot –
in these lines:

> For who that's but a queen, fair, sober, wise,
> Would from a paddock, from a bat, a gib,
> Such dear concernings hide?
>
> (3.4.189–91)

The implication then is that only an honest whore would keep the
secret of Hamlet's madness from Claudius. There is a further

insult to Claudius in the words used to describe him, as they name the common familiars of witches. At any rate the pun on 'queen', either way, is an insult to Gertrude, and further calls into question Hamlet's willingness to be blessed by his 'blessed' mother.

Finally, whatever Gertrude's protestations that she will keep Hamlet's secret, she tells Claudius that he is 'mad as the sea and wind' and there is little to doubt that she really thinks he is homicidal and insane. Claudius has reached the same conclusion: 'Hamlet in madness hath Polonius slain', he tells Rosencrantz and Guildenstern. When we next see Hamlet again he is in custody and with sardonic humour he announces that Polonius is at supper – where he is the main dish for worms. But Claudius does not see any humour in the situation – Hamlet is a threat that must be removed, and in soliloquy he reveals that he has ordered 'England' to put him to death. (The time reference here is perhaps to the remote past when the Danes had control of part of England.)

What then we have seen is a Hamlet who has tried to murder Claudius, just as he said he would, but who has killed Polonius instead, a Hamlet moreover whom Gertrude considered 'idle' at the beginning of the scene and whose behaviour has confirmed her impression. (The full implication of what Gertrude meant by 'idle' can be seen in Q1 viz.

> But Hamlet this is onely fantasie,
> And for my loue forget these idle fits.
> Hamlet. Idle, no mother, my pulse doth beat like yours.
> It is not madnesse that possesseth Hamlet.)

The appearance of the Ghost has merely served to confirm her belief for she has not seen it, and she therefore also rejects Hamlet's claim that his father had been murdered. This Hamlet had also played the priest like Feste and stirred Gertrude's conscience without concern for his own, although in Catholic eyes, and Protestant also, he is in a state of mortal sin, and he ends up 'lugging the guts into the neighbour room'. How then should we characterize him? In Eleanor Prosser's view: 'In this grotesque bit of sardonic brutality and in his eagerness for further knavery, Hamlet is now acting much like the medieval Vice.'[21]

I think it probable that Shakespeare's audience took a similar view. Even the tears that Gertrude says Hamlet shed, and Bradley's claim that Hamlet is like a 'father-confessor ... redeeming a fellow-creature from degradation ... pitiless in denouncing the sin', and Granville Barker's comment – 'a macabre business, this torchlight hue and cry through the darkened castle after a lunatic homicide' ... are included in the symbol of the Vice.[22] Spivack refers to the 'rapid alternation between one mood and another' of the Vice, and that

> to look piteous, to shed tears plentifully, and to howl dismally ... show his affection, his moral refinement; and compose the 'flag and sign of love' behind which evil moves into position for its destructive assault. 'Wepe' urges the stage direction in *Horestes*, and 'O oo oo, you care not for me,' moans the Vice until he brings the hero around to the unnatural destruction of his mother.

Spivack also speaks of the 'pious solicitude' that accompanies the 'grave countenance' of the Vice and quotes the Vice Infidelity in *Mary Magdalene*:

> Lyke obstinate Friers I temper my looke,
> Which had one eie on a wench, and an other on a boke.

And Hamlet's grisly jesting about the body of Polonius, and his 'hide-and-seek', mirror the 'rapid transition between convulsions of simulated grief and genuine hilarity' typical of the Vice.[23]

The question of course that arises is whether the 'antic disposition' shown by Hamlet at this point in the play is feigned or not. Probably as moderns we see no dissimulation here – the death of Polonius is not a joke as far as we are concerned, and Hamlet's concern for his mother's moral welfare appears to be genuine. We might in fact repudiate the notion that there is any trace of an antic disposition here and agree with Bradley that Hamlet's desire is to save his mother's soul and welcome 'that sudden sunshine of faith and love which breaks out'.[24] And we may also believe that Gertrude in saying that Hamlet wept for Polonius is telling a lie to conceal the callousness that her son has shown. But we are not Elizabethans, who probably saw a son driving his mother to despair (and to drink – I shall return to this point later) and who might also have waited with bated breath to see if Hamlet, carried away by anger and disgust at Gertrude's conduct, might kill his own mother, like Nero, whom he alluded to as he entered her bedroom, or Orestes (who, according to Pikeryng, was driven on by the Vice Revenge). We all know the play so well that we may be ignoring what should be obvious – Hamlet's disgust is a possible motive for murder – and so think in terms of psychological instead of dramatic symbols. The Elizabethan ground-

136

ling who knew his Vice may well have the edge on us, and see Hamlet's conduct in terms of the 'antic' disposition or 'natural' disposition of the Vice. Thus I suggest that a Hamlet who wears his Vice's cap in these scenes is dressed for the part he has to play.

7

Ophelia and Laertes

OPHELIA may have derived her name from an Italian source – the *Arcadia* of Sannazzaro, for Montano, a name found in the same piece, is used in Q1 for the later Reynaldo. We cannot be sure that Shakespeare chose the name but we can be certain that he represented her as Catholic, indeed very obviously Catholic. For example, Polonius, with the approval of Claudius, plans to use her as a decoy and gives her a book so that she can pretend to be at prayer. Now as Harold Jenkins points out: 'In iconographic convention a solitary woman with a book represented devoutness . . . The book is of course traditional in pictures of the Annunciation.'[1] But it should be added that both the iconographers and the tradition were Catholic. If we refer to Ernst Gombrich we may find examples of this in Italian art. Simone Martini and Lippi Memmi (1313), Fra Angelica da Fiesole (c.1440) and Gherardo di Giovanni (1474–6) in their paintings of the Annunciation portray the Virgin holding a book.[2] Thus a Catholic woman at her 'orisons' would be following the example of 'Our Lady'. Ophelia however is doing nothing of the kind; she is not praying, she is bent on trickery. Both Polonius and Claudius are aware of the incongruity:

> Read on this book,
> That show of such an exercise may colour
> Your loneliness; we oft to blame in this,
> 'Tis too much proved, that with devotion's visage
> And pious action we do sugar o'er
> The devil himself.
>
> (3.1.44–9)

Polonius's words as we know jog Claudius's conscience, but the point is that no Protestant in Shakespeare's audience would have disagreed because the worship of the 'Blessed Virgin' in the Catholic manner was abhorrent to them and Catholicism itself a sham.

Then, in her first 'mad' song which begins:

138

> How should I your true love know
> From another one?

(4.5.23–4)

a pilgrim wears the garb which lovers, editors assure us, also used as a disguise, and the 'cockle' hat was particularly associated with the shrine of St. James of Compostella in Spain. But Protestants took a less romantic and less pious view. First, on pilgrimages:

> When we were ignorant in God's word, and heard nothing but the sound of a tinkling cymbal; did we not think superstitions to be religion, deceivers true teachers; vanity to be verity; the gospel to be heresy: to gad abroad in pilgrimages from this saint to that saint.[3]

Then there is the pilgrim's hat which was treated with derision and still survives but reduced to the status of a nursery rhyme:

> Mary, Mary, quite contrary
> How does your garden grow?
> With silver bells and cockle shells
> And pretty maids all in a row.

But what of the convention of the lover as a pilgrim? It is true that Romeo and Juliet use the symbolism of the pilgrimage in their wooing, and that the Prince of Morocco describes Portia as 'this shrine, this mortal-breathing saint', but is there not irony here? Portia is no saint – she can be bitchy, as when she discusses her wooers with Nerissa; Wolf Mankowitz calls her 'a cold, snobbish little bitch'.[4] Nor is there anything saintly about Juliet. Why then did Catholic lovers disguise themselves as pilgrims we must ask. Warburton's answer was:

> While this kind of devotion was in favour, love-intrigues were carried on under that mask. Hence the old ballads and novels made pilgrimages the subject of their plots.[5]

Bishop Thomas Percy, whose *Reliques of Ancient English Poetry* are a valuable source of material, says:

> The pilgrimages undertaken on the pretence of religion, were often productive of affairs of gallantry, and led the votaries to no other shrine than that of Venus.[6]

(And his editor Henry B. Wheatley adds (1910):

> Even in the time of Langland, pilgrimages to Walsingham were

139

not unfavourable to the rites of Venus. Thus in his Visions of Pierce Plowman, fo. 1.

> Hermets on a heape, with hoked staves,
> Wenten to Walsingham, and her wenches after.)[7]

I have quoted these two eighteenth-century critics because they seem to be closer to the Elizabethans in attitude although neither can be described as being as hostile to Catholicism as the Elizabethan Protestants were, or the earlier Reformers.

As Ophelia's first song also seems to be connected with Walsingham it seems appropriate to note what Wheatley says about it:

> The shrine of the Virgin at Walsingham was the favourite English resort of pilgrims for nearly four hundred years, and the people of Norfolk were in great distress when their image was taken away from them and the stream of votaries was suddenly stopped.[8]

Bishop Percy tells us why:

> At the dissolution of the monasteries in 1538, this splendid image ... was carried to Chelsea, and there burnt in the presence of commissioners; who, we trust, did not burn the jewels and the finery.[9]

He also says:

> Erasmus has given a very exact and humorous description of the superstitions practised there in his time ... He tells us, the rich offerings in silver, gold, and precious stones, that were shown to him, were incredible, there being scarce a person of any note in England, but who some time or other paid a visit, or sent a present to our lady of Walsingham.[10]

It is perhaps to be expected that there were songs about such a famous place. Peter J. Seng is our authority here:

> Although the source of Ophelia's first song has not survived, there exists an interesting analogue to it in 'As ye came from the holy land of Walsingham,' a ballad which has been handed down in three manuscripts and one printed version.[11]

He then goes on to discuss the question of authorship and the parodies and broadside ballads of the 'Walsingham' genre and concludes:

140

From the text in Shakespeare and from the variety of imitative material which has survived, it is possible to make reasonable conjectures about the lost source of Ophelia's song. It was evidently written in ballad-meter like the fragments in *Hamlet* and most of the parodies and imitations. Since it employs the dialogue device of question and answer it may have been a jig. It is even possible to infer the narrative pattern: a deserted lover meets on the roadway a pilgrim returning from the shrine of Our Lady of Walsingham. The lover's mistress has also gone on a pilgrimage to Walsingham, but has failed to return. The lover inquires of the stranger he has met whether she has been seen on the way. Asked how she can be recognized, he attempts to describe her. This opening, the encounter and the inquiry, seems to be the common mark of 'Walsingham' songs.[12]

It seems that two endings in particular were popular – the literary version such as that ascribed to Sir Walter Raleigh in which 'the old lover deserted by his (apparently) young mistress, takes melancholy refuge from his sorrows by philosophizing on old age and the nature of true love'; and the broadside version in which the lover finds his wife with another man but 'brings her, repentant, home'. But

> Ophelia's song differs from both in being much closer to its source. Moreover, for his own dramatic purposes, Shakespeare has apparently reversed the roles of the lovers: in his song it is the mistress who awaits in longing the return of her pilgrim-lover. From a wayfarer she learns that he has been stayed forever on his pilgrimage by death.[13]

There are two points to be made here. First, to the imitations and parodies in the early seventeenth-century drama we can affix the label 'Protestant'. Then as to the Raleigh version one must doubt whether a 'fervent Protestant' would take it seriously because of its connection with Walsingham which for him was anything but holy. One wonders also what scurrilous versions never found their way into print.

A version of the Walsingham ballad of particular interest is one composed by Bishop Percy himself from fragments of ballads in Shakespeare's plays with 'one small fragment taken from Beaumont and Fletcher'. He entitled it *The Friar of Orders Gray*[14] and it tells the story of a lady in 'pilgrim's weedes' who asks the 'reverend friar' if he has seen her true love 'at yon holy shrine'.

The friar replies that 'he is dead and gone' and tries to console her but is a Job's comforter for he philosophizes that he might have been false to her if he had lived. In the end he confesses that he has fallen in love with her and as he has not taken his final vows there is hope for them both if she in turn loves him. She does of course and says:

> Now farewell grief, and welcome joy
> Once more unto my heart;
> For since I found thee, lovely youth,
> We never more will part.

What is of importance is that Percy's title is taken from a song that Petruchio sings in *The Taming of the Shrew*; Shakespeare gives only the first two lines:

> It was the Friar of Orders gray,
> As he forth walked on his way.
>
> (4.1.148–9)

This is about a love affair between a Franciscan friar and a nun. He gives her a singing lesson after which she prays and then:

> This fryer began the nunne to grope
> inducas
> It was a morsell for the pope
> In temptationibus
> > Inducas inducas
> > In temptationibus
>
> The frere & the nunne whan they had done
> > Inducas
> Eche to theyr cloyster dyd they gone
> > Sine temptationibus
> > > Inducas inducas
> > > In temptationibus
> > > Finis.[15]

According to Seng, Petruchio's song 'is apparently from a lost version of a ballad or carol, probably scurrilous in nature'. The analogue which Seng records dates from c.1500 but in its extant form may be an expanded version of a later analogue dating from about 1550.[16] As it derides the Pope, I would venture to add that it has been re-touched by a Protestant. The question then arises whether the good Bishop Percy who had such an extensive knowledge of ballads knew of its existence. If he did there is no doubt that he took a more lenient view of friars than the Elizabethans did – for them, as John Peter records, 'It seems to have been an Elizabethan saying that an old fornicator was always clothed in a friar's habit'.[17] To this we may add the words that Marlowe put into Faustus's mouth:

> Go and return an old Franciscan friar,
> That holy shape becomes a devil best.
>
> (1.3.25–6)

But of course the association with the Walsingham ballad could be coincidental.

When however we look at Ophelia's allusion to the legend of the baker's daughter who was turned into an owl because she refused bread to Christ, it seems possible that Bishop may have been making more than an unconscious association. According to Chambers the story was 'monkish'[18] in origin, but it seems rather the sort of yarn that a dishonest member of a mendicant order might have used to frighten housewives into giving him alms – someone like Chaucer's Friar for example. There also appears to be a similar legend in gypsy folklore and their word for the owl translates as 'baker's daughter', which may have arisen from a cynical joke, for they too went in for begging.

Then there is sexual innuendo. Harold Jenkins points out that

> Bakers' daughters were traditionally women of ill repute: the Marian martyr John Bradford said of Philip of Spain that 'he must have three or four in one night ... not of ladies and gentlewomen, but of bakers' daughters, and such poor whores'.[19]

As we know that Chaucer's Friar cultivated the 'seleres of vitaille' the baker's daughter according to popular prejudice may have always been ready to 'bake bread in her oven' or 'keep a bun in the oven' for a religious. This is guesswork of course, but Freud records that the oven is a common dream symbol for the uterus and it could be found as a colloquial metaphor in some parts of the Germany of his time and he even discovered it in Herodotus.[20] Steevens's account shows how easily a double meaning could become attached to the original story:

> This is a common story among the vulgar in Gloucestershire, and is thus related. 'Our Saviour went into a baker's shop

where they were baking, and asked for some bread to eat. The mistress of the shop immediately put a piece of dough into the oven to bake for him; but was reprimanded by her daughter, who insisting that the piece of dough was too large, reduced it to a very small size. The dough, however, immediately afterwards began to swell, and presently become of a most enormous size. Whereupon, the baker's daughter cried out: 'Heugh, heugh, heugh', which owl-like noise probably induced our Saviour for her wickedness to transform her into that bird.'[21]

Then Ophelia sings a song about a woman seduced by her lover on St. Valentine's day – the day on which according to tradition the first girl a man saw would be his valentine or true love for the year. It was also popularly believed that it was the day on which the birds chose their mates. Shakespeare alludes to this in *A Midsummer Night's Dream*. Theseus, when the lovers have awakened, says:

> Good morrow friends. Saint Valentine is past:
> Begin these wood-birds but to couple now?
>
> (4.1.145–6)

The song contains words that were unmistakably Catholic, e.g.

> By Gis and by St. Charity
>
> (4.5.57)

According to the *OED* this was a common Catholic oath, 'Gis' being a corruption of 'Jesus'. Harold Jenkins also points out that 'Saint Charity' was not in fact a saint's name,[22] that it was however frequently used in oaths, and quotes from the *Shepheardes Calender*:

> The Catholiques comen othe ... to haue charitye alwayes in their mouth.[23]

Then there is the line:

> By Cock, they are to blame.

'Cock' is a corruption of 'God' and the *OED* gives examples to show that the usage was common before Elizabethan times, and we may presume that this, in keeping with the context, was also characteristically Catholic usage, but in addition, as Jenkins says, 'no doubt there is a thought of the male organ too'.[24] Thus, what we are listening to is a 'dirty' Catholic song – the bawdiness is clearly labelled as Catholic and we are to see then what gross licentiousness Catholics allowed themselves on a saint's day.

Just after this song Ophelia says:

> Come, my coach! Good night, ladies, good night. Sweet ladies, good night, good night. (4.5.70–1)

If we are to associate what she says with what has gone before it may be a reference to Queen Mab, who, as Mercutio in *Romeo and Juliet* tells us:

> Is the fairies' midwife, and she comes
> In shape no bigger than an agate stone ...
> Her chariot is an empty hazel-nut,
> Made by the joiner squirrel or old grub.
> Time out o' mind the fairies' coach-makers.
> And in this state she gallops night by night
> Through lovers' brains, and then they dream of love.
>
> (1.4.55 ff.)

Perhaps this association may be supported by Ophelia's own confused chronology, for she began her song:

> To-morrow is Saint Valentine's day.

Perhaps too the Scottish expression 'away with the fairies' meaning madness may also be relevant.

Thus, while presumably we cannot, and are perhaps not supposed to, understand Ophelia's ravings, they certainly would not endear her to Protestants. If we take her allusions 'vertically' as it were, tracing them separately into the contemporary background, they produce a tantalizing sense of pattern that we cannot complete – the pattern is Catholic certainly but how does it fit together? And there is the same sense of bafflement when we try to connect her remarks in 'horizontal' sequence – we have a series of puzzling leaps of thought coupled with the feeling that there is an underlying coherence. A true love who was a pilgrim is dead – there is a friar's (?) yarn possibly connected with seduction – then a 'real' seduction on St. Valentine's day. But where does Hamlet fit into all this? We have to think in metaphors to make him fit even into the first part of the sequence; he doesn't fit into the second, and it strains credulity to see him as having seduced Ophelia. But what about Polonius? He is a better candidate for he is dead, but what had that to do with the friar (?), the baker's daughter, and St. Valentine's day?

If we turn now to Ophelia's second entrance, Laertes, who has not seen his sister since he left for France, is aghast at her appearance – to him she is a withered flower:

> O rose of May,
> Dear maid, kind sister, sweet Ophelia!

But his choice of words had a wider connotation – the Virgin Mary for Catholics was, and is, also titled 'The Mystical Rose' and 'The Flower of May', so already his words would be treated with derision by Protestants in Shakespeare's audience. In Catholic devotional practice in medieval times most flowers, and herbs also, were associated with the Virgin Mary besides the rose, for instance the lily (cf. the Madonna lily), and the *OED* records such usages which would appear at first glance to be botanical anomalies: 'lent-lily' and 'lenten rose' for the golden daffodil, and Laertes' 'rose of May' for the white narcissus. This latter usage would certainly seem more apt when applied to the poor distracted girl whose face might have been pale (as the Ghost's?). Thus too the association with the Virgin produced the compound 'rosemary' from the Latin 'ros' meaning 'dew' and 'marinus', 'marine', and in what we might describe as the Catholic language of lovers it became a symbol of remembrance.

Some of these associations can be seen in John Skelton's (?1460–1529) poem 'To Mistress Isabel Pennell':

> By Saint Mary, my lady,
> Your mammy and your daddy
> Brought forth a goodly baby!
>
> My maiden Isabel,
> Reflaring rosabel.
> The fragrant camomel;
> The ruddy rosary [rose-bush]
> The sovereign rosemary
> The pretty strawberry;
> The columbine, the nept [mint]
> The jelofer [gillyflower] well set,
> The proper violet:
> Ennewed your colour
> Is like the daisy flower
> After the April shower.[25]

146

Similarly, in French the columbine was 'Our Lady's glove' (le gant de Notre Dame) and the daisy, 'la paquerette' from 'paque', Easter. We may add 'la pensée' from which our 'pansy' is derived, and which in its religious association would refer to meditation – the Italians call it 'viola del pensiero'. Then there is rue which symbolized grace and also repentance – it was put in the holy water, and penitents were also sprinkled with sprigs of it. Sir Edmund Chambers refers to it in his edition of *Hamlet*.[26]

If we turn to *The Winter's Tale* however we find a change. Perdita, who acts as 'mistress of the Feast' and gives presents of flowers, which include rosemary and rue, as Ophelia does, is aware that she is acting like the May Queen, a figure who was the centre of attraction in the May Games whose origin, like the custom of 'maying', is lost in antiquity. She says:

> Come, take your flowers;
> Methinks I play as I have seen them do
> In Whitsun pastorals.
>
> (4.3.132–4)

Florizel identifies her with the Roman goddess Flora (4.3.132–4), and this in turn, as we learn from Douce, links her with Maid Marian:

> Maid Marian not only officiated as the paramour of Robin Hood in the May games, but as queen and lady of the May, who seems to have been introduced long before the games of Robin Hood ... There can be no doubt that the queen of the May is the legitimate representative of the Goddess Flora in the Roman festival.[27]

Ophelia too encourages us to identify her as Maid Marian and as May Queen by singing what one must presume to be a snatch of a bawdy song:

> For bonny sweet Robin is all my joy.

Thus Ophelia, the May Queen and Maid Marian seem to have a distinctly secular air, perhaps with the influence of the Reformation and its hostility to Catholicism. Douce remarks on the May Queen:

> It appears that the Lady of the May was sometimes carried in procession on men's shoulders; for Stephen Batman, speaking of the Pope and his ceremonies, states that he is carried on the

backs of four deacons, 'after the manner of carying [*sic*] whytepot queenes in Western May games'.[28]

Douce thinks that a 'whytepot queene' was a 'kitchem malkin or cook wench'.

If we look again at the meanings of Ophelia's flowers that editors have assigned to them there is evidence of a shift from divine to human love, including its darker side. Skelton's columbine now symbolizes cuckoldry, and his daisy represents dissimulation. The pansies, from referring to religious thoughts, are now thoughts of a lover. So too with violets (as we learn from Brewer); rue loses its connection with holy water, and rosemary in particular for Protestants has no longer any association with the Virgin Mary.

Thus, using the Protestant language of flowers, if we may so term it, following Dover Wilson I assign fennel and columbine to Claudius, as appropriate to a flattering seducer and cuckold-maker; Gertrude gets rue for penitence; Ophelia keeps the dissembling daisy for herself. Most oddly however Ophelia gives Laertes the lover's token of rosemary and pansies – as Harold Jenkins says, 'Ophelia confuses her brother with her lover'.[29] I also agree with him that she would offer him violets to complete the gift, but would add that there is more involved here than faithful love, as we shall see.

But – and I think the point is important – what editors have done without realizing it, and they have ample evidence for what they have done, is switch from the Catholic 'language' that Ophelia has been using to this wholly Protestant usage. I agree with Harold Jenkins in particular that Ophelia may be acting like the May Queen in distributing the flowers as Perdita does, and she sings a snatch of a song that also links her with Maid Marian, and we know from Douce that we are talking about one and the same role. But if we assign a Catholic meaning to the flowers we must also ask ourselves what, in Catholic terms, Ophelia might be seen as doing. The answer is that Shakespeare's audience might think she is the May Queen who represents the 'Blessed Virgin' in what is now called the 'May Procession'. The month of May is sacred to the Virgin Mary and devotions in her honour are widely observed by all Catholics to this day. The 'May Procession' may vary in detail but it is still common for a young girl to be chosen as a May Queen and for her to crown the statue of the Virgin which may or may not be carried in the Procession, and she may also give flowers to bystanders. She may also be accompanied by a retinue of children, dressed as nuns or wearing white dresses, who are to be confirmed. They also may carry baskets of flowers and distribute them like the May Queen. Thus, allowing for local variations, we have a living survival of a widespread medieval custom that all Catholics observed, and it would seem that the role of Ophelia as May Queen is as ambiguous as the connotations of the flowers she carries. It may then be that Shakespeare expected his audience to be aware of the ambiguity of Ophelia's role and of the language she uses – she is both nun and whore, a combination of ideas that we shall encounter again shortly.

Then there is the question of whether Ophelia actually gives flowers or in her madness only 'goes through the motions'. I suggest that she gives straws instead, for straw seems to have been associated with lunacy for centuries. For example, in Dekker's *The Honest Whore* (Part 1) the madmen 'sit and pick the straws' (5.2). Lear says:

> Where is this straw, my fellow?
> The art of our necessities is strange,
> That can make vile things precious.

> (3.2.69–71)

Swift in *A Tale of a Tub* (1704) referred to the current treatment of the insane as 'phlebotomy, and whips, and chains, and dark chambers, and straw'. Hogarth in *The Rake's Progress* shows the bedding in the madhouse consisted of straw, and there is ample evidence of this practice continuing well into the nineteenth century.[30] Besides, Ophelia herself 'spurns enviously at straws' in which action she displays the same sin of ambition as Fortinbras does in his fashion. Ophelia's world is made of straw, the world of Bedlam in which, as Hogarth shows, even crowns were made of it.

The funeral of Ophelia yet again emphasizes her Catholicism. As in *Romeo and Juliet* she is probably 'In . . . best robes uncover'd on the bier' (4.1.110), and flowers, probably rosemary, are strewed around her (5.1.79–80). Similarly, in *The White Devil* (5.4) we find rosemary used in this way. Granville Barker also quotes evidence to substantiate the use of rosemary in funerals in this country.[31] We have then it seems another folk tradition associated with the Virgin which was pre-Reformation. M.C. Bradbrook comments that 'the substitution of the Queen's flowers for marriage-strewings is a powerful theme in old ballads, where

149

the interchange of bride-bed for death-bed gives a strong climax', and she also observes that Paris in *Romeo and Juliet* laments:

> Sweet flower, with flowers thy bridal bed I strew
> O woe! thy canopy is dust and stones.[32]

> (5.2.12–13)

Rue was also used for it represented grace as we have seen, and there is also evidence that its Catholic association was retained in Sussex even as late as 1838 where it was called 'Ave Grace'.[33]

The requiem that is refused Ophelia is the Catholic requiem mass in the opinion of Richmond Noble:

> The Prayer Book makes no provision for a requiem mass, and taken in conjunction with the other features – 'maimed rites' and 'death was doubtful' – the refusal of a requiem would point clearly to Roman usage.[34]

Dover Wilson in discussing this point did not refer to 'dirge', the Q1 reading which was another Catholic name for the requiem. Thomas Nashe, for example, talked of 'Masses, Dirges, or Trentals',[35] and dirges and trentals were also derided in Tarlton's *Newes out of Purgatorie*. 'Dirige', as the *OED* has it, was originally the first word of the antiphon 'Dirige domine deus meus &c' at Matins in the Office of the Dead and the word clearly retained its Roman association into the seventeenth century. For example, in 1642 we find 'a priest to read Masse or Dirigies for the weale of his soule after his decease' (*OED*). Thus also Claudius's:

> With mirth in funeral and with dirge in marriage

> (1.2.12)

would be a clear indication to a contemporary audience that not only was the funeral of Hamlet's father Catholic, but Claudius's marriage had been Catholic as well – a point that, as was previously indicated, the *Brudermord* makes very plain, for the Pope's sanction for the marriage is mentioned.

There is a further point arising from the funeral perhaps worthy of inclusion and that is that Laertes' 'churlish priest' would not have been allowed if he had been addressing an Anglican minister, nor would he have dared to challenge the Church's ruling in such an event. Indeed the Church of Elizabeth had no written code of practice in these matters and would not have welcomed embarrassing questions, as Noble assures us, but the Roman Catholics had canonical rules to which reference could be made, and refusal of a requiem mass would be correct procedure. Dover Wilson's insistence that the funeral is Protestant even contradicts his own stage directions which have, earlier, Ophelia praying before a crucifix.

But if we do not see the pains which Shakespeare has taken to emphasize Ophelia's Catholicism we miss the bitter irony of her death, as Gertrude describes it. For example, the

> long purples
> That liberal shepherds give a grosser name.
> (4.7.168–9)

were known, according to the *OED*, as 'fool's cullions' or 'fooles ballockes' – the botanical name 'orchis' being derived from the Greek word for testicle. Then again, Ophelia with her clothes spread wide is 'mermaid-like', and 'mermaid' was a cant term for a prostitute. The irony is deepened further by her singing 'old lauds' as in Q2, these being, presumably, Catholic hymns sung at Matins, for Lauds had disappeared from the Book of Common Prayer in 1552. There is another point also, that only a religious, such as a nun, would have sung that part of the Catholic liturgy in the Middle Ages. Ophelia then dies a 'nun' – the manner of her death is a kind of dramatic pun, but only to a Protestant audience.

Harold Jenkins has pointed out that the only indubitable literary examples of 'nunnery' meaning 'brothel' occur after *Hamlet* was written.[36] But I think we have to ask ourselves whether this was not a common Protestant joke, and also why it took so long to develop – if it did – so long after nunneries disappeared in 1538. Are we after all dealing with a dirty joke that produced a synonym used so commonly that no one thought fit to write it down? That feelings still ran high in Shakespeare's time can be seen in Burton's comments which were written even later:

How odious and abominable are those superstitious and rash vows of Popish Monasteries, so to bind and enforce men and women to vow virginity, to lead to single life against the laws of nature, opposite to religion, policy, and humanity ... For let them but consider what fearful maladies, feral diseases ... come to both sexes by this enforced temperance. It troubles me to think of, much more to relate, those frequent aborts & murdering of infants in the Nunneries ... their notorious fornications, those male-prostitutes, masturbators, strumpets

151

&c, those rapes, incests, adulteries, mastuprations, sodomies, buggeries of Monks and Friars.[37]

We have to advance the clock to Milton's time to find once again a

> pensive Nun, devout and pure,
> Sober, steadfast and demure

which was of course the sort of nun that Hamlet wished Ophelia to become. But what Protestant in Shakespeare's audience would have shared his sentiments?

But Catholics too would have regarded Ophelia's insanity as connected with Satan, for she has displayed sexual feelings and was, ipso facto, evil and a demoniac – they might have considered that exorcism might have saved her. We are at liberty to forget the connection made between madness and Satan, but Shakespeare's audience however liberal, in the modern sense, that they were then would not have denied the Devil's ability to take possession of a human being. Ophelia has despaired and committed suicide and only Claudius's influence has prevented her from being buried in unsanctified ground.

Yet another ironic note is evident – crowflowers (associated with the 'upstart crow' as a symbol of ambition?), 'crownet' or 'coronet weeds' and the 'envious sliver' may point to ambition as well as 'purples'. Ophelia's desire to be queen may be displayed in this pathetic manner. But crowflowers may also be ambiguous – not only 'buttercups' but 'ragged robins' as well – and because long purples were known also as 'priest's pintle' what we may have here is a form of nun's 'wedding' garland symbolizing her mystical role as a bride of Christ. Even today a Franciscan nun wears a rose crown when she becomes a postulant and a crown of thorns when she takes her final vows.

All this, it is true, is a far cry from Bradley:

> Coleridge was true to Shakespeare when he wrote of 'the affecting death of Ophelia – who in the beginning lay like a little projection of land into a lake or stream covered with spray-flowers quietly reflected in the quiet waters but at length is undermined or loosened, and becomes a fairy isle, and after a brief vagrancy sinks almost without an eddy'.[38]

But, sad to say, we can share these sentiments only if we shut our eyes to what the words meant in Elizabethan times, to the misogynistic feelings that stemmed from the Church's teaching about Eve[39] and which, coupled with the belief in the Devil, led to the death of thousands of women as witches.[40] We have also to allow for the reaction of a Protestant audience to Ophelia's Catholicism – even her last exit before the eyes of the audience is made with a Catholic blessing on her lips, which would keep her at arm's length from them, and all the more so when, being guilty of 'self-slaughter', she was damned and on the way to Hell, there to meet another 'bonny sweet Robin':

> Miss Margaret Murray points out that one of the many names of the witch-god, the god of fertility, is Robin, that Robin is in fact, almost a generic name for the Devil, who in many of the witch trials is described as wearing a hood, whence 'Robin with a hood' or 'Robin Hood'.[41]

∽o∽

When we first meet Laertes he asks permission to return to France from which he had come 'willing' to 'show [his] duty' in attending the coronation. We also learn that, like Polonius, he condones the incestuous marriage. As to his purpose in returning we are left to guess, if we must. But from the instructions that Polonius gives Reynaldo, Laertes is bent on sowing some more wild oats in Paris, which, according to Brantôme, was notorious for the scandals of the Court. Paris was also associated with the massacre of the Protestants there in 1571 – which Marlowe had dramatized.

A.L. Rowse also records that

> the English regarded the French as . . . essentially unreliable and treacherous. (Henry of Navarre's desertion of Protestantism and conversion to Rome gave the Queen much concern, religious as well as political; the English distrust over oath-breaking is a contemporary theme of *Love's Labour's Lost*.)[42]

Then again, according to the *Encyclopaedia Britannica*, France was notorious for duelling – between 1589 and 1608 more than 8,000 gentlemen were killed in duels, although Henry IV tried to restrain his countrymen. In 1610 duelling was on the increase again and Lord Herbert of Cherbury, the British ambassador in Paris, reported that 'there is scarce a Frenchman worth looking on who has not killed his man in a duel'. In 1626 Richelieu tried to clamp down on it, and we may remember the excitement of Dumas's *The Three Musketeers*.

Laertes fits this setting, for Claudius tells us that Lamord

> the brooch indeed
> And gem of all the nation

had given him a 'masterly report' for his skill with the rapier. And

> The scrimers of their nation
> He swore had neither motion, guard, nor eye,
> If [he] opposed them.
>
> (4.7.99–101)

The formal duel however, as Bowers points out, had not by 1603 affected English society.[43] But the reputation for fencing and horsemanship that the French had acquired is reflected in the character of Monsieur le Bon in *The Merchant of Venice* who boasts of his expertise on horseback and who will 'fence with his own shadow'. Lamord however does not share his comic aura, indeed his name has a distinctly apocalyptic ring to it.

The Laertes then that we first see should be dressed in such fashion as would suggest the French duellist and he should wear a long rapier. The name Laerters occurs in Ovid's *Metamorphoses* in the context of the death of Achilles and it is possible that Shakespeare chose the name as suitable for a man who would match Hamlet in swordsmanship. Polonius is aware of his son's love of fencing, for this is one of the 'slight sullies' that Reynaldo is allowed to put on Laertes, and he associates it with gaming, drinking, swearing, quarrelling and drabbing. Polonius indeed repeats most of this list:

> There was 'a gaming, there o'ertook in's rouse,
> There falling out at tennis, or perchance,
> 'I saw him enter such a house of sale.'
> Videlicet, a brothel, or so forth.
>
> (2.1.56–9)

What are 'slight sullies' to Polonius were in fact examples of the Seven Deadly Sins recognized to this day by the Catholic Church, and were familiar also to the Elizabethans. For example, Marlowe's Wrath says:

> I am Wrath! I had neither father nor mother; I leapt out of a lion's mouth when I was scarce an hour old, and ever since have run up and down the world with these case of rapiers, wounding myself when I could get none to fight withal: I was

154

born in hell, and look to it, for some of you shall be my father.
(2.2.133–8)

If then we look again at Hamlet's words:

> Up, sword, and know thou a more horrid hent,
> When he is drunk asleep, or in his rage,
> Or in th'incestuous pleasure of his bed,
> At game, a-swearing, or about some act
> That has no relish of salvation in't,
>
> (3.3.87–91)

it becomes obvious that Polonius's ideas of what constitutes mortal sin are all his own and that the mocking laughter of Shakespeare's audience is what we should hear at this point. It may be added that being killed in a duel was a certain way to be denied Christian burial – whether Protestant or Catholic. For example, Cornelia in *The White Devil* (5.4.105) says:

> They would not bury him 'cause he died in a quarrel;
> But I have an answer for them:
> Let holy church receive him duly,
> Since he paid his church-tithes truly.

This Catholic practice seems to have continued during the early part of the Reformation, for an authority on the Book of Common Prayer says: 'Persons not receiving holy sacrament, at least at Easter, or such as were killed in duels, tilts or tournaments, were formerly excluded from burial', and it seems that this was the official attitude of the reformed Church until 1661.[44]

The point is that if dramatists like Webster and Marlowe could use the concept of deadly sins in their plays we can surely assume that an Elizabethan audience were aware of the religious attitude to them and to their consequences. Webster also illustrates how 'falling out at tennis' was a means to damnation:

> That while he had been bandying at tennis,
> He might have sworn himself to hell, and struck
> His soul into the hazard!
>
> (5.1.72–4)

In France in Shakespeare's time it would have been easy to do so, for Henry IV favoured tennis and in the Paris of 1596 there were said to be 250 tennis courts. An English visitor in 1598 attested its popularity when he claimed that there were more tennis players than all the ale-drinkers in France.[45]

Gambling also seems a rather innocuous pursuit to us, but Chapman's Valerio in *All Fools* illustrates a similar itinerary for a 'rake's progress', for he is skilled in 'dice, cards, tennis, wenching, dancing, and what not'. Thus Laertes, even if he had never plotted to kill Hamlet, was heading for Hell anyway by leading the life of a gallant in Paris, and while Ophelia fears that he may become 'a puffed and reckless libertine' his life style in contemporary Paris would make this a certainty.

Laertes' character becomes more obviously Catholic, and more evil, as the play progresses. When we meet him on his return to Denmark he is a rebel who has stirred up a mob who want him to be king

> as the world were now but to begin

thus recalling Satan, the first Rebel; in Milton's words:

> This pendent world, in bigness as a star
> Of smallest magnitude close by the moon.
> Thither, full fraught with mischievous revenge,
> Accursed, and in a cursed hour, he hies.

Laertes' rebellion is also 'giant-like', recalling the Titans, and his commitment to Satan and to revenge is complete:

> To hell allegiance, vows to the blackest devil,
> Conscience and grace to the profoundest pit!
> I dare damnation. To this point I stand,
> That both the worlds I give to negligence,
> Let come what comes, only I'll be revenged
> Most throughly for my father.
>
> (4.5.131–6)

The association of revenge with Hell is quite unequivocal. And he uses the symbol of the pelican, the symbol of Christ himself in the Middle Ages, in a blasphemous vow to welcome his 'good friends' who will help him to encompass his revenge. Skelton has the lines:

> Then said the Pellycane,
> When my byrdis be slayne
> With my bloude I them reuyue
> Scripture doth record
> The same dyd our Lord,
> And rose from death to lyue.

According to Sir Edmund Chambers, 'both the Catholic concep-
tions of the Eucharist and the symbolism in religion fell into
disfavour, and the pelican became thenceforth an emblem of self-
sacrifice generally, and in especial, of true kingship'. Lyly, for
instance, called Queen Elizabeth 'that good Pelican'.[46] But for
Catholics the pelican has retained its original symbolic meaning,
and some Protestants in the seventeenth century also still clung to
the remnants of Catholic ceremonial – in baptism for example. In
1643 and 1644 one William Dowsing was appointed by the Earl
of Manchester 'for demolishing the Superstitious Pictures and
Ornaments of churches', and he recorded 'a glorious Cover over
the Font, like a Pope's Tripple Crown, with a Pelican on the Top,
picking its Breast, and gilt all over with Gold'.[47] Thus it is possible
that even a Protestant groundling was aware of the association of
the pelican with Catholic baptism and might have seen Laertes as
having renounced his baptism in order to follow the satanic path
of vengeance.

T.J.B. Spencer comments:

> No-one, as far as I can discover, has yet suggested that Laertes,
> with his arms stretched out in the form of a cross and with the
> blood flowing from his wounded breast, is a Christ figure. Yet
> the religious metaphor seems clear: Laertes's image of himself
> feeding his father's friends with his own blood is offensive
> bombast, typical of the man.[48]

When Laertes asserts that he is prepared to cut Hamlet's throat
'i' the church' the context is to be seen as Catholic and Laertes puts
himself in the same category as Thomas à Becket's murderers.
And Dover Wilson has also seen quibbles on Laertes' words
'anoint' and 'unction' which may then refer to the Catholic rite of
Extreme Unction. It may also be added that the 'mountebank'
from whom the poison was bought was associated by the
Elizabethans with Italy and Venice – Sidney refers to them in his
Apology for Poetry (1586). This Italianate allusion is in keeping with
the belief that 'poison, a weapon at once secret and safe, was the
traditional means of Italian vengeance', as Fredson Bowers puts it
and goes on to quote Fines Moryson:

> The Italyans aboue all other nations, most practise reuenge by
> treasons, and espetially are skillful in making and giuing
> poysons ... In our tyme, it seemes the Art of Poysoning is
> reputed in Italy worthy of Princes practice.

There is, incidentally, an engraving by Giacomo Franco dated 1609 of mountebanks in the Piazza San Marco in Venice.

The Catholic note is again evident in Claudius's reference to a 'chalice' which will also be poisoned, for this was a mass vessel that was ordered to be removed from churches in the early years of Elizabeth's reign. The chalices were replaced by 'communion cups' that were less ornate but larger.

The Grave Scene is also marked as Catholic. The Second Clown's oath 'Mass' would perhaps alone have left the audience in no doubt, but there are other indications that the setting is to be regarded as pre-Elizabethan. For example, the discussion, comic though it is, of the legalities of Ophelia's funeral seems to stem from a real case of suicide in 1554. Then there is the First Clown's song, which appeared in *Tottel's Miscellany* in 1557. There is also the possibility that the First Clown's 'even-Christen' was archaic in Shakespeare's time, for there is a gap of fifty years between the usage in *Hamlet* and the previous example recorded in the *OED*, and no recorded usage after *Hamlet*. And finally, Hamlet's reference to 'equivocation', a Jesuit doctrine of which much was heard in 1600–1, ensures that the 'maimed rites' are to be seen in the context of Catholicism, and that spells corruption in the state of Denmark.

The image of the Titans who piled Pelion on Ossa to reach Olympus is continued in the Grave Scene. Like the rebel angels under Satan they were cast down to 'Hell' – the Tartarus of the *Aeneid* (Book VI), which was a well-known text. Other sources which were easily accessible were Ovid's *Metamorphoses* (Book I) and Heywood's translation of *Hercules Furens*. In particular, Virgil's Aeneas sees 'the two sons of Aloeus, giants in stature, who had assaulted the vast heaven in an attempt to tear it down with their own hands and thrust Jupiter from his empire on high'.[49] But why did Shakespeare see the struggle in the grave in this fashion? What is the point of alluding to Otus and Ephialtes (who was also the demon of nightmare)? The link would appear to be ambition, and if so we may regard Hamlet and Laertes as contenders for the throne of Denmark – we may remember the rabble shouting:

> 'Choose we, Laertes shall be king! ...
> Laertes shall be king, Laertes king!'
>
> (4.5.106–8)

But we may well ask: is Hamlet ambitious? We have heard him

say he is and we have heard him praise ambition, but we may not be convinced. But is our 'modern' attitude right? If it is, why does Hamlet when he leaps into the grave call himself 'Hamlet the Dane', i.e. King of Denmark – compare Claudius's

> You cannot speak of reason to the Dane,
> And lose your voice.
>
> > (1.2.43–4).

Both Quincy Adams and Dover Wilson have drawn attention to Hamlet's assumption of the title. If then Hamlet is sane at this point he is certainly ambitious – in the Elizabethan sense – and the only way to refute this charge is to call him mad, and so agree with Gertrude:

> This is mere madness,
> And thus awhile the fit will work on him.
>
> > (5.1.278–9)

It may help to clarify matters here if we remember Malvolio's presumption and the humour that Shakespeare's audience apparently derived from it, for the same sort of audience may have found humour too in the mention of Hercules, in whose 'vein' – 'Ercles' vein' – Bottom claimed he could give a masterly performance. It was a part to tear a cat in. The old actor in Greene's *Groatsworth of Wit* (1592) says, 'The Twelve labours of Hercules have I terribly thundered on the stage'. Thus the ranting of Hercules, 'the voyce of one that playeth Hercules in a play', was well known to theatre audiences, as Chambers points out. Sir Edmund Chambers also puts him in the same category as the Herod of the Miracles, and in Chaucer's time Pilate was just as noisy.[50] Herod as a stage character antedates the Vice, but his outrageous blustering must have been a source of amusement. For example, in the Chester play of *The Slaughter of the Innocents* he says:

> For I am kinge of all mankinde, ...
> I maister the moone, take this in mynde
> > That I am moste of mighte,
> I am the greatest above degree,
> That is, that was, that even shalbe,

while in the Coventry version of 1534 'Erode' boasts that he has the powers of God and is God's cousin as well as

159

Prynce ... of Purgattory, and cheff capten of Hell!

I wonder then if it is fanciful to hear in Hamlet's ranting challenge:

Woo't drink up eisel? eat a crocodile?

(5.1.270)

an echo of the Miracles in which Christ is offered vinegar in a sponge at his crucifixion? The Salisbury Primer (1555) has: 'Blessed Jesu ... I beseech thee for the bitterness of the aysell and gall that thou tasted.'

We may refer here once more to Stubbes's denunciation of stage performances, and of the Vice in particular: 'if you will learn to play the Vice, to swear, tear and blaspheme both heaven and earth'. To 'tear' in this context is synonymous with blasphemy of course, but Hamlet's 'woo't tear thyself', while it probably refers to the Old Testament custom of tearing one's clothes as a sign of grief, may also refer to a fool's trick of tearing his garments, as in *Robert the Devil* Robert 'taere hys clothes and gnewe hys shyrte'. And as it is probable that Herod was played by the 'King' at the Feast of Fools we may see the Grave Scene as tragi-comic, and Hamlet doing his best to 'out-Herod Herod'.

Another point, following John Vyvyan's identification of 'Lamord' with one of the Four Horsemen of the Apocalypse, is the verse:

And said to the mountains and rocks, fall on us, and hide us from the face of him that sitteth on the throne, and from the wrath of the Lamb. (Revelation 6:16)

For in desperation first Laertes cries:

Now pile your dust upon the quick and dead,
Till of this flat a mountain you have made,

(5.1.245–6)

and later Hamlet shouts:

And if thou prate of mountains, let them throw
Millions of acres on us.

(5.1.274–5)

The 'doomsday' note it may be said has already been sounded in this scene by the gravediggers (5.1.59) and the priest's 'last trumpet' (5.1.224).

Finally then the impression we gain of Laertes before the last movement of the play begins is that of a fiery, quarrelsome bravo

hell-bent on revenge who embodies what the Elizabethans regarded as the worst features of the French and the Italians – he
is both duellist and poisoner – and he is a Catholic who would not
hesitate to wreak vengeance even in the sanctuary of the church.
He also knows that he is following the path to damnation but is
desperate and does not care. We are looking at a villain cast in the
mould of Cesare Borgia.

8

The Last Act

SOME COMMENTATORS have found a calmness in Hamlet on his
return to Denmark and regard this as proof of his sanity. His
cross-talk with the First Clown certainly, as far as a modern
audience is concerned, seems to show that Hamlet has all his wits
about him. But he has not abandoned his role as Vice because the
graveyard is a place of humour where the clowns joke and Yorick,
dead though he is, is still 'good for a laugh'. The theme of *memento
mori* was popular in the writing and painting of the time. Thomas
Nashe, for example, pays tribute to the fair sex in much the same
way as Hamlet:

> Your morn-like crystal countenances shall be netted over and
> (masquer-like) caul-visarded with crawling venomous worms.
> Your orient teeth toads shall steal into their heads for pearl; of
> the jelly of your decayed eyes shall they engender them young.[1]

Even Andrew Marvell thought it neither indelicate nor morbid to
remind his coy mistress that worms were waiting to devirginate
her. Mary Queen of Scots had a watch in the shape of a skull
and the skull and crossbones was a symbol commonly used in
Scotland on gravestones in the early nineteenth century. We also
have to remember Gray's *Elegy* and realize that modern attitudes
to death were not those of our ancestors – Evelyn Waugh's *The
Loved One* satirized them in their most extreme form. So we may
exaggerate the graveyard as a symbol of decay and corruption in
Denmark – Death for Shakespeare and Elizabethans could be an
'antic' and the *memento mori* a source of humour as we see from
Falstaff's comments on Bardolph's face:

> I make as good use of it as many a man doth of a Death's head,
> or a *memento mori*: I never see thy face but I think upon hell-
> fire. (3.3.33–6)

Hamlet's musings do not apparently have any spiritual effect on
him. He mention Cain, but does not comment on the injunction
of God not to take revenge on him or see any connection with

Claudius. Hamlet also refers to the 'pate of a politician', but it does not remind him of Polonius. And his thoughts on 'a courtier' do not prompt him to a confession of the murders of Rosencrantz and Guildenstern. Even his observations on Alexander and Caesar inspire him to compose a jig as an end piece to their tragic tale, just as a clown was expected to do:

> Imperious Caesar, dead and turned to clay,
> Might stop a hole to keep the wind away.
> O, that that earth, which kept the world in awe,
> Should patch a wall t'expel the winter's flaw!
>
> (5.1.207–10)

This then is the same Hamlet who composed a jig after the Gonzago play. In a sense too he is Yorick's heir, upon whose back he rode as a child, just as the Vice did to the Devil. And his outburst at the grave of Ophelia confirms that Hamlet too can be a 'whoreson mad fellow'. When he bellows in 'Ercles' vein' he is dressed like a sailor in a gown of coarse cloth and probably has a dagger at his belt – if then the sea-gown is a little too big for him he would look like a Vice who was often dressed thus except that his dagger was wooden.

The more sinister side of Hamlet's role as Vice appears in the next scene when he tells Horatio how like a mutineer (a word which connoted rebellion and hence Satan) he stole the commission that Rosencrantz and Guildenstern were carrying and, having discovered that it was his death warrant, wrote one for them instead. The moral he says is that

> There's a divinity that shapes our ends
>
> (5.2.10)

and, that being so, heaven was 'ordinant' in ensuring that he had a copy of the royal seal of Denmark in his purse and thus the order to execute Rosencrantz and Guildenstern was apparently given the king's sanction. In order words God enabled him to bring about the deaths of Rosencrantz and Guildenstern whose crime was, at worst, sycophancy, as there is no evidence that they knew what the original commission contained. The 'divinity' concerned could in Elizabethan times only be the 'divinity of hell' of Iago – 'a favourite theme of Shakespeare's and other sixteenth century writers, based on the Devil's citation of Scripture during the Temptation (Matt. IV. 6)', as Alice Walker records.[2] Hamlet did not feel that his victims were 'near' his conscience, and he also considers it is 'perfect conscience' to kill Claudius. This it may be observed makes him worse than Laertes who says later that it is 'almost 'gainst' his conscience to kill Hamlet, whose conscience ceased to function after he killed Polonius. Thus, far from becoming rational, Hamlet by the time he returns to Denmark is convinced that God has licensed him to commit murder, and we cannot make a plea in mitigation on his behalf because his crime is premeditated. I do not suggest that Hamlet forfeits entirely the sympathy of the audience, but that he has broken the moral law – specifically the Sixth Commandment – would be obvious to every groundling. We may if we wish substitute for 'divinity' a more complex notion and less circumscribed philosophical idea such as 'Destiny', but we cannot expect an Elizabethan to accept any agency other than the Devil to have been involved in murder, because God had himself written in his tables that murder was contrary to his law, and for an Elizabethan to have thought otherwise would have been atheism.

The appearance of Osric introduces another be-feathered fool – there is editorial agreement that 'water-fly' suggests that he has 'a hat with antennae-like plumes', as J.H. Walter puts it. And there is a quibble on 'vice' in ''tis a vice to know him' similar to that in *Othello*, as William Empson comments:

> It is not, I think, dangerously far-fetched to take almost all Shakespeare's uses of fool as metaphors from the clown, whose symbolism certainly rode his imagination and was explained to the audience in most of his early plays. Now Iago's defence when Othello at last turns on him ... brings in both Fool and the Vice used in *Hamlet* as an old name for the clown.[3]

The by-play at the beginning of *The Malcontent* points to Christopher Sly as having played Osric. That he is a 'fool' also may point to his having been derived from the 'Phantasmo' of the *Brudermord* (assuming of course that 'Phantasmo' was in the *Ur-Hamlet*). Phantasmo is more Vice-like than Osric however, for he knows about the poisoned drink and the poisoned sword, but both act as umpire in the duel. That Osric is however close to Laertes is suggested by his choice of vocabulary – 'continent', for example – which causes Hamlet to let loose a stream of words which could have had a French pronunciation – 'semblable' and 'umbrage' in particular. An affected French accent would perhaps fit Osric's role as umpire in what is in effect a French duel of the kind that was playing havoc with the gentry of France. Osric is also a 'chough' and a 'lapwing', as befits his be-feathered state. Indeed the character who comes closest to wearing 'a forest of feathers' in the play is Osric whom, I repeat, ''tis a vice to know'. There may also be a pun here because a 'chuff' could mean a 'boor' – a man with money who lacked the necessary qualities to be considered a 'gentleman'.

Hamlet's dazzling display of verbal fencing leaves Osric disarmed and bewildered, and this coupled with the complications of the duel has perhaps prevented editors from recognizing its more serious moral implications. First there is to be a wager and any gamble that involved money was forbidden to the Elizabethans both by the Law and by the Church. In his *A Declaration of the Ten Commandments* Bishop Hooper, expatiating on the Eighth Commandment, says:

> Here is forbidden also all games for money, as dice, cards ... and other; which is very theft, and against charity, that would rather augment his neighbour's goods, than make them less: so the diminution of any man's fame; as when for vain glory any man attribute unto himself the wit or learning that another brain hath brought forth, whereof many hath complained, as this of Virgil:
> > Hos ego versiculos feci, tulit alter honores.
> They make a fair shew with another bird's feathers, as Aesop's crow did.[4]

It is a rather strange coincidence that Osric, who is an 'upstart crow' of sorts should be the one to persuade Hamlet to gamble. At any rate Hooper's attitude to gambling was probably representative of the Protestant Church as a whole because Thomas Becon considered 'gamesters, dicers &c who would overreach and win of their neighbours, are thieves'.[5]

This is of immediate relevance to the play because being killed 'at game' as Hamlet himself assures us had 'no relish of salvation in it', and was one of the situations in which he might dispose of Claudius. If then, as seems likely, Elizabethans were warned as children against gambling when they were taught their Catechism, they would immediately be aware that Hamlet was embarking on a course of action which imperilled his very soul and would thus have endorsed their picture of him as an impenitent murderer heading for damnation.

There was such a thing as 'wager by battle' which we also know as 'trial by combat', but this kind of wager too was not allowed by

the Church, Catholic or Protestant. Here, for example, is Brother
Francisco Maria Guazzo whose *Compendium Maleficarum* dates
from 1608:

> But this sort of combat provides no proof; for it is against all
> law according to the unanimous opinion of the Doctors.

Indeed the Catholic Church regarded this as duelling and

> that duels are forbidden by the law of God is proved by every
> argument which forbids us to tempt God, and by the
> commandment that we shall do no murder.[6]

On the Protestant side Bishop Hooper would have agreed:

> God in this commandment [the Sixth] forbiddeth not only the
> murder done with the hand, but also the murder of the heart
> and of the tongue ... In the murder done of the hand is
> forbidden all private revenging between private persons that
> will be judges in their own dance; which begins with blows,
> then followeth hurting of some members of the body, or clean
> destruction of it, at the last, murder of the whole body. Some
> kill with the sword, some with poison, some with enchant-
> ments; some dissemble, as though they played, and so in
> bourding [mock-fighting] putteth him out of the way that he
> hateth.[7]

Also, as we have already seen, the Church in England, Catholic
and Protestant, denied Christian burial to the participants and
according to Guazzo the general Catholic position had not
changed after the Reformation:

> Those who engage in duels, and they who act as seconds
> thereto, let them be punished with excommunication and the
> confiscation of all their goods and perpetual disgrace, and may
> they for ever be deprived of ecclesiastical burial like murderers
> etc.[8]

There was therefore no relish of salvation in the course that
Hamlet was following. The point is that even if Hamlet had not
killed Polonius or Rosencrantz and Guildenstern and had been
killed by Laertes' trick, he would still have been damned
according to the ideas of the time. And we can also now
understand a little better the spiritual status, as it were, of the
Ghost who had fought a duel with Fortinbras's father but also
gambled his kingdom on the outcome. A king who took such a

risk with the lives and well-being of his people was not fit to govern – oddly enough we find confirmation of this in Chaucer:

> A gambling prince would be incompetent
> To frame a policy of government,
> And he will sink in general opinion
> As one unfit to exercise dominion.[9]

We must bear all this in mind when we look again at Hamlet's 'gain-giving as would perhps trouble a woman' (5.2.213–14) before the duel, for he is in fact dismissing what had been the Church's teaching for centuries – it is a rejection of Christian doctrine similar to 'coward conscience'.

Hamlet's frame of mind at this juncture prompted Bradley to refer to 'that kind of religious resignation which however beautiful in one aspect really deserves the name of fatalism rather than that of faith in Providence, because it is not united to any determination to do what is believed to be the will of Providence'.[10] Hamlet, like Caesar, denies in effect the existence of God and the Law of God. We may detect the same note in Marlowe's Guise in *The Massacre at Paris*:

> Yet Caesar shall go forth
> Let mean conceits and baser men fear death:
> Tut, they are peasants. I am Duke of Guise;
> And princes with their looks engender fear.

Hamlet says that he defies augury, which sounds like a religious sentiment, for the Church forbabe fortune-telling, but in fact he is shutting his eyes to the inevitable consequences of his proposed actions – Hell and damnation. He says 'the readiness is all', but as L.C. Knights says:

> All that Hamlet is now ready for is to meet his death in playing the part of the avenger, the part imposed on him by that Ghost whose command had been for a sterile concentration on death and evil.[11]

Hamlet's words:

> If it be now, 'tis not to come – if it be not to come, it will be now – if it be not now, yet it will come (5.2.218–20)

are a more elaborate way of saying:

167

> Let come what comes

(4.5.135)

which is what Laertes said after thundering:

>   vows to the blackest devil,
>   Conscience and grace to the profoundest pit!
>   I dare damnation.

(4.5.131–3)

or what Faustus said – 'Che sarà, sarà' (1.1.46) – before he made his pact with Mephistopheles and so secured his damnation. And of course we see a similar fatalism in Hieronimo's speech:

>   Fata si miseros iuvant, habes salutem:
>   Fata si vitam negant, habes sepulchrum.
>   If destiny thy miseries do ease,
>   Then hast thou health, and happy shalt thou be:
>   If destiny deny thee life Hieronimo,
>   Yet shalt thou be assured of a tomb:
>   If neither, yet let this thy comfort be,
>   Heaven covereth him that hath no burial.

All these are examples of what to an Elizabethan was 'despair', and it did not matter whether he was a Protestant or Catholic; a modern Catholic Catechism defines despair as 'a want of confidence in God', and that is what Hamlet suffers from. Article XVII of the Thirty-Nine Articles is concerned with predestination, a theological doctrine of which there were several interpretations in Shakespeare's time, which were almost certainly beyond the reach of most of Shakespeare's audience – except perhaps for ministers of the gospel. It is astonishing therefore to find in Q1 the lines:

>   there's a predestinate providence
>   in the fall of a sparrow.

It sounds more like the regurgitation of a gobbet of religious instruction that has been swallowed whole, a remembered phrase picked up from a sermon, and of course it may not be Shakespearean. If then we assume that a minister had read out Article XVII to his congregation without exposition I would guess that the only immediately comprehensible part would be:

> ... so for curious and carnal persons, lacking the spirit of Christ, to have continually before their eyes the sentence of

168

God's predestination, is a most dangerous downfall, whereby the devil doth thrust them either into desperation, or into wretchlessness of most unclean living, no less perilous than desperation.

The danger lay, as the Church saw it, in a man feeling that his fate was pre-determined and so making no attempt to lead a good life to ensure his salvation. That is Hamlet's attitude and it is shared by yet another contemporary dramatic figure – Bussy d'Ambois – who is also a duellist:

> Fate is more strong than arms and sly than treason
> And I at all parts buckled in my fate.

The Church's concern about despair was underlined in the Injunctions of 1559, for the clergy were exhorted to 'have always in a readiness such comfortable places and sentences of Scripture as do set forth the mercy, benefits, and goodness of Almighty God towards all penitent believing persons [in order that] the vice of damnable despair may be clearly taken away'. And again, at the Hampton Court Conference:

> The Bishop of London took occasion to signifie to His Majestie, how very many in these daies, neglecting holiness of life, presumed too much of persisting of grace, laying all their religion upon predestination, If I shall be saved, I shall be saved; which he termed a desperate doctrine, showing it to be contrary to good divinity and the true doctrine of predestination, wherein we should reason rather ascendendo than descendendo, thus, 'I live in obedience to God, in love with my neighbour, I follow my vocation, etc.; therefore I trust that God hath elected me, and predestinated me to salvation'; not thus, which is the usual course of argument. 'God hath predestinated and chosen me to life, therefore though I sin never so grievously, yet I shall not be damned; for whom He once loveth He loveth to the end.'[12]

As the Church's preaching against despair never varied for more than fifty years, the probability is that the Elizabethans were thoroughly indoctrinated and it is more than probable that if Pasfield had thought that Hamlet's attitude would have corrupted any member of the audience he would have banned the play. Yet Hamlet has agreed to fight Laertes in a fencing match that is likely to develop into a duel, and a wager is also involved – both courses of action which would lead to damnation if they ended in death. So how could Pasfield, presumably agreeing with Hooper's reading of the Sixth and Eighth Commandments, license the play for the stage unless he thought it was clear to all that Hamlet would in fact be damned? Pasfield knew about 'predestinate providence' and the dangers of its misinterpretation and must have been in full agreement with the words above of Bishop Bancroft, for he probably not only heard them at the Hampton Court Conference but certainly, in his capacity as corrector, 'allowed' them. So, far from the Elizabethan audience dwelling on the profundities of human existence and the mercy of God, it is more likely that they saw clearly and simply that Hamlet was heading closer to Hell as his course was 'desperate'.

His attempts to obtain a reconcilement with Laertes are a failure. He claims, rightly, that he is

> punished
> With a sore distraction

that his 'madness' is to blame for having wronged Laertes (Ophelia, it should be remembered, was also 'distract' (4.5.2), so that 'madness' here means 'insanity'). Thus if we allow ourselves a snap judgment we may accept that Hamlet at this point is desperate, but lucid according to modern standards. Laertes however is desperate too and fobs off Hamlet with talk of honour, which has already been linked by Hamlet with 'divine ambition' and so, as we have seen, with Satan. Laertes' argument in fact is based on what he considers his natural right to revenge himself when his honour is at stake – even

> to find a quarrel in a straw

no doubt. This is the duellist's code. Monsieur in *Bussy d'Ambois* speaks the same language as Laertes:

> Justice will soon distinguish murtherous minds
> From just revengers: had my friend been slain
> His enemy surviving, he should die,
> Since he has added to a murthered fame,
> Which was in his intent, a murthered man.

But in the end they patch up their quarrel, at least for the time being, and Hamlet accepts this 'brother's wager', an allusion that is doubly ironic for it emphasizes the essential immorality of betting and also recalls the story of Cain and Abel which is again

170

of relevance in Hamlet's figure of firing an arrow over a house and hitting his brother.

Claudius calls for 'stoups' of wine to be placed on the table. According to the *OED* this held at least a quart, and no smaller quantity is recorded in England. This would be in keeping with the gross drinking habits in the Denmark of the play. Claudius then drinks to Hamlet and the match begins with the promise that he will put a pearl in a cup if Hamlet scores in the first three exchanges. If we ask what Gertrude is doing at this time the answer is that she is probably drinking also. She is Claudius's partner in incest and his drinking companion too, for when Claudius does place the poison in the cup meant for Hamlet Gertrude 'carouses' to Hamlet. In modern terms this is the equivalent of saying 'bottoms up' and if she has already drunk greedily her action is that of a seasoned toper and fits in with the dissolute image that we are surely meant to have of her. The Bedroom Scene might well begin with Gertrude fortifying herself for her ordeal with a drink, and her description later of Ophelia's garments as 'heavy with their drink' fits a woman who may enter with a 'stoup' in her hand – drowning her own sorrows. Her words may also form part of the unconscious, grisly humour of Laertes' 'Too much of water hast thou Ophelia' – which he of course associates with tears. If then Gertrude is played as a 'lush' and dies when she is tipsy at least, there is no relish of salvation in her death, but as in addition she is guilty of incest she is bound for Hell – she meets the requirements for damnation that Hamlet outlined for Claudius.

Laertes is killed by the very poison meant for Hamlet. Before he dies he 'exchanges forgiveness' with Hamlet and in modern terms this may be taken as a manly gesture, but to the Elizabethans – Protestant or Catholic – Laertes has misused the little time left to him in order to repent and make his peace with God. Only Christ could forgive sins, and without sincere repentance damnation inevitably followed. Laertes' gesture, therefore, in Elizabethan eyes, does nothing to avert his fate – like Gertrude, Hell is his destination.

In the same way Hamlet's apparently pious

> Heaven make thee free of it!

> (5.2.330)

is ironic, if not downright blasphemous, for he is responsible for the deaths of Polonius, Rosencrantz and Guildenstern, and

Claudius. He has also shown 'rage', fought a duel and been 'at game' – so how can he speak on God's behalf? His preventing Horatio from committing suicide is commendable in modern eyes, but his motive is to prevent his name being 'wounded' – and this is precisely one of Laertes' major concerns, for he wishes to keep his name 'ungored' (5.2.247). If Hamlet were as noble as we would wish him to be it is difficult to account for his naming Fortinbras as his successor. Yet this same Fortinbras, bloodthirsty as he is, is shaken by the carnage that Hamlet has left behind him.

When the ambassadors from England arrive to notify Claudius that Rosencrantz and Guildenstern have been executed Horatio's reactions are curious – he does not reveal that Hamlet is responsible in spite of his promise to 'truly deliver'. Indeed C.E.M. Joad made a point that no one else seems to have noticed:

> For my part, I cannot help thinking that all this [the substitution of the original death warrant] is rather shabby on Hamlet's part, an opinion apparently shared by the good Horatio, who, though we are explicitly told that he was made privy to what Hamlet had done, nevertheless is so ashamed of it that right at the end of the play he feels constrained to tell lies about it, assuring the English ambassadors that Hamlet never commanded the death of R. and G.[13]

It is a possible interpretation, as there is an apparent parallelism in these lines:

> Not from his mouth
> Had it th'ability of life to thank you
> (5.2.370–1)

and:

> And from his mouth whose voice will draw on more
> (5.2.390)

Whatever the answer may be Horatio links this 'bloody question' with the 'Polack wars'.

Horatio's love (as we would have it today) for his dead friend also leads to the famous lines:

> Now cracks a noble heart. Good night, sweet prince,
> And flights of angels sing thee to thy rest!
> (5.2.357–8)

But these words may be compared with the Latin version of the antiphon of the Catholic burial service which was used until the decrees of the Second Vatican Council (1965):

> In paradisum deducant te angeli … Chorus angelorum te suscipiat … aeternam habeat requiem.

Thus it is doubtful whether they would have aroused much sympathy from an Elizabethan audience because they were to prepare Hamlet's soul to enter Purgatory, not Hell.

Thus Fortinbras, puffed with 'divine ambition', who rebelled against his king, is left in control of Denmark. He is clad in armour like the Ghost at the beginning of the play – he not only acts like Satan, he looks like him. Elizabethans would have had no difficulty in seeing the parallel. Fortinbras loves the sound of cannon as did Claudius, for they make him feel omnipotent:

> And let the kettle to the trumpet speak,
> The trumpet to the cannoneer without.
> The cannons to the heavens, the heaven to earth …
>
> (5.2.273–5)

Like Claudius, he feels that he controls the 'earthly thunder', that he is a god with the power of life and death in his hands (G. Wilson Knight referred to the 'ominous discharge of ordnance … once before Hamlet sees the Ghost, and twice in Act V').[14] The wish to play God was Satan's sin, and this had led to the Fall, after which, as R.M. Frye says:

> Power succeeds upon love, and as it does so, the next successive result within the saga is Cain's murder of Abel. The fatherhood of God having been repudiated, fratricide replaces brotherhood … Violence, oppression and 'sword law' … are exalted as Satan's demonic view of war and slaughter, which he styles 'the strife of glory', becomes the governing order of human relations … As the Satanic perversion spreads through human society, the greatest 'glory' of man is seen in destruction and the force of war, as man, patterning himself on the image of the demonic rather than the divine, 'to glory aspires Vain-glorious, and through infamy seeks fame.[15]

Frye of course is commenting on Milton's *Paradise Lost* which is an accurate reflection of medieval attitudes to the Devil, whose aspiration is 'to become power without love'.

But this has a familiar ring to it, a contemporary ring. Back in 1944 E.M.W. Tillyard wrote:

173

In *Hamlet* if anywhere in Shakespeare we notice the genealogy from the Miracle Plays with their setting of Heaven, Purgatory, and Hell ... *Hamlet* is one of the most acutely modern of Shakespeare's plays.[16]

If we glance quickly at the modern scene:

> Power is in inflicting pain and humiliation. Power is in tearing human minds to pieces and putting them together again in new shapes of your own choosing ... In our world there will be no emotions except fear, rage, triumph and self-abasement. Everything else we shall destroy – everything. There will be no love ... There will be no laughter, except the laugh of triumph over a defeated enemy.

It sounds like Satan, but of course it is George Orwell's O'Brien in *Nineteen Eighty-Four* (pp. 214–15). Both believe in 'power without love' and in Orwell's nightmare we find the same moral inversions as in the medieval formulation – 'foul is fair', and in particular love becomes hatred. Then too there is distortion of 'right reason' (the 'oratio recta') and two and two make five in Orwell's 'Airstrip One'. What is also fascinating is that Orwell may have reached this conclusion empirically through his personal acquaintance with, and study of, totalitarianism, particularly the Stalinist model, and not primarily by following Milton, who was one of his favourite writers – 'bad' politics and not lack of Christianity are the chief causal factors. For while there is an apparent similarity between the medieval and modern attitude there is also a world of difference – Orwell's 'love' included the sexual and did not necessarily include the supernatural, whereas the medieval standpoint eschewed sexuality and emphasized the primacy of the divine in human relations – the love of Christ. Thus we may say Fortinbras was 'evil' and that O'Brien was 'evil', but unless we see them both in their respective contexts we begin to confuse the literal and the metaphorical. In particular we detach Fortinbras from Satan and the literal Hell which the Elizabethans feared.

There is however a point of similarity between the endings of *Hamlet* and *Nineteen Eighty-Four*, for I believe that they were both propagandist rather than reflections of their authors' pessimism. Shakespeare's message was anti-Catholic and Orwell's (primarily) anti-Stalinist. L.C. Knights maintained that 'Hamlet's way of knowing the world is not Shakespeare's own'[17] and

Bernard Crick doubted that Orwell's illness made him share his Winston Smith's despair.[18] But while Orwell's political bias is evident enough the medieval, and Elizabethan, homiletic strain in *Hamlet* has been somewhat neglected – Herman Ulrici's misgivings about the morality of Hamlet's revenge (1839) were ignored until fairly recently. But Fortinbras's rebelliousness and ambition were precisely what 'An Homily against Disobedience and Wilful Rebellion', which had been inspired by the rebellion in 1569, specifically condemned, and which were specially associated with Catholicism:

> The anti-Catholic theme is also greatly expanded. The main causes of rebellion are ambition and ignorance; and in European history the ambition of the Papacy for temporal power.[19]

Fortinbras is greedy for power – he has 'sharked up a list of lawless resolutes' to feed his ambition – just like the chief henchman of Satan who in Elizabethan eyes was the Pope himself.

If we see Fortinbras as a hungry shark then Horatio is a kind of 'remora', a parasitic sucker-fish who will soon attach himself to him. Horatio is a sycophant by nature who will 'sweet lord' Fortinbras as much as he did Hamlet, who, although he affected to scorn dog-like devotion – 'let the candied tongue lick absurd pomp' (3.2.58) – welcomed it in Horatio. Hamlet prides himself that he does not need to flatter anyone and that his compliments therefore are sincere:

> For what advancement may I hope from thee,
> That no revenue hast but thy good spirits
> To feed and clothe thee?
>
> (3.2.55–7)

But where does that leave Horatio? How sincere is he? He may be held to worship Hamlet, a false God whose favour must be sought. He is conscious always of the difference in their status in spite of being Hamlet's 'fellow-student' and Hamlet is still the 'sweet prince' that his 'candied tongue' is ready to lick at the end. Denmark – Catholic Denmark – is an unweeded garden indeed and Horatio's 'love' for Hamlet would be as acceptable to Elizabethans as Claudius's 'love' for Gertrude. Horatio's love is tainted with ambition and he may have been played with homosexual overtones for good measure – homosexuality having been linked with Catholicism and with Italy in particular.

And so the play ends. The rest is not silence; there is the sound of cannon, the harbinger of further wars, of Armageddon, of the Apocalypse. And in our day when our demi-gods see each other as possessing 'power without love' and have a 'nuclear capability' instead of 'earthly thunder', we may well ask ourselves what this love is that we lack, for if it has no literal existence, divine or human, how can we use it to cure the symptoms of 'pure power' so well known both to us and to the Elizabethans?

Epilogue

IT WOULD BE premature, as well as presumptuous, at this stage for me to attempt to pass judgment on what I have been suggesting is the Elizabethan *Hamlet*. I see my role rather as a picture-restorer who has found traces of an earlier portrait underneath, as it were. I intend therefore merely to look briefly at evidence which marks the transition from Shakespeare's play to that to which we have become accustomed, an obvious starting point being the detachment of the drama from its original religious background.

By 1736, as we may see from *Some Remarks on the Tragedy of Hamlet* which was probably written by Sir Thomas Hanmer, Purgatory was no longer understood and it no longer evoked the scorn and condemnation that it formerly had. Moreover, we may see also the beginnings of the attitude that revenge was just:

> Hamlet's speech upon seeing the King at prayers, has always given me great offence. There is something so very Bloody in it, so inhuman, so unworthy of a Hero, that I wish our poet had omitted it. To desire to destroy a Man's Soul, to make him eternally miserable, by cutting him off from all hopes of Repentance; this surely, in a Christian Prince, is such a piece of Revenge, as no tenderness for any Parent can justify. To put the Usurper to Death, to deprive him of the Fruits of his vile Crime, and to rescue the Throne of Denmark from Pollution, was highly requisite; But there our young Prince's Desires should have stop'd, nor should he have wished to pursue the Criminal in the other World, but rather have hoped for his Conversion, before putting him to Death; for even with his Repentance, there was at least Purgatory for him to pass through, as we find even in a virtuous Prince, the Father of Hamlet.

It is also evident however that Hanmer was aware of the enormity of trying 'to destroy a Man's Soul'.

Similarly, Warburton in 1747 did not know of the legendary connection between St. Patrick and Purgatory:

177

How the poet comes to make Hamlet swear by St. Patrick I know not. However, at this time all the whole northern world had their learning from Ireland; to which place it had retired, and there flourished under the auspices of this Saint.[1]

Then again, nuns and nunneries were no longer the subjects for scurrilous jokes. Richard Lovelace in 1646 wrote to his Lucasta:

> Tell me not, sweet, I am unkind,
> That from the nunnery
> Of thy chaste breast and quiet mind
> To war and arms I fly.

And Milton in his *Il Penseroso*:

> Come pensive Nun, devout and pure,
> Sober, steadfast, and demure.

Thus Johnson more than a hundred years later could speak of 'Ophelia, the young, the beautiful, the harmless, and the pious'.[2] Nor did the eighteenth-century editors connect her song with Walsingham. Also, while Milton could still be nasty about friars and 'eremites' in Book III of *Paradise Lost*, his friar in *Il Penseroso* belongs more to the world of fairy-tale and romance, as does Bishop Percy's in his version of the Walsingham ballad, as we have seen.

Then there are the changes in attitude to the Vice and to the Ghost. Hanmer was unaware of the Vice:

> Hamlet's light and even ludicrous expressions to his companions, his making them swear by his sword, &c., are all circumstances certainly inferior to the preceding part.

Coleridge in his *Lectures on Shakespeare* reveals that he knew something of the dramatic tradition of the Vice, but he too did not recognize that Hamlet plays Vice to the Ghost's Devil, or that Hell lay under Shakespeare's stage:

> The subterraneous speeches of the Ghost are hardly defensible:
> – but I would call your attention to the characteristic difference between the Ghost as a superstition connected with the most mysterious truths of revealed religion, – and Shakespeare's consequent reverence in his treatment of it, – and the foul earthly witcheries and wild language in Macbeth.

Then, if we move on rapidly to Sir Edmund Chambers we find the same mixture as before:

I cannot help thinking that some of the rude humour in the latter part of this scene is a survival from the older play, and was retained to please the groundlings. It can, of course, be treated as having dramatic value.[3]

Similarly, Dover Wilson did not recognize the Vice dialogue, although in *What Happens in Hamlet* he admits that Hamlet is talking to the Ghost as if it were a devil, and he identifies the Cellarage as Hell only in his Additional Notes on the play. How curious that he saw Hamlet as playing the 'natural' and talking to a devil beneath the stage yet never made the final identification.

The evidence that the Ghost scenes were misunderstood we can therefore trace back to Hanmer at least, and it can be explained in terms of ignorance of Roman Catholicism and Elizabethan stage-practice, and also of course the gradual decay of religious symbols into poetic metaphors. And coupled with the fact that scholars had not identified let alone clarified the religious issues in the play there is the astonishing fact – as Eleanor Prosser shows – that there is a very strong probability that Shakespeare's play 'vanished' from the stage in 1642 and did not reappear until

F.R. Benson's six-hour version of the Folio at the Lyceum in 1900. Between these dates the play had been cut and re-written as producers and actors imposed their own interpretation upon it. In Ducis' 1769 version there is no Ghost and in 1785 George Frederick Cooke deleted 'Ghost beneath' in the cellarage scene and noted his objection to the old tradition of having the Ghost sink through the trap.[4]

More subtle changes that are difficult to chart took place in the attitude to madness. There was much argument about Hamlet's insanity last century, as we have seen, but very little about compassion for his mental state. Compassion for the mad is a modern development. Even a man of Sir Thomas More's enlightenment had ordered a lunatic to be bound to a tree and soundly beaten with rods,[5] and even as late as the beginning of last century the king himself – George III – was subjected to 'mechanical restraint' like a common lunatic.[6] Today we are also offered precise diagnoses of the mental illnesses exhibited in the play. Dr. R.D. Laing says of Ophelia: 'Clinically she is latterly undoubtedly a schizophrenic.'[7] Dr. Scott, as we have seen, sees Hamlet as hypomanic. As a layman I cannot argue with these diagnoses, but a glance at a psychiatric textbook description of hypomania is of interest. Hypomanic behaviour is described thus:

179

Many hypomanic patients are mischievous, boisterous, and full of pranks, indulge in risqué remarks and coarse and unseemly jokes and make facetious comments about some object, or especially some person in the environment ... Unbridled criticism and bluntness of speech, even to the point of impudence, are common ... the stream of thought is character-ized by loquaciousness and rapid association of ideas. Frequent-ly the patient speaks with a crispness and vigour of articulation, with emphatic accents and frequent changes of pitch. His style of phrasing may be pompous, and his speech may assume the character of theatrical declaration ... As the hypomanic state passes into acute mania, the pressure of speech develops into a flight of ideas with rhyming, play upon words, and 'clang' association of words having similar sounds but no relation in meaning.[8]

These symptoms bear some resemblence to Hamlet's behaviour, and there is no doubt that Shakespeare, because those suffering from mental illness in his time were not, apart from a small minority, institutionalized, could have observed madness at first hand. And it is also possible that the Vice as he exhibits the swings in mood of a cyclothymic personality may have been modelled in part on 'naturals' who were manic-depressive – the laughter and the tears of the clown are nearly proverbial. But how far then are we back to Bradley in effect? For we are treating the dramatis personae as real and not characters governed by dramatic art. Most important however is what is missing in our modern approach – the brutal humour that madness evoked in the Elizabethans. John Corbin in 1895 pointed this out, but claimed in the face of the evidence, that Shakespeare's final version was free of it.[9] I do not think it is. I see no reason to assume that Shakespeare's view of the mad was any more compassionate than Sir Thomas More's, and his treatment of Ophelia is particularly savage. Corbin's rather lame conclusion however illustrates the difficulty that any commentator on *Hamlet* experiences – the enormous weight of traditional criticism, the gravitational pull of other minds. But we have to consider what we ourselves have added to Shakespeare's play, and whether as a result we have enhanced or distorted his creation.

Then there is the problem of identifying oneself with Hamlet. This seems to have begun with William Hazlitt in 1817, and the latest commentator to share his views is Clive James.[10] Jung too I

Epilogue

believe suggested that Hamlet was one of the universal symbols of the Self, and Freud and Ernest Jones saw in him the Oedipus Complex at work. Is there then in *Hamlet* some sort of basic psychological ingredient, some sort of essence that we all possess, or, as C.S. Lewis put it, is it 'a certain spiritual region through which most of us have passed'?[11] Or, and I emphasize that I speak in terms of analogy only, is *Hamlet* like a Freudian dream with a 'latent content' which is permanent but the 'manifest content' of which can vary from age to age? I ask these questions but I do not know the answers. If I attempt an answer of some kind I think I would follow the lead of C.S. Lewis and opt for a spiritual region, a region I would add in which there is no love human or divine. In the end Hamlet's concern is for his reputation, he cannot love anyone, including himself, or God. L.C. Knights says:

> In King Lear, where so many lines of Shakespeare's thoughts converge, Lear only comes to 'see better' through a purgatorial progress of self-knowledge which enables him finally to respond to love. Perhaps we may say that Hamlet's consciousness is not unlike the consciousness of the unregenerate Lear, full of the knowledge of bitter wrong, of evil seeming inherent in human nature. But Hamlet, unlike Lear – even if, initially, he is less greatly sinning – cannot break out of the closed circle of loathing and self-contempt, so that his nature is 'subdued to what it works, like the dyer's hand'. The awareness that he embodies is at best an intermediate stage of the spirit, at worst a blind alley.[12]

I cannot put it better than that. I would also point out that Hamlet as Vice, in the sense that I have suggested, inhabits the same region as the Vice in Heywood's *Play of Love* who is 'the vyse nother louer nor beloued'.

For the Christian of course there is always God and in Elizabethan eyes Hamlet was a 'fool' to have forgotten that. For those of us who are not Christians, if we cannot look forward to a heaven, depriving us of love nevertheless gives us a taste of hell. And if Hamlet 'goes through hell' in the play we go with him, but we come out again into the sunlight which is all the brighter because we have been in the dark.

APPENDIX A

Of Rosencrantz, Virgin Crants and Coronet Weeds

As HAS BEEN suggested, flowers and plants seemed to have been the special care of the Virgin in Catholic Europe. Marina Warner says, 'as a mother, she is associated with joy, with songs, with dancing and flowers', and quotes Gerard Manley Hopkins's *May Magnificat*, one verse of which goes:

> All things rising, all things sizing
> Mary sees, sympathising
> With that world of good,
> Nature's motherhood ...[1]

She also points out that

> as early as the tenth century, the intimate association between the aromas of herbs and flowers and the victory of Mary over death was celebrated in the ritual of the feast of the Assumption. Medicinal herbs and plants were brought to church on that day. Periwinkle, verbena, thyme and many other ingredients of the herbalist's art were laid on the altar, to be incensed and blessed. Then they were bound into a sheaf and kept all year to ward off illness and disaster and death.[2]

I shall return to this 'Flora' role of the Virgin later, but first I wish to focus on the rose in particular because its symbolism is intrinsic to the language of the rosary and to 'Rosencrantz', for that is what the name means.

The origins of the rosary are obscure, its development complex and its theological implications are beyond my compass. Thus, at the risk of oversimplification, I shall concentrate only on its linguistic aspects which in themselves present difficulties. First then I turn to the *New Catholic Encyclopedia*:

The origins are traceable to the Marian devotions to Jesus and Mary that arose in the 12th century, and to the desire to give the unlettered faithful closer participation in the liturgy ... Strings of beads called 'paternosters' were used to count these prayers. Marian devotion followed a similar trend. Mary's clients celebrated her joys by saluting her with liturgical antiphons, especially Gabriel's aves, believing that when they did so she relived the joys of the Annunciation. Hence they multiplied their Hail Marys, especially in 'chaplets' of 50 mystical crowns placed on Mary's brow.

These coronets were thought of as being composed of roses, as the various languages show. In French, 'chaplet' is 'chapelet' and refers to a garland of roses. In German it was rendered as 'rosenkranz' and in Danish as 'rosenkrans'. In the Eastern Church a similar symbolism was employed – the beaded, mainly monastic, rosaries such as the Russian 'chotki' and the Greek 'kombologion' mean 'chaplet'.[3] In England 'garland' seems to have been in more common use, but I have been given a Scottish Catechism used by Catholic children in 1932 which instructed them to think of 'the rosary [as], as it were, a chaplet of the most beautiful prayers and meditations wherein the chief mysteries of our holy religion are wreathed like fragrant roses'. The name 'chaplet' too is preserved in the heraldic symbol which consists of a circlet of four roses.

When the term 'rosary' became attached to the original 'paternoster' the chaplet of roses as symbol seems to have been preferred to that of the 'rose garden' which the *New Catholic Encyclopedia* dates c.1409:

> Soon after 1409 Dominic of Prussia linked 50 phrases referring to Jesus and Mary to 50 Aves, undivided by Paters. Such a series of points was called a *rosarium* (a rose garden), a common term used to designate a collection of similar material.

In English, as Eric Partridge records, 'rosary' derives from the neuter form of the adjective, i.e. 'rosarium' meaning a rose garden whence in turn it became, in medieval Latin, 'a rose garland for crowning the Virgin'.[4] In French too there was a similar development – 'rosaire' is glossed in *Petit Larousse* as 'guirlandes de roses' and as 'Grand chapelet de quinze dizaines d'avés, précédées chacune d'un pater'. It would seem then that 'rosary', formally approved by the Pope in 1520, and attached to the form of the prayers in use today, was 'grafted' on to the earlier symbolism which consisted as we have seen of chaplets of roses (the modern chaplet is one third of the rosary) with which to crown the Virgin.

This being so it is surprising that a crown of roses does not seem to feature in Byzantine art, nor is it prominent in the medieval iconography. Instead, the Virgin is crowned with gold. But in the woodcuts of the late fifteenth century, as Marina Warner points out, 'there are signs of mass devotion to the rosary [in which] the Virgin appears ringed with roses'.[5] Then there is Dürer's *Festival of the Rose Garlands* which shows 'Dürer himself, as well as the Emperor Maximilian and Pope Julius II and other figures offering wreaths of roses to the Virgin' and also Veláz-quez's picture of the Virgin crowned in roses by the Holy Trinity.[6] And of course there is Stefan Lochner's *The Virgin in the Rose Bower* (c.1440), but her crown is golden. Thus if we ask ourselves why the rose is so prominent in the rosary and so inconspicuous in the iconography, and look for an answer which allows for an illiterate although devout peasantry, we may find it in the practice of placing a garland on the statue of the Virgin – the painter felt no need to record what was a purely mundane and common occurrence; his representation in the 'world before perspective' (as Lamb called it) aided and added to its extra-terrestrial, supernatural quality. Moreover, gold and blue pigments cost money and required wealthy patronage, whereas a plaster or wooden madonna was altogether cheaper and more accessible to the poorest. ('Blue' madonnas are increasingly evident in the medieval iconography.)

Another flower, absent from the Byzantine iconography, makes its appearance in the medieval painting – the white lily (latterly called the 'Madonna lily'). One of the best-known examples is *The Annunciation* by Simone Martini and Lippo Memmi (1313) in which a vase of lilies is placed near the Virgin's feet. In others, according to Brewer's *Dictionary of Phrase and Fable*, 'St. Joseph holds a lily-branch in his hand, indicating that his wife Mary was a virgin'. Marina Warner says:

> In pictures of the Annunciation Gabriel greets her with a lily staff, and its heady perfume filling her chamber symbolizes her incorruptibility. Pots of lilies often decorate her room. Lilies or roses spring up in paintings of the Assumption, like Pinturic-chio's mille-fleurs evocation in the Borgia Apartments of the Vatican.[7]

As with the rose, however, the lily may have been used in Byzantine times in vases at the foot of her statue, for both flowers had been potent mythological symbols to the Greeks, as the *Encyclopaedia Britannica* (1970 edn.) records:

> Mythologically the white lily (rosa junonis) called 'Madonna' in the late 19th century was fabled to have sprung from the milk of Hera ... As the plant of purity it was contrasted with the rose of Aphrodite.

C.S. Lewis also when remarking on the *Contention of the Lily and the Rose* (ninth century) by Sedulius Scotus notes 'the beginning of the floral symbolism of the allegorical débat, both of which count for much in later poetry'.[8] The Virgin, as indicated above, has certain appellations and titles and these include 'Rose of Sharon' and 'Lily of the field'.

Chaucer of course uses this symbolism. In the *Second Nun's Prologue* St. Cecilia's garlands are 'rose and lily laden' and in the *Invocacio ad Mariam* we also find St. Cecilia's name translated as 'Lily of Heaven'; then the angel gives a 'coronal' of roses to Valerian and a similar one of lilies to Cecilia. And of course his Squire (in Nevil Coghill's version)

> was embroidered like a meadow bright
> And full of freshest flowers, red and white
> Singing he was or fluting all the day;
> He was as fresh as is the month of May.

This stylized red and white floral symbolism was also familiar to the Scottish poets. For example, H. Harvey Wood in *The Poems and Fables of Robert Henryson* compares Robert Henryson's 'quhyte and reid' flowers in *The Taill of the Lyon and the Mous* to a line from Douglas's Virgil:

> of blomit branchis and flowris quhite and rede

and comments:

> The actual flowers are usually lilies and roses, and have several contrasted significations – the lily-white symbolizing chastity, loyalty, modesty &c; the rose-red symbolizing courage, pride lust, youth.[9]

In the work of William Dunbar (c.1460–c.1520) who was a Franciscan friar, the Marian association is more clearly evident:

Sweet rose of vertue and of gentleness,
Delightsome lily of every lustiness,
Richest in bounty and in beauty clear,
Except onlie that ye are mercyless.
Into your garth this day I did pursue;
There saw I flouris that freshe were of hew;
Baith whyte and reid most lusty were to seyne,
And halisome herbuis upon stalkis greene;
Yet leaf nor flower find could I nane of rue ...

Then the association of the rose and the lily appears in the anonymous poem 'The Bridal Morn' (in *The New Oxford Book of English Verse*, ed. Helen Gardner (1972), p. 19).

The maidens came
   When I was in my mother's bower;
I had all that I would.
   The bailey beareth the bell away;
   The lily, the rose, the rose I lay.
The silver is white, red is the gold;
The robes they lay in fold.
   The bailey beareth the bell away;
   The lily, the rose, the rose I lay.
And through the glass window shines the sun.
How should I love, and I so young?
   The bailey beareth the bell away;
   The lily, the rose, the rose I lay.

It is worth nothing also that in the Marian symbolism we have two sets of 'synonyms': (1) rose–red–gold and (2) lily–white–silver, which may help to explain why in medieval literature gold is always 'red' not yellow, as one would have expected because of their common etymological ancestry. We may also add that if we include Franciscan usage in Florence c.1400 gold was also 'glory' (recalling the coronation of the Virgin perhaps) and silver meant 'grace'.[10]

Even Edmund Spenser, Protestant though he was (he reminded his readers in his 'Gloss' to *The Shepheardes Calender* (March) that Flora 'the Goddesse of flowres' was 'indede ... a famous harlot'), used this symbolism in *Epithalamion*:

And let them also with them bring in hand
Another gay girland

For my fayre love of lillyes and of roses
Bound truelove wize with a blew silk riband.

But the Marian symbolism, though it entwined with the secular
even in the early Middle Ages, was not in the end secularized, as
we may see when we turn our attention to the 'virgins' garlands'
dated 1734, 1736 and 1751 which were still hanging in the church
at Minsterley, Shropshire, last century. Charlotte Sophia Burne
described them thus in 1883:

> At Minsterley there are no less than seven of these garlands ...
> Projecting from the upper part of the interior walls of this
> church are several short iron rods with heart-shaped escut-
> cheons at their ends ... To these iron brackets the garlands or
> crowns were originally attached, but seven of them now
> depend against the gallery walls. Each measures a full foot in
> height, and is thus constructed. The lower part consists of a
> hoop of thin wood about 9½ inches in diameter, to which are
> secured two arches of the same material, intersecting each other
> at the top, and steadied by a second hoop placed in mid-height.
> This wooden framework is covered with linen, and on it are
> sewed *lilies and roses of two sizes, made of pink and white paper*.
> From the lower circle descend short paper streamers, principal-
> ly blue and white; but in one instance there is the addition of
> strips of *red cloth*. Within these *crowns* are hung three pairs of
> gloves cut out of white paper. [my italics][11]

That the Marian influence is still apparent need not surprise us
because there had been a Franciscan presence at Shrewsbury
nearby since the thirteenth century.[12] Harold Jenkins has shown
that these virgins' garlands were 'certainly widespread in Elizabethan England' and the custom survived even into the eighteenth
century. Originally a floral wreath had been used but this was
replaced by a less perishable artificial structure; surviving and
recorded examples show characteristically:

> A frame of wood shaped like a crown, twelve or more inches
> high, covered with cloth, or paper, adorned with artificial
> flowers (or occasionally black rosettes), and hanging from it
> ribbons, a pair of gloves, and sometimes a collar or kerchief.[13]

Jenkins also says, 'for women of rank this might be a chaplet of
pearl or gold and silver filigree'. Samuel Johnson however took a
different view of their antiquity:

I have been informed by an anonymous correspondent that crants is the German word for garlands, and I suppose it was retained by us from the Saxons. To carry garlands before the bier of a maiden and to hang them over her grave is still the practice in rural communities.[14]

As we have already encountered the use of rosemary at both weddings and funerals, for the purpose no doubt of invoking the blessing of the Virgin, it is interesting to compare the 'garland' worn by an Italian lady at her wedding in 1400:

> On her head she wore a high, elaborate head-dress, called a 'garland' – mounted on a crimson *mazzocchio* or support which held her hair together and supported her heavy head-dress, embroidered in gold and adorned with no less than 240 carved gilt beads, golden leaves, and enamel flowers.[15]

The 'garland' mentioned was presumably a 'corona' in Italian and linked to the 'Coronarius' or wreath maker of the Romans, whose lineal descendant today is the 'coronario' or maker of funeral garlands. I have been informed by a Benedictine source that *rosa gallica*, the French rose, was popularly used in earlier times as it was 'coronarias' – suitable for making chaplets. Rosemary too apparently had this useful property – the *OED* has an entry dated 1635 for 'garland' which reads: 'Rosemarie which some call the garland rose, or in Latine Rosmarinus coronaria'. We may also add the carnation which the *OED* records was used in chaplets and was classified as 'betonica coronaria' from whence the name 'coronation', widely used as an alternative in the sixteenth century, was probably derived. (In modern Corsica the white carnation is specially associated with the Virgin Mary and with her Assumption and Coronation.) Campion also referred to the flowers as being shaped like 'little crownets'. Thus the crown of roses of the rosary might in the past have had a wider application than the coronation of the statue of the Virgin and been applied also to weddings and to the burial of the dead. Jenkins also records that virgins' garlands were used throughout Northern Europe and that he himself had seen some still being used in Norway. The continuation of a Catholic custom in Lutheran countries may be explained by Luther's toleration of Marian worship. Charlotte Sophia Burne also added that in her time virgins' garlands were used at funerals in Tsarist Russia – in Livonia and Courland which were then presumably following the practice of the Lutheran Church – so that again Marian influence may be inferred.

Traces of the more generalized 'Flora' role of the Virgin are also observable in the folklore of Shropshire. (I am indebted to Charlotte Sophia Burne.) The gloves mentioned above by Jenkins may be 'les gants de Notre Dame' which at Ellesmere appears to have been translated as 'lady-glove' – the French being the medieval name for the foxglove, which at Clun was also known as 'ladies' fingers', perhaps from 'les doigts de la Vierge'. This is reminiscent of the genteel Prioress of Chaucer's *Prologue* whose French was not Parisian. Lungwort also became 'the Virgin Mary's cowslip' and 'the Virgin Mary's honeysuckle'. Other plants showing a Marian association were the 'lady-smock' and, the 'lady-grass', which was also called 'lady-ribbons'. Then there is the marigold, which was called 'the Mayflower' – a rendering of 'the Flower of May' which we have already encountered as an appellation of the Virgin. Marigold seems to be a simple combination of Mary and gold; Shakespeare called them 'mary-buds', as we see in *Cymbeline* (2.3.26). Wreaths of marigolds were apparently hung on doors during May – a custom also observed in Co. Donegal and therefore indubitably Catholic. Elsewhere in Salop the mayflower is the blossom of the white hawthorn – associated in ancient times with the Roman Flora – and is still sacred to the Virgin 'in many of her sanctuaries in Ireland'.[16]

The floral symbolism as it affects the rosary and the virgins' garlands is still preserved to some extent in the devotional practices of the modern Franciscan nun at three particular stages of her service. These are postulancy (when she joins the Order), profession (when she takes her final vows), and at death. As a postulant, when she takes her preliminary vows, the relationship is similar to an engagement to marry – a betrothal *de futuro* as it was called in Shakespeare's time. At this stage the ceremonial includes the wearing of a wreath of roses – the 'chaplet', or 'rosenkranz' if you will. At profession she is solemnly crowned, following a ritual which is very ancient. Marina Warner gives an example of this:

In one ancient form of the ritual, the nun was crowned with a garland: 'Accipe signum Christi in capite,' said the celebrant, 'ut uxor eius efficiaris, et si in eo permanseris, in perpetuum coroneris.' (Receive this sign of Christ on your head, that you

189

may be his wife, and if you remain in that state, be crowned for all eternity.)[17]

This in essence is marriage, at which the nun becomes a Bride of Christ, and accordingly she wears a garland of thorns on her head to symbolize the union and her dedication to the *via crucis*. And then at death the crown of thorns is worn again – the wedding and the funeral employ the same symbolism with which we are now familiar. The Poor Clares however, who are today an enclosed Order of Franciscans, use instead the generalized Marian flower symbolism. The postulant wears a chaplet of any flowers that are seasonal, and they need not be garden flowers. At profession however the crown of thorns is worn and yet again at death.

Just what a Franciscan nun wore in England prior to the Dissolution of the Monasteries is not known and can only be guessed at, but it seems more likely that the ritual of the Poor Clares was used because roses are seasonal here to a greater degree than in the Mediterranean, and also because the beaded rosary, called the Franciscan Crown Rosary, which they employed as distinct from the Dominican, originated in and incorporated the symbolism of the Mystic Rose. It has also been suggested to me that the wedding ceremonies of the maiden and the nun were nearly identical, particularly when their common lot was poverty.

If then we look at the 'coronet weeds' that Ophelia hangs on the tree we must see them through Catholic eyes. First there are the 'crow flowers' which Harold Jenkins is correct in identifying as the cuckoo flower or ragged robin – if we follow the strict Elizabethan botanical classification. But the crow flower was also the lady-smock to which elsewhere Shakespeare makes reference. But why then does he use two different names for the same flower? Personally I do not think he does and I therefore follow Onions and Dover Wilson in preferring the buttercup. This flower was regarded as symbolic of the Chalice – the cup containing the wine at Mass. Its openness also symbolized its receptivity to divine grace. The daisy, which was Chaucer's favourite flower, was for the nun a symbol of humility. Long purples were 'supposed to grow beneath the Cross, and the spots on its leaves have been explained as drops of blood which fell from Christ when He was crucified'.[18] Nettles were used penitentially in monastic practices and had a religious association. They were emblematic of thorns; the 'dead nettle' was dedicated to St.

Michael the archangel, and yet another was called 'the archangel'. In short Ophelia's 'coronet weeds' look like the equivalent of the crown of thorns – as a whole they represent the Passion of Christ.

The Protestant attitude to this is of course implicit in the description 'coronet weeds'. But to the Franciscan nun who eschews wealth and possessions and who shares the intense love of nature and 'all creatures great and small' of her illustrious founder, to wear such a garland or be strewed with buttercups and daisies as she prostrates herself at Profession is to enter into a mystic union with Christ. Poor Ophelia however in her madness becomes a 'coronario' and churns out these wreaths because the nun, to the Protestant, had more than one 'bridegroom', the second and human one being her father confessor – hence perhaps the origin of long purples as 'priest's pintle' ('pintle' meaning penis – a name Robert Burton, cleric that he was, did not hesitate to use).[19]

We cannot then understand the medieval attitudes to flowers and plants if we think in terms of botany or even more crudely by classifying them as flowers and weeds. All had a religious association, usually Marian, but there was acknowledgement also of God who 'fathers-forth' and of the saints.[20] And if there were 'dialectal' variants in the main floral language they were all derived from the same spiritual root-stock. The Reformation made some changes, as we have seen, but in the main the old Catholic associations probably persisted and even when they did not, the same flowers were still used in weddings and funerals. For example, while the pansy became a love token, Milton included it in the flowers he chose for Lycidas, and rosemary was used similarly long after invocation of the Virgin had ceased. In *Hamlet* the Catholic association would be unmistakable because Rosencrantz is Catholic and Shakespeare's audience to whom 'crants' was an unfamiliar word would have associated them with him. So too the 'coronet weeds' would have been familiar to them because they knew about and derided the whole idea of 'Brides of Christ', treating them instead as unrepentant Magdalenes or as devotees of the pagan 'harlot' Flora. As Basil Willey pointed out, 'the divine order, the order of Grace, was felt to be wholly separate from, and in a sense opposed to, "Nature"'.[21] During the Renaissance, in Petrarch for example, a change in the attitude to Nature is observable, a change which gathered momentum to the extent that Sainte-Beuve, commenting on this passage from Montaigne, charged him with having forgotten 'le mal d'Adam':

How much more fitting to strew their classrooms with flowers and leaves than with stumps of blood-stained willows! I would portray there Joy, Sprightliness, Flora, and the Graces. (Of the Education of Children)[22]

In essence these attitudes are Franciscan, but Elizabethan Protestants would have none of this and it took until Wordsworth's time for Nature to be enjoyed spontaneously without a feeling of guilt and remembering Eden.

APPENDIX B

Ophelia as 'Nun'

FURTHER QUESTIONS arise when we suppose that Ophelia's Catholicism would have been treated with derision by most of Shakespeare's audience. First then there are the lauds that she sings. As has been pointed out these would have been sung by a nun – in Latin also it may be added. Philip Edwards in the New Cambridge Shakespeare edition of the play (1985) is in agreement on the specifically Catholic nature of these hymns: 'lauds is an unusual word, not frequently used outside its technical reference to the second of the canonical hours in the Catholic breviary'.[1] He justifies his reading in preference to the Folio's 'tunes' on the grounds that 'crazy hymn-singing might well have marked Ophelia's death'.

Thus, if we accept that she thinks she is a nun when she sings them, and also hangs up the floral chaplets that Franciscan nuns might have worn at Profession, her nun-like role can easily be extended to her distributing flowers earlier because nuns would almost certainly have done this at some time during May (which Hopkins called 'Mary's month') when the Virgin in her Flora-role was coronated with flowers. In Sicily even today children at confirmation echo the ancient rituals connected with the Brides of Christ: 'lace dresses or miniature nuns' habits, palm branches, flowers are called for at confirmations'.[2] A fresh look at the first 'mad scene' seems therefore to be called for.

The more information that accumulates about the medieval shrine at Walsingham the less likely it is that there is any allusion that is other than derogatory. Marina Warner records that

at Walsingham ... there was a replica of the Holy House at Nazareth, which drew pilgrims from all England and Europe for three hundred years and fattened the clergy. During the reign of Edward the Confessor, the Virgin had appeared to a devout widow of Walsingham ... and had led her in spirit to Nazareth ... and asked her to build 'England's Nazareth' ... Miracle cures were claimed to have taken place as a result but

193

[the] cult [of the Virgin] excited precisely those excesses of external idolatry with their accompanying hollowness of the Spirit, that horrified the men who pressed for reformation. Among them was Erasmus [who] was scathing about the shrine at Walsingham and others.[3]

If then we acknowledge that Ophelia's role in distributing heartily of the destruction of the shrine and its image – or idol, as they would have regarded it – who in Shakespeare's audience, not to mention Pasfield, the corrector, would have looked for sincere love and romance in Ophelia's song? The love associated with pilgrimages to Walsingham was illicit – even in the Raleigh version the lover is deserted by his mistress, and this tradition of a sex-romp rather than a religious pilgrimage goes back as we have seen to Langland. Thus, even among Catholics, pilgrimages to Walsingham involved 'Mariolatry' – excessive veneration of the Virgin Mary – and sexual licence.

Then Philip Edwards also records that in other versions of the legend of the owl and the baker's daughter it was a beggar who asked for and was refused bread, and that the beggar was Jesus – which supports my guess that the yarn was used by a friar mendicant. And it may be added that the gypsies' sense of humour which I have supposed made them nickname the owl a 'baker's daughter' was also displayed in their giving religious hermits the soubriquet of 'highwaymen', as the *OED* shows. In Scotland, even in John Buchan's time, the 'tinkers' took a professional pride in their skill as beggars.

If then we acknowledge that Ophelia's role in distributing flowers, making floral coronets and singing lauds is nun-like, I propose that we adopt a simple hypothesis – call it a leap in the dark – and imagine that Ophelia is dressed as a nun in her 'mad scenes'. Hamlet has told her to go to a nunnery, and in her madness she adopts that garb. All she would need would be a white shift, and her hair would be unbraided (to wear her tresses up in braids was a sign of virginity and associated with St. Catherine) as befitted a postulant on the eve of Profession. At this point the Q1 stage direction may be relevant:

Enter Ophelia playing on a Lute, and her haire downe singing.

(Like Chaucer's Prioress, nuns sang the divine service and accompanied themselves on musical instruments as part of their devotions.)

Then if she sings of her 'true love' Shakespeare's audience would automatically assume that her lover was a friar, according to the popular, and scurrilous, tradition:

> As a nail to his hole, the cuckold to his horn, as a scolding quean to a wrangling knave, as the nun's lip to the friar's mouth; nay as the pudding to his skin

as the clown puts it in *All's Well that Ends Well* (2.2.27–30).

Thus if the Walsingham song refers to a friar the association is continued in the owl and the baker's daughter, as we have seen, and if we go on to the seduction on St. Valentine's day, remembering that Ophelia might well have been regarded as a Poor Clare, the strictest sect of Franciscan nuns like Isabella in *Measure for Measure* (and the wanton nun Angelica in *The Devil's Law Case*), and remembering also that the birds were supposed to choose their mates for the coming year on that day and that St. Francis preaching to them was a commonplace in the popular iconography, then the seducer, her 'valentine', is a friar. Percy's friar proposes marriage, so that may have been part of the popular tradition too.

But the point is that Ophelia confuses her 'true love' with Polonius, her father. Her 'friar' is her 'father' too – Isabella addresses the disguised duke thus in *Measure for Measure* (e.g. at 3.1.248 and 4.1.66) – and Claudius's 'conceit upon her father' after hearing her tell of the owl and the baker's daughter may have been taken by the audience as a pun, for their benefit, on 'father'. Philip Edwards points out that 'there is a constant reference to a hidden meaning in Ophelia's utterances, introduced first by the Gentleman's speech'.[4] But what is the hidden meaning? I suggest that she is talking about incest, real or imaginary, committed with Polonius. If not, what else is she talking about? The idea is startling, and repellent, because we have been brought up to believe in an innocent, romantic Ophelia, patient and submissive to her father's will, but this is Denmark, the unweeded garden possessed by things rank and gross in nature where the very king and queen are guilty of 'damned incest'. Thus, even if what Ophelia hints at is untrue, who in Shakespeare's audience, with its anti-Catholic prejudices, would give her the benefit of the doubt? Nor does Ophelia's 'imagination' stop there because she gives Laertes, her own brother, a love-token of rosemary and pansies and regrets not being able to give him violets too (which betokened her virginity), which she associates with the death of her father. If then we were 'fervent Protestants' we might be inclined to see a parallel between Ophelia and Lucrezia Borgia, who was also seduced by her father, and by her brother – Laertes certainly is nasty enough to take his place beside Cesare Borgia in the rogues' gallery (but it is true that he does not suspect Polonius). Thus too Polonius, whom Hamlet calls a 'fishmonger', a pimp or brothel-keeper, might have been associated with Pope Alexander VI, the keeper of the keys of St. Peter, the patron saint of fishmongers.

The incest may not have taken place but Hamlet doubts Ophelia's 'honesty', i.e. her virginity:

> If thou dost marry, I'll give thee this plague for thy dowry – be thou chaste as ice, as pure as snow, thou shalt not escape calumny; get thee to a nunnery, go, farewell. (3.1.137–40)

After all, his own mother is guilty of incest so why not Ophelia? Then too he calls Polonius 'Jephtha' and he cannot be paying him a compliment – on the contrary Jephtha was the son of a harlot and he sacrificed his own daughter, who, before dying, 'bewailed her virginity'. If then Hamlet thinks Ophelia has lost hers, her father and brother are in Hamlet's eyes the most obvious culprits. Polonius is a fishmonger, and as for Laertes:

> Let her not walk i' th' sun. Conception is a blessing, but as your daughter may conceive, friend look to't. (2.2.184–6)

I am aware that the pun on 'sun' is usually taken to refer to Hamlet himself but it seems more apt if applied to Laertes. I also believe that the average Elizabethan play-goer was as prone to accept stereotypes as we are today, and that the Borgias represented for them the ultimate in Catholic and Papal villainy, thus enabling Barnabe Barnes to produce his pot-boiling *The Devil's Charter* in 1607.

The doubts of the audience about Ophelia's chastity would also add irony to her funeral, at which she is allowed her 'virgin crants', and of course to her hanging up the floral chaplet which betokens that she is a virgin Bride of Christ. It is all very nasty but then Satan is behind it all – Satan who committed incest with his own daughter (according to Milton, called 'Sin'), the result of their union being Death, whose 'sport is the rape of his mother', as R.M. Frye puts it.[5] Thus I think it is wrong to distort the pattern

196

of motivation in the play by ignoring the Satanic, and Catholic, background which lies behind it. *Hamlet* is a study in evil, but for the Elizabethan audience he was not Everyman, he was Every-Catholic who was *ipso facto* a follower of Satan, whose arch-priest was the Pope himself.

Notes to the Text

NOTES TO THE INTRODUCTION

1. A.C. Bradley, *Shakespearean Tragedy* (1957 edn.), pp. 17, 141.
2. Fredson Bowers, *Elizabethan Revenge Tragedy* (1966 edn.), pp. 263–81.
3. Eleanor Prosser, *Hamlet and Revenge* (1971, 2nd edn.), p. 72.
4. L.C. Knights, *An Approach to Hamlet* (1964 edn.), especially pp. 31–5.
5. G. Wilson Knight, *The Wheel of Fire* (1960 edn.), p. 42.
6. Philip Edwards, 'Tragic Balance in Hamlet', *Shakespeare Survey 36* (1983), p. 45.
7. Richmond Noble, *Shakespeare's Biblical Knowledge* (1935), p. 45.
8. Caroline Spurgeon, *Shakespeare's Imagery* (1935), p. 20.
9. *Early Writings of John Hooper D.D.*, Parker Society (1853), p. 368.
10. Prosser, *Revenge*, p. 13.
11. Alexander Nowell, *A catechism written in Latin with the same catechism translated into English by Thomas Norton*, Parker Society (1853), pp. 133, 201.
12. Prosser, *Revenge*, p. 22.
13. Bowers, *Revenge Tragedy*, pp. 13–14.
14. Ibid., p. 20.
15. F.H. Drinkwater, *The Abbreviated Catechism with Explanations* (1977), p. 41,
16. Robert Bolt, *A Man for All Seasons* (1978, Heinemann edn.), p. xv.
17. Anne Barton, *Hamlet* (*The New Penguin Shakespeare*) (1983 edn.), p. 36.
18. *Hamlet*, ed. Harold Jenkins (1982), p. 155.
19. Edwards, *Survey*, p. 48.
20. J.H. Walter, ed., *Hamlet* (1972, Heinemann edn.), p. 334.
21. *Mer. V.* 2.1.74; *The Honest Whore* Part 1, Act, Sc. 2.
22. Noble, *Biblical Knowledge*, p. 121.
23. C.T. Onions, *A Shakespeare Glossary* (1919, 2nd edn.).
24. Nigel Alexander, *Poison, Play and Duel* (1971), pp. 45–6.
25. Ibid., p. 47.
26. Barton, *Hamlet*, p. 35.
27. Alexander, *Poison*, p. 33.

NOTES TO CHAPTER ONE

1. John Dover Wilson, *What Happens in Hamlet* (1935), p. 65.
2. Bowers, *Revenge Tragedy*, p. 73.
3. Charles Edward Whitmore, *The Supernatural in Tragedy* (1915), p. 233.
4. Dover Wilson, *What Happens*, p. 56.
5. G.K. Hunter, *English Folly and Italian Vice* (*The Jacobean Theatre*), ed. John Russell Brown (1960).
6. M.C. Bradbrook, *Themes and Conventions of Elizabethan Tragedy* (1960 ed.), pp. 25–6.
7. Thomas Marc Parrott, *The Revenge of Bussy d'Ambois* (1910). See footnote on 5.5.133 ff.
8. George R. Kernodle, The Open Stage: 'Elizabethan or Existential?' *Shakespeare Survey 12* (1959), pp.

2–3.

9. John Dover Wilson, ed., *Hamlet* (Cambridge, 1964 edn.), p. 297.
10. Prosser, *Revenge*, p. 105.
11. Dover Wilson, *What Happens*, p. 84.

NOTES TO CHAPTER TWO

1. Sir Edmund Chambers, *The Elizabethan Stage* (1923), Vol. 3, p. 161.
2. Ibid., p. 167.
3. Edward Arber, *A Transcript of the Registers of the Company of Stationers of London* (1875).
4. W.W. Greg, *Marlowe's Doctor Faustus* (1950), e.g. p. 85; F.S. Boas, *The Tragical History of Doctor Faustus* (1932), pp. 32–3.
5. Arber, *Stationers*, Vol. 3, pp. 163, 450.
6. Dover Wilson, *What Happens*, pp. 62, 83.
7. Edgar C.S. Gibson, D.D., *The Thirty-Nine Articles of the Church of England* (1902), pp. 37, 80.
8. *The Scottish Catechism of Christian Doctrine.*
9. Samuel Harsnett, *A Declaration of Egregious Popish Impostures* (1963), p. 157.
10. A.C. Southern, *Elizabethan Recusant Prose* (1950), pp. 66, 380, 537.
11. Arber, *Stationers*, Vol. 3, p. 155.
12. Ibid., p. 189.
13. Ludwig Lavater, *Of Ghostes and Spirites Walking by Nyght* (1572), ed. John Dover Wilson and May Yardley, Shakespeare Association (1929), Introduction.
14. Arber, *Stationers*, Vol. 3, p. 279.
15. J. Strype, *Annals of the Reformation* (1824), Vol. 1, Part 1, p. 364.
16. Southern, *Recusant Prose*, pp. 35–6.
17. *Tarlton's Jests and News out of Purgatory*, ed. J.O. Halliwell

(1844).

18. Ibid., p. 107.
19. Arber, *Stationers*, Vol. 3, p. 163.
20. John Peter, *Complaint and Satire in Early English Literature* (1956), p. 199.
21. Reginald Scot, *The Discoverie of Witchcraft*, ed. Brinsley Nicholson (1886), p. 153.
22. *The Works of Thomas Nashe*, ed. Ronald B. McKerrow (1904), Vol. 2, p. 161.
23. Robert Burton, *The Anatomy of Melancholy*, ed. Floyd Dell and Paul Jordan Smith (1955), p. 169.
24. Dover Wilson, *What Happens*, p. 56.
25. G.M. Trevelyan, *English Social History* (1946 edn.) pp. 180–1.

NOTES TO CHAPTER THREE

1. Dover Wilson, *What Happens*, p. 55.
2. I.J. Semper, 'The Ghost in *Hamlet*: Pagan or Christian?' *The Month*, IX (1953), pp. 222–34.
3. Dover Wilson, *What Happens*, p. 84.
4. Roy W. Battenhouse, 'The Ghost in *Hamlet*: A Catholic "Linch-pin"?' *Studies in Philology*, XLVIII (1951), pp. 161–92.
5. Prosser, *Revenge*, pp. 102, 104, 115, 123, 141–3, 173.
6. Philip Hughes, *The Reformation in England* (1954), Vol. 2, pp. 122–3.
7. John Dover Wilson, *Life in Shakespeare's England* (Penguin, 1954), p. 354.
8. Horace Howard Furness, *Hamlet* (*A New Variorum Edition of Shakespeare*) (1963, Dover edn.), Vol. 2, p. 241.
9. Ibid., p. 123.
10. Bradbrook, *Themes*, p. 15.
11. 1.3.21; 3.2.86–7. And see Prosser, *Revenge*, p. 121.
12. C.S. Lewis, *Hamlet: The Prince or*

the Poem? British Academy Shake-speare Lecture (1942).

13. *The Plays of John Marston*, ed. H. Harvey Wood (1939), Vol. 3, p. 65.
14. François Rabelais, *Gargantua and Pantagruel*, trans. J.M. Cohen (1963), p. 355.
15. A.R. McGee, 'Macbeth and the Furies', *Shakespeare Survey 19* (1966), p. 57.
16. *A Midsummer Night's Dream* (*The Warwick Shakespeare*), ed. Sir Edmund Chambers, Appendix A.
17. R. Trevor Davies, *Four Centuries of Witch-beliefs* (1947), pp. 26, 44, 45, 104.
18. Christopher Marlowe, *Complete Plays and Poems*, ed. E.D. Pendry (1976).
19. Prosser, *Revenge*, p. 120.
20. Strype, *Annals*, Vol. 3, Part 2, p. 270.
21. Jenkins, ed., *Hamlet*, p. 436.
22. Enid Welsford, *The Fool* (1968 edn.) pp. 22–3.
23. McKerrow, ed., *Works of Nashe*, Vol. 1, p. 38.
24. Glynne Wickham, 'Hell-Castle and its Door-Keeper', *Shakespeare Survey 19* (1966), pp. 68–74.
25. John Marston, *Sophonisba*, Act 4, Sc. 1.
26. *The Ecclesiastical Polity*, ed. Benjamin Hanbury (1830), Vol. 3, p. 494.
27. Ibid., Vol. 2, p. 199.
28. Gibson, *Thirty-Nine Articles*, pp. 357–8.
29. Nevill Coghill, *Shakespeare's Professional Skills* (1964), p. 11.
30. Irving Ribner, *Patterns in Shakespearean Tragedy* (1962 edn.), p. 83, sees the 'mole of nature' as 'original sin which beclouds man's reason and makes it so difficult for him to learn what Hamlet must learn before he can combat evil'.
31. Trevor Davies, *Witch-beliefs*, p. 99.
32. *An Approach to Hamlet* (1964),

p. 30.
33. Ibid., p. 47.
34. Bradbrook, *Themes*, p. 151.
35. Helen Gardner, *The Theme of Damnation in 'Doctor Faustus'* (1948), reprinted in *Marlowe, Doctor Faustus, A Casebook*, ed. John Jump (1969), p. 96.
36. And see Prosser, *Revenge*, p. 109, quoting Le Loyer IV, 301–2.
37. Furness, *Hamlet*, pp. 245–6.
38. Prosser, *Revenge*, p. 115.
39. Gibson, *Thirty-Nine Articles*, p. 109.
40. Wickham, *Hell-Castle*, p. 71.
41. Southern, *Recusant Prose*, p. 255.
42. *The Shakespeare Allusion Book*, ed. John Monro (1909, re-issued 1932), Vol. 1, p. 364.
43. Ibid., p. 169.
44. C.E.M. Joad, 'Hamlet as a Literary Struldbrug', in *Points of View*, ed. M. Alderton Pink (1966), pp. 51–62.
45. *The Book of Common Prayer*, ed. Archibald John Stephens, Parker Society (1854), Vol. 3, p. 1578.
46. Jenkins, *Hamlet*, pp. 456–7.
47. Noble, *Biblical Knowledge*, p. 202.
48. Philip Stubbes, *The Anatomie of Abuses* (1583); Dover Wilson, *Life*, p. 229.
49. Dover Wilson, *What Happens*, p. 82.
50. Francis Douce, *Illustrations of Shakespeare* (1839), p. 455.
51. Coghill, *Professional Skills*, p. 10, says 'Let us pause to consider the meaning of this Latin phrase; it is to be translated "here and everywhere" of course: but who in the universe can be both here and everywhere? Only God and the Devil: certainly not a ghost.'
52. *Shakespeare Allusion Book*, Vol. 1, p. 351.
53. Leslie Hotson, *Shakespeare's Motley* (1952), p. 116; George Rylands, *The New Clarendon Shakespeare* (1947), p. 203; Jenkins, ed., *Hamlet*, p. 458.

54. Nashe, *Works*, Vol. 3, p. 348.
55. Harsnett, *Popish Impostures*, Introduction.
56. Bernard Spivack, *Shakespeare and
the Allegory of Evil* (1958), p. 255.
57. James Russell Lowell, *Among my
Books* (1870).
58. Spivack, *Allegory*, pp. 167, 168,
179, 181, 187.
59. Harsnett, *Popish Impostures*, pp.
114–15.
60. Spivack, *Allegory*, p. 132.
61. Chambers, ed., *MND* – note on
3.2.421.
62. Elmer Edgar Stoll, *Art and Artifice
in Shakespeare* (1963 edn.), pp.
91–2n.
63. Prosser, *Revenge*, p. 113.
64. *Hamlet*, ed. Samuel Johnson and
George Steevens, *The Plays of
William Shakespeare* (1793), p. 75.
65. Jenkins, ed., *Hamlet*, p. 154.

NOTES TO CHAPTER FOUR

1. Paul S. Conklin, *A History of
'Hamlet' Criticism, 1608–1821*
(1957 edn.), pp. 12–16.
2. Furness, *Hamlet*, p. 226.
3. W.I.D. Scott, *Shakespeare's Melancholics* (1962), p. 100.
4. Prosser, *Revenge*, p. 151.
5. Ibid.
6. Daniel Hack Tuke, *Chapters in the
History of the Insane in the British
Isles* (1882), pp. 32–3, 43–4.
7. E.M.W. Tillyard, *The Elizabethan
World Picture* (1963 edn.), p. 131.
8. Jenkins, ed., *Hamlet*, p. 226.
9. Welsford, *Fool*, p. 167.
10. Ibid., p. 24.
11. Ibid., p. 26.
12. Douce, *Illustrations*, p. 82.
13. M.C. Bradbrook, *Shakespeare:
The Poet in his World* (1978), p. 50.
14. Robert Armin, *Fools and Jesters*,
Shakespeare Society (1842), p. 12.
15. Ibid., p. 3.
16. Welsford, *Fool*, pp. 132, 134, 138,

143–4, 147, 148, 159, 163, 164.
17. Spivack, *Allegory*, p. 135; Welsford, *Fool*, p. 281.
18. Spivack, *Allegory*, p. 137.
19. Welsford, *Fool*, pp. 123–4.
20. Ibid., p. 125.
21. *The Merry Conceited Jests of George
Peele* (1809). This appears to be a
re-issue of the original edn. of
1602. No editor is listed.
22. Joseph Quincy Adams, *Chief Pre-
Shakespearean Dramas* (1924), pp.
332–8.
23. *The Marriage of Wit and Wisdome*,
ed. J.O. Halliwell, Shakespeare
Society (1846), p. 20.
24. Hotson, *Motley*, p. 78.
25. F.P. Wilson, *Shakespearean and
Other Studies* (1969), p. 116.
26. Hotson, *Motley*, p. 68.
27. Thelma Niklaus, *Harlequin
Phoenix* (1956), p. 32.
28. Welsford, *Fool*, p. 47.
29. Sir Edmund K. Chambers, *The
Medieval Stage* (1903), Vol. 2,
p. 204.
30. Welsford, *Fool*, p. 281.
31. Hotson, *Motley*, p. 56.
32. Chambers, *Medieval Stage*, Vol. 1,
p. 387.
33. Hotson, *Motley*, p. 58.
34. Douce, *Illustrations*, p. 510.
35. Hotson, *Motley*, p. 58.
36. Spivack, *Allegory*, p. 199.
37. *Antonio's Revenge*, ed. W. Reavley
Gair (1978), p. 123.
38. Welsford, *Fool*, p. 282.
39. Spivack, *Allegory*, p. 199.
40. *Henry the Fourth (The New Clarendon Shakespeare)*, ed. Bertram
Newman (1964 edn.).
41. Jenkins, ed., *Hamlet*, p. 325.
42. Dover Wilson, *What Happens*,
p. 213.
43. Jenkins, ed., *Hamlet*, p. 510.
44. Dover Wilson, *What Happens*,
pp. 96–7.
45. J. Isaacs, 'Shakespeare as Man of
the Theatre', in *Shakespeare Criticism 1919–1935* (1949 edn.),
p. 320.

46. Welsford, *Fool*, pp. 153, 156.
47. Chambers, *Medieval Stage*, Vol. 1, p. 388.
48. Ibid.
49. Dover Wilson, *What Happens*, p. 244.
50. M. Channing Linthicum, *Costume in the Drama of Shakespeare and his Contemporaries* (1935), pp. 243–4. There is a single reference to 'razed' (meaning 'raised') pantofles by Stubbes (1580) but no mention of 'rac'd' ('slashed') shoes.
51. Jenkins, ed., *Hamlet*, p. 509.
52. It may be that the traditional costume of the old Vice was preserved in puppet-shows, as he was still appearing there in Samuel Johnson's time (see Johnson and Steevens, eds., *Plays of Shakespeare*, Vol. 4, p. 146, and note Hamlet's reference to puppets at 3.2.247.
53. A.J.A. Waldock, *A Study of Critical Method* (1931), extract in *Shakespeare's Tragedies*, ed. Laurence Lerner (1963), pp. 84–5.
54. Dover Wilson, *What Happens*, pp. 95–6
55. Harry Levin, *The Question of Hamlet* (1970 edn.), p. 124.
56. Ibid.
57. Welsford, *Fool*, p. 269.
58. Noble, *Biblical Knowledge*, p. 250.
59. Nowell, *Catechism*, p. 31.
60. McGee, *Survey*, pp. 64–5.
61. Knights, *An Approach*, p. 83.
62. Nowell, *Catechism*, p. 167.
63. Knights, *An Approach*, pp. 71–9.
64. Georg Brandes, quoted in Dover Wilson, ed., *Hamlet*, p. 191.
65. T.J.B. Spencer, *The New Penguin Shakespeare*, p. 268; Ribner, *Shakespearean Tragedy*, p. 73.
66. Knights, *An Approach*, pp. 76–7.
67. Prosser, *Revenge*, p. 168; Jenkins, ed., *Hamlet*, p. 491.
68. Nowell, *Catechism*, p. 178.
69. Noble, *Biblical Knowledge*, p. 43.
70. Burton, *Melancholy,* p. 964.
71. Tillyard, *Elizabethan World*, p. 13.
72. *Coleridge's Essays and Lectures on Shakespeare* (1911, Everyman edn.), p. 136.
73. Edwards, *Survey*, p. 45.
74. Burton, *Melancholy*, p. 342.
75. Kenneth Muir, *Shakespeare's Sources* (1957), pp. 120–1.
76. Dover Wilson, *What Happens*, p. 315.
77. Prosser, *Revenge*, p. 6.
78. *The Two Liturgies*, Parker Society (1844), p. 469.
79. Scott, *Melancholics*, p. 24.
80. Jenkins, ed., *Hamlet*, p. 483.

NOTES TO CHAPTER FIVE

1. Coleridge, *Essays*, p. 149.
2. Armin, *Fools and Jesters*, p. 49.
3. Hotson, *Motley*, p. 91.
4. Isaacs, *Man of the Theatre*, p. 321.
5. George Bull, *Venice* (1980), p. 79. And see also p. 63 – Coryat's reference to 'chapineys' c.1608.
6. Jenkins, ed., *Hamlet*, p. 478.
7. Douce, *Illustrations*, pp. 460–1.
8. Welsford, *Fool*, p. 292; Chambers, ed., *MND*, p. 148.
9. Bradley, *Tragedy*, p. 109.
10. John Wain, *The Living World of Shakespeare* (1966, Pelican edn.), p. 173.
11. Ibid.
12. Dover Wilson, *What Happens*, pp. 170–1.
13. *Macbeth* (*The Arden Shakespeare*), ed. Kenneth Muir (1965), pp. 29–30.
14. E.M.W. Tillyard, *Shakespeare's History Plays* (1962 edn.), p. 132.
15. K.M. Briggs, *Pale Hecate's Team* (1962), p. 156.
16. Walter, ed., *Hamlet*, p. 188.
17. Prosser, *Revenge*, pp. 183–4.
18. Burton, *Melancholy*, p. 151.
19. Hotson, *Motley*, p. 98.
20. Nowell, *Catechism*, pp. 132–3.
21. Tillyard, *History Plays*, pp. 20, 66–9, 84.

22. Charles Lamb, *Tales from Shakespeare* (1807).
23. Quoted by Steevens in *Plays of William Shakespeare*, Vol. 15, p. 177.

NOTES TO CHAPTER SIX

1. Sir Ernst Gombrich, *The Story of Art* (1950), p. 157.
2. Prosser, *Revenge*, p. 187.
3. Burton, *Melancholy*, p. 943.
4. L.A. Cormican, 'Medieval Idiom in Shakespeare', *Scrutiny*, XVII (1950), p. 311.
5. Nowell, *Catechism*, p. 185.
6. Walter, ed., *Hamlet*, p. 212.
7. Jenkins, ed., *Hamlet*, p. 135.
8. Bradley, *Tragedy*, p. 108.
9. Prosser, *Revenge*, p. 189.
10. Kenneth Muir, ed., *Othello* (*The New Penguin Shakespeare*) (1971), p. 16.
11. Bowers, *Revenge Tragedy*, p. 52, quoting Gentillet.
12. Drinkwater, *Catechism*, p. 68.
13. Prosser, *Revenge*, p. 191.
14. Ibid., pp. 188, 193.
15. Jenkins, ed., *Hamlet*, p. 515.
16. Fred Reinfeld, *Treasury of the World's Coins* (1955), p. 123.
17. Nowell, *Catechism*, p. 141.
18. Prosser, *Revenge*, p. 195.
19. Welsford, *Fool*, pp. 132–6.
20. Jenkins, ed., *Hamlet*, p. 323, footnote.
21. Prosser, *Revenge*, p. 204.
22. Bradley, *Tragedy*, p. 110; Harley Granville-Barker, *Prefaces to Shakespeare* (1963 edn.), p. 127.
23. Spivack, *Allegory*, pp. 161–3.
24. See 22 above.

NOTES TO CHAPTER SEVEN

1. Jenkins, ed., *Hamlet*, p. 276.
2. Gombrich, *Story of Art*.

3. Strype, *Annals*, Vol. 2, p. 119.
4. Wolf Mankowitz, *Shakespeare in Perspective*, ed. Roger Sales (1982), Vol. 1, p. 212.
5. Johnson and Steevens, eds., *Hamlet*, p. 260.
6. Thomas Percy, *Reliques of Ancient English Poetry*, ed. Henry Wheatley (1910), p. 10.
7. Ibid.
8. Ibid., p. 87.
9. Ibid.
10. Ibid., pp. 86–7.
11. Peter J. Seng, *The Vocal Songs in the Plays of Shakespeare* (1968, 2nd printing), p. 140.
12. Ibid.
13. Ibid., p. 141.
14. Percy, *Reliques*, Vol. 1, p. 242.
15. Seng, *Vocal Songs*, pp. 4–5.
16. Ibid., p. 3.
17. Peter, *Satire*, p. 82.
18. Chambers, ed., *Hamlet*, p. 199.
19. Jenkins, ed., *Hamlet*, p. 533.
20. Sigmund Freud, *Introductory Lectures on Psychoanalysis*, ed. James Strachey and Angela Richards (Pelican, 1982), p. 196.
21. Johnson and Steevens, eds., *Hamlet*, p. 262.
22. Jenkins, ed., *Hamlet*, p. 351.
23. Ibid.
24. Ibid.
25. Helen Gardner, *The Oxford Book of English Verse* (1975 edn.), p. 33.
26. Chambers, ed., *Hamlet*, pp. 201–2.
27. Douce, *Illustrations*, pp. 589–90.
28. Ibid., p. 591.
29. Jenkins, ed., *Hamlet*, p. 538.
30. Tuke, *Insane*, pp. 37, 73, 95, 343.
31. Granville-Barker, *Prefaces*, p. 148.
32. Bradbrook, *Poet*, p. 163.
33. Henry N. Ellacombe, *Plant Lore of Shakespeare* (1896), p. 276.
34. Noble, *Biblical Knowledge*, p. 85.
35. Nashe, *Works*, Vol. 2, p. 161.
36. Jenkins, ed., *Hamlet*, p. 494.
37. Burton, *Melancholy*, pp. 356–7.
38. Bradley, *Tragedy*, p. 133.

39. See C.S. Lewis, *The Allegory of Love* (1969 edn.), p. 14: 'According to the medieval view passionate love itself was wicked.'
40. Gregory Zilboorg in *A History of Medical Psychology* (1941) quotes from Guazzo's *Malleus Maleficarum* (1608): 'All witchcraft comes from carnal lust, which is in women insatiable.'
41. F. Marian McNeil, *The Silver Bough* (1959), Vol. 2, p. 79.
42. A.L. Rowse, *The Elizabethan Renaissance : The Cultural Achievement* (1972), p. 339.
43. Bowers, *Revenge Tragedy*, p. 30.
44. Stephens, ed., *Common Prayer*, Vol. 3, p. 1578.
45. *Encyclopaedia Britannica* (1970 edn.)
46. Chambers, ed., *Hamlet*, p. 200.
47. Stephens, ed., *Common Prayer*, Vol. 1, p. 364.
48. Spencer, ed., *Hamlet*, p. 317.
49. Virgil, *Aeneid*, trans. W.F. Jackson Knight (1956), pp. 164–5.
50. Chambers, ed., *MND*, p. 109.

NOTES TO CHAPTER EIGHT

1. Thomas Nashe, *Life in Shakespeare's England*, p. 174.
2. Alice Walker, *Othello (The New Shakespeare)* (1957 edn.), p. 177.
3. Wm. Empson, *Shakespeare's Tragedies*, ed. Laurence Lerner (1963), p. 113.
4. Hooper, *Early Writings*, p. 393.
5. Thomas Becon, *Early Works*, Parker Society (1843), Vol. 2, pp. 108–62).
6. Francisco Maria Guazzo, *Compendium Maleficarum* (1608), ed. Montagu Summers (1929), p. 149.
7. Hooper, *Early Writings*, p. 368.
8. As 6 above.
9. *The Canterbury Tales*, ed. Nevill Coghill (1977 edn.), p. 266.
10. Bradley, *Tragedy*, p. 116.
11. Knights, *An Approach*, p. 89.

12. Gibson, *Thirty-Nine Articles*, pp. 484, 484n.
13. Joad, *Struldbrug*, p. 54.
14. Wilson Knight, *Wheel*, p. 42.
15. R.M. Frye, *God, Man and Satan* (1960), pp. 63–4.
16. E.M.W. Tillyard, *Shakespeare's Problem Plays* (1950), p. 30.
17. Knights, *An Approach*, p. 91.
18. Bernard Crick, *George Orwell: A Life* (1980), p. 397.
19. Tillyard, *History Plays*, p. 68.

NOTES TO THE EPILOGUE

1. William Warburton, *Hamlet*, ed. Johnson and Steevens, p. 84.
2. Ibid., p. 360.
3. Chambers, ed., *Hamlet*, Note on 1.5.112.
4. Prosser, *Revenge*, pp. 243–5.
5. Tuke, *Insane*, p. 41.
6. Ibid., p. 100.
7. R.D. Laing, *The Divided Self* (1960), p. 214.
8. Arthur P. Noyes M.D. and Lawrence C. Kolb M.D., *Modern Clinical Psychiatry* (1963), pp. 307–8.
9. John Corbin, *The Elizabethan Hamlet* (1895).
10. Clive James, *Shakespeare in Perspective*, Vol. 1, p. 178.
11. Lewis, *Prince or Poem*.
12. Knights, *An Approach*, pp. 90–1.

NOTES TO APPENDIX A

1. Marina Warner, *Alone of all her Sex* (1976), p. 281.
2. Ibid., p. 100.
3. *Encyclopaedia Britannica* (1970 edn.)
4. Eric Partridge, ed., *A Short Etymological Dictionary of Modern English* (1966 edn.).
5. Warner, *Alone*, p. 307.
6. Ibid., p. 321.
7. Ibid., p. 99.
8. Lewis, *Prince or Poem*.

9. *The Poems and Fables of Robert Henryson*, ed. H. Harey Wood (1965 edn.), p. 242.
10. Iris Origo, *The Merchant of Prato* (1984), p. 324.
11. Charlotte Sophia Burne, *Shropshire Folklore* (1883), p. 312.
12. Dom David Knowles, *The Religious Orders in England* (1950), p. 141.
13. Jenkins, ed., *Hamlet*, p. 555.
14. Johnson and Steevens, eds., *Hamlet*, p. 314.
15. Origo, *Merchant*, p. 191.
16. Warner, *Alone*, p. 283.
17. Ibid., p. 128.
18. *Field Guide to the Wild Flowers of Britain* (Reader's Digest Association, 1981), p. 400.
19. Burton, *Melancholy*, p. 564.
20. Keith Thomas, *Man and the Natural World* (Penguin, 1984), reaches a similar conclusion on more extensive evidence (p. 82), and the Marian association is evident in his list of common medieval garden flowers: 'a heavy concentration on roses, lilies, gillyflowers (pinks) [which were also sometimes referred to as carnations], cowslips, marigolds, and violets'. He says also (p. 84), 'The old names were also disliked by Protestants when they had Popish associations with the Virgin or with saints, or indeed if they had any religious implication at all'.
21. Basil Willey, *The Seventeenth Century Background* (1962 edn.), p. 35.
22. Ibid., p. 38.

NOTES TO APPENDIX B

1. Philip Edwards, ed., *Hamlet (The New Cambridge Shakespeare)* (1985 edn.), p. 212.
2. Dana Facaros and Michael Pauls, *Mediterranean Island Hopping* (1981), p. 112.
3. Warner, *Alone*, pp. 295–6.
4. Edwards, ed., *Hamlet*, p. 195.
5. Frye, *God, Man and Satan*, p. 37.

Quotations from *Hamlet* are taken from: John Dover Wilson, ed., *Hamlet* (Cambridge, 1964 edn.). All others in the canon are taken from: W.J. Craig, ed., *The Complete Works of William Shakespeare* (Oxford, 1952 edn.).

Index

Cooke, George Frederick 179
Corbet, Bishop 53
Corbin, John 180
Cormican, L.A. 125
Cornelius 57
Coryat, Thomas 130
Cotgrave, Randle 86
Crick, Bernard 175
Cushman, L.W. 79
Cymbeline 189

Dante Alighieri 64
Davies, R. Trevor 54, 200
Deacon and Walker 29
Dekker, Thomas: *Old Fortunatus*
(1600) 38; *The Honest Whore* (1604)
9, 39, 77, 149; *News from Hell* (1606)
22; *Lanthorne and Candlelight* (1609)
71; *The Witch of Edmonton* (1623) 5,
114, 128
Despair (theological) 62, 99, 101, 115,
167–8
Dickens, Charles 87
Diet of Worms, The 56
Douce, Francis 68, 77, 83, 85, 106,
147, 200–1
Drayton Michael: *The Barrons Warres*
(1603) 114; *The Merry Devil of
Edmonton* (1608) 65
Drinkwater, F.H. 198, 203
Ducis, J.F. 179
Dumas, Alexandre 154
Dunbar, William 185
Dürer, Albrecht 184

Edwards, Philip 2, 7, 100, 193–5
Edwards, Richard 105
Eliot, T.S. 65
Ellacombe, Henry N. 203
Empson, William 164, 204
Encyclopaedia Britannica 185, 204
Erasmus, Desiderius 120, 194
Eulenspiegel, Till 84
Evelyn, John 106

Facaros, Dana (and Michael Pauls)
205
Falstaff, Sir John 86, 99, 162
Faustbook 56
Field Guide to the Wild Flowers of Britain
205
Fletcher John: *The Woman Hater* (1607)
64
Florio, John 85
Flower symbolism 146–51, 182–93
Fools (*see also* Vice): madness of 78–9;

dress 81–9; 'transformations' 82;
feathers of 83–4, 88–9; synonyms
85–6, 90–1
Fortinbras 50, 172–3, 175
Francisco 48–9
Franco, Giacomo 158
Freud, Sigmund 143, 181, 203
Friar of Orders Gray, The 141, 203
Frye, Roland Mushat 173, 196, 204
Fulke, William 29
Furness, Horace Howard 199, 200, 201

Gardner, Helen 62, 203
Gee, John 55
Gertrude 112, 116, 129–36, 171
Ghost, The 43–74, 117, 132–3, 135,
178–9
Gibson, Edgar C.S. 60, 199, 200, 204
Golden Legend, The 46
Gombrich, Sir Ernst 124, 138, 203
Granville-Barker, Harley 112, 128,
135, 149
Greene, Robert: *A Looking Glass for
London* (1587–9) 16; *Alphonsus, King
of Arragon* (1587–8) 16; *Friar Bacon
and Friar Bungay* (1589–92) 16, 89;
Greene's Groatsworth of Wit (1592)
77, 114–15, 159
Greg, Sir Walter 26
Grim the Collier of Croydon (c.1600) 35,
46
Guazzo, Brother Francisco Maria 166,
204
Guérin 87
Guildenstern 94, 117, 119, 120, 122,
163, 171, 172

Hampton Court Conference 27, 69
Hanmer, Sir Thomas 177, 178
Harlequin (*see also* Arlecchino) 83, 107,
125
Harsnett, Samuel 28, 41, 69, 70, 199,
201
Hazlitt, William 180
Henry IV, King 61, 68, 85
Henry IV (of France) 107, 153, 155
Henry V, King 84
Henry VI, King 85
Henry VIII, King 83
Henryson, Robert 185, 205
Heywood, Jasper 41: translation of
Troas (1559) 14; translation of
Hercules Furens (1561) 104, 158
Heywood, John 181
Heywood, Thomas 107: *The Captives*
(1624) 5, 22

211